Extraordinary
Investments
for Ordinary
Investors

OTHER BOOKS BY WAYNE F. NELSON

How to Profit From the Money Revolution

How to Buy Money

Extraordinary Investments for Ordinary Investors

Choosing the Best From the New Money Packages

Wayne F. Nelson

G P. PUTNAM'S SONS / *New York*

G. P. Putnam's Sons
Publishers Since 1838
200 Madison Avenue
New York, NY 10016

The author gratefully acknowledges permission from the following sources to reprint material in their control:

American Association of Individual Investors for chart entitled "IRA Breakeven Holding Periods" reprinted from American Association of Individual Investors Journal, March 1984.

The Donoghue Organization, Inc., for Central Asset Account checklist.

E. P. Dutton, Inc., for material from *The Tao Jones Average*, by Bennett Goodspeed, copyright © 1983 by E. P. Dutton, Inc.

Forbes Inc., for chart entitled "At the Head of the Class" reprinted from *Forbes* Magazine, August 27, 1984, copyright © 1984 by Forbes Inc.

William J. Grace for material from *The Phoenix Approach* by William J. Grace, copyright © 1984 by Bantam Books, Inc.

The Investment Company Institute for chart entitled "The Tax-Exempt Edge of Municipal Bonds."

McGraw-Hill Book Company for material from *Winning* by Sully Blotnick, copyright © 1984 by McGraw-Hill Book Company.

Medical Economics Company Inc. at Oradell, N.J. 07649, for chart entitled "What Compounding Can Do for Your Contributions," copyright © 1983 by Medical Economics Company Inc.

Merrill Lynch, Pierce, Fenner & Smith Inc. for chart entitled "The Tax-Exempt Edge of Municipal Bonds" reprinted from *You and Your Money—A Financial Handbook*, copyright © 1984 by Merrill Lynch, Pierce, Fenner & Smith Inc.

The No-Load Fund Investor, Inc., for material from *The Handbook for No-Load Investors* by Sheldon Jacobs, copyright © 1983 by The No-Load Fund Investor, Inc.

Norwood Securities for graph entitled "Performance of Commodity Funds."

T. Rowe Price Associates for graph entitled "The Long-Term Bond Rate Versus the Rate of Inflation."

Random House, Inc., for material from *Street Smart Investing* by George B. Clairmont and Kiril Sokoloff, copyright © 1983 by Random House, Inc.

Simon & Schuster, Inc., for material from *Creating Wealth* by Robert Allen, copyright © 1983 by Robert Allen.

Robert A. Stranger & Co. for charts entitled "Leverage Real Estate Partnerships" and "Unleveraged Real Estate" from *The Stranger Register* by Robert A. Stranger & Co., copyright © 1983 by Robert A. Stranger & Co.

Watkins, Meegan, Drury for chart entitled "Alternative Minimum Tax."

Library of Congress Cataloging in Publication Data

Nelson, Wayne F.
   Extraordinary investments for ordinary investors.

   1. Investments—United States—Handbooks, manuals, etc. 2. Investment trusts—United States—Handbooks, manuals, etc. I. Title.
HG4921.N44   1984   332.6'78   84-11679
ISBN 0-399-12991-X

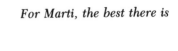

For Marti, the best there is

Contents

Extraordinary
Investments
for Ordinary
Investors

Introduction

FOR YEARS, Louis Appleby invested in one oil and gas program after another. Mr. Appleby, a successful automobile dealer, was delighted with the tax savings resulting from his investments and was convinced that he was building wealth. The reports from his various partnerships were glowing. One gigantic oil find after another was reported by the general partner. It wasn't until after he had retired and the tiny distribution checks began arriving that Mr. Appleby realized how poor an investment he had made. It was then that he learned how unfairly his oil and gas program had been "structured." Everyone made money but the limited partner, and even the massive oil finds would never return his original investment.

Don Struck's research and development partnership was equally unsuccessful. Unlike Mr. Appleby, Mr. Struck never understood anything about his investment. He jumped into it when he learned that Irving Smith, a highly respected, and certainly one of the most wealthy investors in his city, had bought several units of that partnership. Mr. Struck was not without company. At least twenty others had invested for the same reason. The list of losers resembled Who's Who of the city elite. None of them had studied the investment or even showed it to their accountants. All had rushed into it because

Mr. Smith was involved and because they were scared to death of being left out.

Fortunately not everyone's investment experience mirrors those of Messrs. Appleby and Struck. I've worked with many people who can boast of fortunes made with Wall Street's products. One is Edna Rouse, who began investing $50 a month in a diversified common stock mutual fund over thirty years ago. She invested whether the market was up or down without ever missing a payment. When she retired in early 1984, her mutual-fund investment had grown to over $1,000,000.

There are others who use Wall Street's money tools for other purposes. Henry Beane used a unit trust to simplify his decision about what to do with his AT&T common stock. Woody and Alice Clark have invested happily in tax-free unit trusts for over ten years, and there are legitimate ways to get a substantial tax write-off without inviting an IRS audit.

In the investment world all of these deals are called *financial products* or *financial packages*. They are designed, created, and operated by some of the most brilliant characters for whom money has ever been a motivator. Some of these extraordinary investments represent your best opportunity at quality, professional money-management and at building wealth. Some are clunkers. Their variety is almost without limit. They include every type of mutual fund (including the money-market funds) tax shelter, and unit trust. And they are likely to dominate all of our financial lives in the 1980s and beyond. George Ball, president of Prudential-Bache Securities, estimates that over $1.4 trillion will be invested in these personal financial tools in this decade alone. That is a staggering amount of money when we consider that in 1970 every share of stock of every company listed on the New York Stock Exchange could have been purchased for that amount.

As an individual investor so much of your money will be involved in these money tools that you must learn to deal with them. This is a book about just that. It is a book about choices—thousands of them—each designed to make your life as an investor easier. But, if you have ever invested in a mutual fund, unit trust, tax shelter, or annuity, or considered investing in one, you know that a limitless universe of choices does anything but make your life easier. In fact, the mind-boggling array of choices makes investment decision-making an almost impossible task for all but a financial junkie. For most people the opportunities are too many and too confusing. I know that because I see it in the faces of so many investors with whom I come into contact as a stockbroker. And I hear it in the voices of the thousands of callers who turn to my radio talk-show (and to the dozens like it throughout the country) for financial help. It is the reason why Money Magazine, *Changing Times,* and the money sections of major newspapers are so popular.

It is also the reason why one of the fastest-growing businesses in America is financial planning. People who are otherwise knowledgeable and successful just plain need hand-holding when it comes to making investment decisions. The financial-products industry today is the automobile industry before Henry Ford, the sewing machine industry before Singer, and the computer industry before IBM. The choices aren't buyer-friendly. Most investors can't understand them or how they should be arranged in a financial plan. Most don't know which are most suitable for their needs. They can't determine when is the right time to buy. Few of those who sell the products bother to explain what problems the buyers are likely to run into, or how to address those problems. Only the clairvoyant seem to be able to make it all fit together. And everyone struggles with the question, Where do I go for some unbiased help?

Personal investments should not be an invitation to frustration. The idea behind most of these financial innovations was to provide you with expert money-management help so that you would have the time to pursue what you do best and/or enjoy most. Professional money-management should mean that money experts are wisely handling your investments to allow you more time for your professional and personal life.

Unfortunately, it hasn't worked out that way. The simple task of picking the right experts and choosing the most desirable financial arenas in which to invest has become as difficult as picking such individual investments as the right common stocks or the best pieces of investment real estate.

There are well over a thousand mutual funds. There is

every variety of unit trust imaginable. There are tax shelters that allow you to own a piece of almost anything. For relatively small sums you can be a part owner of oil wells, windmills, racehorses, skyscrapers, computers, helicopters, shopping centers, box or hopper cars, post offices, motion pictures, farms, or satellites. You can also play your hunches by investing in specialized mutual funds to capitalize on whatever economic, social, or political turn you might foresee. For example, you can place your money in groups of energy stocks, health-management organizations, Japanese businesses, airline corporations, or any other specialized niche of the financial market.

Business Week reported that there are 1430 different savings certificates with varying combinations of maturities and interest rates.* J.C. Penney and Montgomery Ward are selling insurance, Kroger is selling mutual funds, and K-Mart offers a money-market fund. There are furniture stores in the banking business and banks in the tax-shelter business. The result is a bewildered public forced to make altogether too many time-consuming, difficult choices.

But let's be realistic. The reason I told the Louis Appleby and Don Struck stories was to make the point that not all money tools are good ones. Some are losers from the moment they are conceived. Some are replays from the original amateur hour. Others are not properly designed. Some are much too expensive. Some were once well managed but are limping along now out of memory. Too many were simply created for the benefit of the creator. But along with all of these there are some truly extraordinary investments, and they are available to all of us extraordinary and ordinary investors alike.

That is why I wrote this book. It is to show you how to make the best choices without making a career out of the selection process. I also want to help you organize your financial life, using the assistance of all the expert money managers available to you. In this book I will show you all the money tools available today, and how to evaluate each. But *it is not enough* to provide a descriptive list of the choices available to you. That may be more confusing than helpful. *And it is unrealistic for*

---

*"The Golden Plan of American Express," *Business Week*, April 30, 1984.

you to evaluate everything. Most people have neither the time nor the interest to undertake that tedious chore. It has been estimated that over fifty million bewildered Americans have parked a trillion dollars in out-of-date savings and investment accounts because they are too confused to move them. Everyone, from Wall Street's brokers to Main Street's bankers, has deals for you and each is more difficult to evaluate than the next.

In my opinion the days of marketing complex financial products to an audience of semiprofessional investors are over. It seems that the vast majority of consumers want straightforward investment products and services, easily arranged. They are not inclined to orchestrate a sophisticated financial program. Such activity is not fun, it is drudgery! The investors whom I work with want help putting together a financial program using only the best of the money tools that abound.

Certainly there are greater opportunities than have ever before existed. The purpose of my book is to help you match these opportunities to your needs, goals, and personality. And if your investment needs, goals, and personality remain mysteries to you, I'll help you uncover them. I want you to understand yourself as an investor so that you are able to choose an investment program that is appropriate for you at this stage of life. That is why the first step in the selection process has nothing to do with investments. It has to do with understanding yourself and knowing who you are as an investor.

When I was going through training school to become a stockbroker, Lindsay Hirkness, a very successful broker, was asked to give a lecture to my class about how he became so successful. He talked for an hour, and I'm certain he passed on a great deal of helpful information, but the one piece of advice I will always remember was, "Before you give any investment advice, sit down with yourself and determine just who you are as an investor. You will never be able to make any intelligent investment decisions until you understand yourself." I am going to help you find the answer to that critical question. The book is designed to help you manage your choices just as I help my clients manage their choices every day of my working life.

I bring to you my experience as a stockbroker who must

every day help people with decisions about their money. Over the years I've seen great successes and great failures. The lessons from each are a part of this book.

Change is very difficult to recognize as it is taking place, just as the turning of the tide is difficult to recognize when sitting on the beach. But there is change going on, indeed. The explosive growth of the new financial products, with which you must deal, is the most significant development in personal finance in the history of money. And it will continue at a mind-boggling pace. Your choices will become more rather than less complex as the number and variety of these money tools multiply. That, in fact, is the first of the major money-trends that will affect your life in this decade and well beyond. Bennett Marshall, one of Merrill Lynch's most successful stockbrokers, describes it as a lazy susan of financial products and services that exists for you to choose from. This trend is so significant that it has caused brokers and bankers to redefine their role in your life. They no longer view themselves primarily as money managers. They now describe their job as one of creating ideas that will move you to action.

There are other major trends already under way in the financial markets that will significantly impact your financial life—and make understanding your investment choices even more important. From my vantage point these are the trends to which I think you should pay close attention.

The second trend has to do with the dominant role in your life that will be played by financial supermarkets. It will have as much impact on financial life as the advent of grocery super-markets and shopping malls had on your day-to-day purchasing habits.

The third trend has to do with your tax bill. It will continue to increase, forcing you to pay as much attention to the tax consequences of your investments as to the potential economic consequences. There is no other practical way for the federal government to reduce its mammoth deficit.

The fourth trend is that you and I will have more income available for investment than middle- and upper-middle-class Americans have *ever* had to work with before. This means that you *must* learn to invest. You can't avoid it any longer. Managing your money will be as important to you as earning it.

The fifth trend involves your Individual Retirement Account, known as the IRA. I believe that you will see the contribution limits (now at $2000 per salaried person annually) increase dramatically, along with the variety of IRA investment opportunities. Your IRA will become one of the most important investment programs that you ever manage. I say this because I believe when you are saving money for retirement you are doing more than saving money—you are working to protect your *dignity* in your old age. A lot of money can buy a great deal of dignity in America.

The sixth major trend involves the common-stock market. The Dow Jones Industrial Average will soar over 3000 in the 1980s and top 5000 by the year 2000. A compelling case can be made for this lofty prediction about the common-stock market for a number of down-to-earth reasons. America is undervalued. Most of its corporations can be bought on the stock exchanges cheaper than they can be rebuilt. That is why so many mergers are occurring. The earning power of these corporations is awesome, as is the amount of money available for investment in common stocks. Productivity is on the rise. Inflation is stalled at a moderate rate. Interest rates are artificially high, and reflect every conceivable worry about future inflationary flare-ups. Once investors recognize these new realities, the stock market will roar. And I believe common-stock investors will do as well as those who invested in real estate in the inflationary 1970s. People will make fortunes. Your goal should be to be one of them. The best way to do that will be to own the right common-stock mutual fund.

Mutual-fund sales are setting new records almost every month. More money is invested in them than in any other type of money tool—over $500 billion. If you are now an investor, it is probably a safe bet to assume that you have money in a mutual fund or at least have considered buying one. Since there are over one thousand choices, picking the right ones can be a bit of a challenge even for seasoned investors. Sadly, some investors have ignored mutual funds because they don't understand them.

I had finished speaking at a trade association luncheon when the newly elected association president turned to me to ask, "How much money do you need to hire an asset manager to run your money?" I told him that mutual funds were managed assets and that he could employ some of the best talent in the business with as little as $500 to invest. He shrugged and shook his head. "No," he said. "I mean a real money manager like the ones wealthy people use."

It's funny how we all have images about the way we think things are. His was that only small-time investors use mutual funds. People with serious money to invest hire personal asset-managers. In the association president's mind these money gurus work in dimly lit, oak-paneled offices into which all sorts of privileged information flows. Because they shun publicity, their names are known only to investment-world insiders. And undoubtedly, in his view, these secretive gnomes of Wall Street consistently outperform the impersonal mutual-fund managers. Personal asset-managers, after all, run their few select accounts with Solomon's judgment, Job's dedication, and Moses's determination. While that is a flattering image, it certainly is far from the truth. Good asset-managers like to run large pools of money because it is a much harder job to manage lots of small accounts. They don't enjoy the hassle of hunting for new business. If they were good salesmen, they would make more money as stockbrokers. Asset managers are paid based on the number of dollars they manage and most enjoy being paid well. For all these reasons most good asset-managers manage money for mutual funds. And you can have access to the best with a relatively modest amount of money. Your task is to learn how to make intelligent choices.

In this book, I'm going to take you inside one of the best-managed mutual-fund organizations in America. I'm going to show you how mutual funds work, how they manage money, and then how to choose the right funds for you. I'll tell you to forget the idea that you should consider only "no-load" funds, that is, those that can be purchased without a sales fee. Sales fees have nothing whatever to do with performance. If you eliminate load funds, you eliminate over half your choices. And when picking a mutual fund I will show you that it is not enough to evaluate the fund's past performance. In fact, that might be the most misused selection technique. It doesn't tell you, for instance, if the people now guiding the fund are the same ones responsible for its past performance. There are much better ways to pick mutual funds that will best serve your purposes.

The key point is that you *can* master your financial life. Your choices *can* be made manageable. You *can* make money and have a great deal of fun doing it. There are some wonderful investment opportunities that you should know about. There are some brilliant money managers that you can hire. There are some investments that really can help you become financially independent. Your challenge is to find them. Mine is to help you.

How much time will it take to become a confident and successful money-tool selector? How much is it worth to you? How much time does it take for you to earn, say, $10,000? A week? A month? Two months? Are you willing to spend that much time if $10,000 would be the result of better money decisions? You will be relieved to know that you won't need to spend nearly that much time, but you must be prepared to spend some.

Investing is not a social event. To do it properly you must have time to select and monitor your investments. And if you lack the proper instinct, you must at least adopt and follow a system. If you have neither the time nor a system you should get some professional help.

Carefully selected money tools are the answer. There are some extraordinary ones available to you. They can put you in touch with investment opportunities that were once available only to the very wealthy or well-connected. And while those fortunate few will still have their choice of many of the best deals around, there are plenty left for the rest of us. This book will teach you the act of gathering around you more practiced investment hands. When you have finished you will see that you are not dealing with thousands of choices at all, but with only a carefully selected number of meaningful ones. From this short list making the right choices is a manageable task indeed—even if you consider yourself only an ordinary investor.

1

Why Aren't You Rich?

YOU WILL NEVER BE RICH until you understand why you aren't. You will never be a successful investor until you understand why success is eluding you now, and you will never be able to pick appropriate investments until you understand yourself.

Some people wander through life making bad decisions because they confuse themselves with the image of a person they've never met. Robespierre said that "No man can climb out beyond the limitations of his own character." Willie Nelson, a more contemporary philosopher and sometime country singer, says that a person can be, "sadly in search of, and one step in back of, himself and his slow-moving dream." Do you really know who you are? Have you ever had an honest talk about your strengths and weaknesses? I can tell you from experience that if you haven't spent the time it takes to figure out who you are, you will never be able to figure out how to be a good investor. How do you react under pressure? Are you a worrier? Are you a gambler? Are you impulsive? Does it bother you to lose money? Can you live with more uncertainty?

John Bradshaw*, a brilliant motivator and psychologist who

*5003 Mandell, Houston, TX 77006, (713) 529-9437.

counts among his clients many of the rich and famous as well as numerous international corporations, designed an exercise for me to use in this book. It is a series of questions that should help you understand more about yourself as an investor.

According to Mr. Bradshaw, the most important step in making that determination is to ask yourself the right questions. Think about that. When you walk into a clothing store, a salesperson will inevitably appear to ask whether you need help. Instinctively most people will say, "No!" Or, "I'm just looking." Or, "Not at the moment." Or, "I'll ask for you if I need you."

Have you ever thought about why people respond that way? Mr. Bradshaw says that it is because if you say "yes," a good salesperson will keep asking questions until you have put yourself in a corner and are forced to buy something—maybe many somethings.

SALESPERSON: "Can I help you?"
CUSTOMER: "Yes, I'm looking for a scarf."
SALESPERSON: "What color scarf would you like?"
CUSTOMER: "Blue."
SALESPERSON: "We have scarfs that range in color from a beautiful royal blue to a soft baby-blue. Do you have a specific shade of blue in mind?"
CUSTOMER: "Royal blue, please."
SALESPERSON: "And the fabric?"
CUSTOMER: "Silk, if you have one under fifty dollars."

Now what are you going to say when the salesperson shows you a royal-blue silk scarf that sells for $39 on sale from $75? Are you going to say that is not what you were looking for? I doubt it. Good salespeople are good because they know how to ask the right questions.

Sometimes we avoid asking ourselves the right questions because we are afraid of the answers—or even because we have a sense of what those answers are, and we don't like them. If that is the case, the value of Mr. Bradshaw's exercise lies in exposing those answers so that we can deal with them. These are his questions:

QUESTION ONE: WHAT IS IT THAT YOU REALLY WANT AS AN INVESTOR?

One of the difficulties in answering this question is that all of you are not the same. Each of you is made up of many different parts. Some parts of you demand sensible, high-quality, risk-free investments. Other parts of you are right at home in front of a slot machine in Las Vegas. Some part might be impulsive, another indecisive, and still another might be hopelessly selfish. Different investments appeal to different parts of you. You may discover that the wrong parts are dominant. The trick is to discover which parts are causing you to be a lousy investor and then make some changes. Perhaps there are certain things that you don't like about yourself as an investor. They may cause you to make the same mistakes over and over. What do you do when you catch yourself doing it again?

Mr. Bradshaw tells the story about an American in Paris who asks a kindly old Frenchwoman on the street corner for the directions to a library. The American speaks no French and the little lady speaks no English. It doesn't take long for bystanders to figure out that when the American says "Where is the library?" the Frenchwoman has absolutely no idea what he is talking about. So the American raises his voice an octave and asks again, "WHERE IS THE LIBRARY?" She still doesn't understand. The American can continue to raise his voice to a shout, but until he finds a different way to respond to the situation the result is going to be the same. Abraham Maslow said that "if the only tool you have is a hammer, you tend to see every problem as a nail."

The lesson to be learned from this is that if you are not already as successful an investor as you want to be, if you are going to get to be any better, and if you don't want to make bad worse, there must be some things that you are now doing that should be changed.

Each of our personal histories is a combination of moments we would like to live over—a significant number differently from the last time. You can never have a better tomorrow if you spend all your time lamenting about yesterday, but you can have a fantastic tomorrow if you can *learn* from what went wrong yesterday.

Thomas Edison is said to have worked on 50,000 experiments resulting in 50,000 failures. When a friend of his heard this, he remarked to Mr. Edison that he must be terribly disappointed in obtaining no results for all of his labors. "Why, man," Edison replied, "I have gotten plenty of results. I now know fifty thousand things that won't work."

The first step in making changes is to spend some time quietly thinking about your primary investment objective. After you have defined it, write it down so that you can test every investment decision you ever make against it.

In his excellent book *Creating Wealth*, Robert G. Allen also advises that investors set goals and write them down. He wrote:

"A study at Yale pointed out the value of goals. The 1954 Yale University graduating seniors were asked if they had set any specific written financial goals at the time of graduation. Only 3% had done so. About 10% had specific goals but hadn't committed them to paper. The rest had no specific goals. Twenty years later, they were resurveyed. Guess which group was most successful. You guessed it. The 3% outperformed the other 97% combined!

"Now, I'm not suggesting that you can't become wealthy without goals, nor that you will automatically 'make it' if you do have goals. But, as the survey suggests, they certainly help.

"Why write your goals down? A goal that is not written down is a wish. A daydream. When you are serious enough to commit your goals to paper and read them regularly, you energize your commitment and creativity."

You may find that you want to change that objective over time. There is no rule against that. I only suggest that your investment objective be an important one, that it be specific, and that it be a written commitment that you have made with yourself. You will be surprised by how many investment deals you can ignore simply by requiring them to match your primary investment objective.

QUESTION TWO: HOW WOULD YOU KNOW IF YOU GOT IT?

I mentioned before that if you expect to achieve any investment objective you must first know yourself. Adam Smith wrote, "If you don't know yourself the investment world is an expensive place to find out."

Coming to know oneself is not a simple process. Accepting what we come to know might be even harder. Each of our parts is a force that plays a role in our decision-making process. The whole might look something like the combination of interwoven circles in Chart 1-1.

CHART 1-1

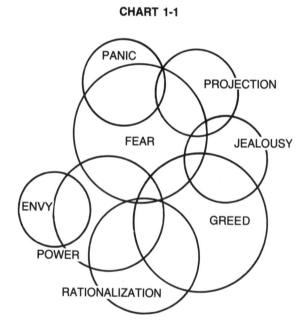

Each of us is different. That is why I've drawn circles of different sizes. Larger circles are intended to show that some characteristics have more influence on our decisions than others.

Some of us have characteristics that play a role that we don't even recognize in our investment decision-making process. Fear and greed are represented by large circles because together they play a role in 90 percent of all investment decisions ever made by mortal man. There is the fear of being left out of an investment. There is the fear of losing money. And of course there is the greed of making a killing, and after that is done the greed of wanting even more. Recognize that since these emotions work on all of us, we must learn to deal with them.

The second step in becoming a better investor is to understand your investment personality. It will affect every decision you make, and it certainly influences the kinds of investments that are best suited to you. I've always maintained that the best investment is sleep at night. If your investments are causing you to worry or to be uncomfortable, you should change them.

Sometimes worry is caused by lack of understanding. In my first book, *How to Buy Money*, I made a point that there is a difference between fear and ignorance. Many people fear what they don't understand, but by gaining knowledge about investments they can overcome that fear. It should be every investor's goal to improve his or her knowledge to put themselves in the position to make better investment decisions. As that happens, your investment personality will change. Every investor can become more confident and comfortable. For some the progress is quicker than for others.

QUESTION THREE: WHEN DO YOU WANT IT?

It takes three ingredients to make money:

1. You must have some money to invest.
2. You must put it into something that will be successful.
3. And you must give the investment *time* to work.

Many people have unrealistic expectations. Let me remind you right here that by any historical measure a better than 15 percent return a year is quite impressive. Most investors fail because they want too much too soon and because we all keep making the same mistakes. I've listed the ten most common after Question Five.

QUESTION FOUR: WHAT IS IT ABOUT WHAT YOU ARE DOING NOW THAT YOU ENJOY?

Let's face it, if you weren't comfortable doing what you are doing you would already have made some changes. There is something about the way you are running your investment life right now that you enjoy. What is it? According to John Bradshaw, unless you find something in the new investment program that is equally satisfying, your efforts to change will be sabotaged from the beginning. Somehow you are going to have to accommodate what you *like* doing with what you *should* be doing. To do that you must identify what it is. Then write it down. Many times when we are forced to put our reasons down in writing, they seem less compelling and perhaps easier to change.

QUESTION FIVE: WHAT IS STOPPING YOU?

You must get out of your own way. What is it that you are now doing that is preventing you from making the changes you want to make?

Be careful not to blame someone else. It has been said that "Every man is the painter and the sculptor of his own life."

Richard Greene, one of Wall Street's most successful stockbrokers of all time, frequently reminds investors that "You have to paddle your own canoe." *You* are responsible for whatever investment success you might or might not enjoy in your lifetime, not some unidentified villain. Sometimes to make this point I will tell the story about the three crows on a railroad track. When they spotted the train approaching, two of them took a notion to fly away. How many of the crows do you think were killed by the train? The answer is all three. You see, two crows only *took a notion*.

WHY AREN'T WE BETTER INVESTORS THAN WE ARE? THE TEN REASONS MOST INVESTORS LOSᴌ MONEY

1. Selling at the Wrong Time

Most investors operate on Father Flanagan's theory—that there is no such thing as a bad investment. In his classic book about investment psychology, *Winning: The Psychology of Investing*, *Forbes* columnist Srully Blotnick put it this way: "We may be skeptical about the economy, or about the market, but when it comes to a particular company we are always ready to believe the best." We have been conditioned to do that from birth. "Things will always get better," we are constantly reminded, "it is the American way." President Jimmy Carter tried to tell the American public that it wasn't necessarily true that there would always be a better future for Americans. He tampered with our vision of the American dream, so the voters threw him out of office. America stands for hope, for optimism, for a determined spirit and a better tomorrow. No wonder we hate to sell an investment. Selling is an act of defeat. It is raising the white flag. It is giving up. It is downright anti-American. As a result, many investors suffer with investment portfolios that are truly red, white, and blue. They are red from the embarrassment of foolish choices, white with the lifelessness of their prospects for recovery, and blue from the bruises suffered in market tumbles.

To be a successful investor we must first face the fact right from the beginning that we are going to lose money in the process. Not all of our choices are going to be good ones. Some will be made for the silliest reasons. Some out of fear, and others from greed. As a consequence there will be some weeds among the roses. As soon as you can identify them, they must be pulled. Problem is, most investors don't do it. Remember this: *Above all else, protecting against the downside is everything.* If you lost 50 percent of your investment, what is left needs to double just to break even. Think about it. Your overall performance will always be a reflection of your worst mistakes.

It will drag the results of your successes into the ground. That is why you must learn to cut losses early if they occur. Or, as Dick Greene advises, "Learn to take some pleasure out of winning by selling stocks before your profits slip away." Establish a mental "safety net" below which you won't allow the value of your investments to fall before you sell. The net may trip you up occasionally, but since it will save you more times than it will trip you, it is the best you can expect of any rule about investing.

2. Coming to the Market With Unrealistic Expectations

A lady who had never invested called me one Sunday on my radio call-in talk show. She had decided to buy a stock. Her strategy was to let it double and then sell it. She devised this strategy because, as she said, "I don't want to be greedy." The same lady is probably delighted with the modest return she is earning on her money in a money-market fund or savings certificate. But when it comes to investing in the stock market, those same people always seem to expect Hialeah-type results. In order to try to get those results, investors frequently turn to the most speculative plays and hope for miracle performances.

As Srully Blotnick sagely pointed out in his book *Winning: The Psychology of Investing*, "the market has shown us time and again that it is unwilling to accommodate our enthusiasm for quick results." Such a game plan points to disaster from the start, and yet it remains the favorite of the majority of inexperienced investors.

3. Buying on Rumor

A rumor is usually worth every penny you pay to hear it. As a stockbroker I usually hear at least one very interesting rumor a day. Rumors are generally about takeovers that are imminent, gigantic contracts that are about to be let, wonder products about to be released, or gigantic earnings announcements that will surprise everyone. In most cases, of course, no one is surprised, because by the time you hear the rumor so has everyone else. The best advice I can offer when you act on a rumor is to sell as soon as it becomes apparent that the reason you made the investment was wrong. If the reason turns out to be right, God bless you, but if it doesn't it is usually a mistake to hold your breath waiting for a miracle to bail you out.

4. and 5. Overtrading or Undermanaging Your Account

Some investors can't make decisions and others can't do anything but make decisions. Both methods of money management are wrong. I have yet to find a security that should be bought and shoved to the back of some musty safe-deposit box. Circumstances change. An investor must continually monitor his or her investments and move when a move is prudent. No investment is right for all seasons. But there are times when doing nothing is the most appropriate course of action. Some people have trouble accepting that, and will even replace advisers who recommend a conservative "do as little as necessary approach" with a go-go type who has a new suggestion a week. Some investors don't have a grain of patience. Others don't have any plan other than to be patient. Neither type will be successful.

6. Having the Wrong Help

People pick their financial adviser for the strangest reasons—most of them having nothing to do with whether the adviser can help them make money. And isn't that the reason you have a financial adviser at all? Friends are rarely good choices, and there is even less reason to pick neighbors. Some people rely on the luck of the draw when they settle for the "broker of the day" at the most convenient stockbrokerage firm. Others begin these very intimate financial relationships by mailing a coupon or answering a salesperson's phone call. Of course it is possible to stumble onto the right adviser that way, but the odds are against it.

7. Acting Too Late

The art of consistently acting too late is often called herd instinct, and every trend has its tail-enders. Try not to be one of them. It's very difficult not to be swept up in whatever is popular and on everyone's mind at the moment. It is also part of the American custom of doing things. We all try to dress to be trendy, to belong to the right clubs, to go to the right schools, to meet the right people, to lead our lives like other right-minded Americans. Unfortunately, when people carry this behavior over to the investment world, their timing can be way off. "Too many people," Ed Mathias, the president of the T. Rowe Price New Horizons Fund, warns, "try to do the fashionable thing too late." By the time the housekeeper is wearing designer jeans, they are no longer the fashion. Of course it's not such a big deal when you buy designer jeans just as they are going out of style. Only a few dollars are involved. However, it can be disaster when you lead your investment life that way and buy gold at $800 an ounce or invest heavily in oil stocks just as the world discovers an oil glut.

The classic example of trendy investing was tulip mania. In 17th century Holland tulips became as popular as Cabbage Patch dolls for Christmas, 1983. Maybe even more popular! Absolutely everybody wanted tulips, tulip bulbs, and tulip roots. Because of this incredible demand the price shot up. Otherwise sensible, reasonable people began speculating in tulips, pushing their prices to extremes. People left their jobs to grow them and there were "stock exchanges" organized to trade them. Everyone from noblemen to chimneysweeps knew his or her road to riches was paved with tulips. People sold their homes to buy them, and for a while it was unthinkable to suspect the price of tulips would ever fall. But fall it did, plunging thousands of people into bankruptcy and nearly ruining the Dutch economy. The pattern happens with such regularity that you will no doubt recognize the curve that I have drawn in Chart 1-2 to depict its various stages.

8. Being Closed-Minded

Some people don't deserve the future! They can't adjust to changes and won't adopt new methods even though there isn't a reasonable argument against them.

These are the people who get into comfortable ruts, pat-

CHART 1-2

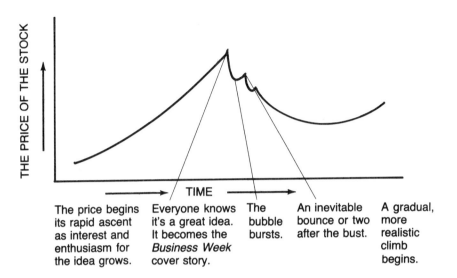

THE PRICE OF THE STOCK

TIME

| The price begins its rapid ascent as interest and enthusiasm for the idea grows. | Everyone knows it's a great idea. It becomes the *Business Week* cover story. | The bubble bursts. | An inevitable bounce or two after the bust. | A gradual, more realistic climb begins. |

terns, or habits that may cost them a small fortune. They may go as far as coming to an intellectual agreement to change, but inevitably they put it off and fall back into their well-established routine.

These were the last to discover money-market funds, the last to discover central-asset accounts, and will be the last to discover every other financial innovation that comes along. I call them financial basket-cases.

9. Having No Goals and Only Sketchy Plans

This will be covered in detail later in this chapter. Let it be sufficient to add that no successful business can operate without concrete goals. Your financial life can't operate without them either.

10. Overlooking the Obvious

Bennett Goodspeed tells this story in his fascinating book *The Tao Jones Averages*. "Several years ago an agent who monitored Russian newspapers at the CIA notices an anomaly: A small town's soccer team, which was the perennial last-place team, suddenly began winning their games by lopsided scores. Intrigued, the reader persuaded the agency to fly a U-2 plane over the town to take detailed photographic mapping. These pictures revealed that a well-camouflaged military installation had been built in the town. Though the Russians went out of their way to hide the plant, they didn't realize that the technicians imported to manage the facilities would improve the town's soccer team. This unintended message proved to be a clue to the new reality."

Some of the best investments you may ever consider are staring you right in the face. They are frequently so close that you look right by them. They may be businesses you understand best, companies you deal with, companies in your hometown. I've met builders who know the products they work with so well that they can spend an entire conversation telling me what is good and bad about the companies that make those products. They know what is new, they understand the competition, the market, and the regulatory environment. They know more about those companies than Wall Street's finest industry analysts. They should be investing in them. What do they do? They ignore their knowledge and put their money in California computer stocks, Texas oil wells, and other more exotic-sounding investments they know nothing about. Not very smart, is it? You shouldn't ever invest in anything you don't understand. You should invest in companies you do.

The authors of the *Dow Jones Irwin Guide to Mutual Funds*, Donald D. Rugg and Norman B. Hale, did extensive research about why investors fail. They concluded that most make the same nine mistakes. They are:

1. Failure to develop a sound strategy
2. Bearing too much or too little risk
3. Poor investment selection

4. Poor timing
5. Inadequate diversification
6. High transaction costs
7. Poor advisers
8. Failure to control emotions—especially greed and fear
9. Paying excessive taxes

Our lists are similar. Most lists in most investment books will be. As investors we haven't made an original mistake in some time. The purpose is not to dwell on past mistakes—simply to learn from them.

2

The Art of
Getting to Yes

As a radio financial talk-show host the most common
question that I hear begins something like this: "Wayne, I have
ten thousand dollars to invest. What should I do?" The amount
of money that the various callers have to invest is unimportant.
Some have a few hundred dollars; some have many multiples of
$10,000; and I will probably always remember the lady with
$14,000,000 who called to ask that very question.

My suggestions will vary based on the differing circumstances of the callers, but in order to find out about those
differing circumstances I need to ask some follow-up questions.
I'd like to share with you how I go about questioning a potential
investor. It is a method not unlike the ones used by experienced investment advisers all over the country. It is how a
successful stockbroker can sell you what you want to buy. The
stockbroker's goal is to find out what you really want by letting
you tell him. After all, it is much easier to sell someone what he
wants than what he doesn't want. In the investment business it
is called "the art of getting to yes."

After we have reached that basic level of understanding
about ourselves, I'm going to take you through a far more
sophisticated exercise. This one is designed to help you understand your investment motives and goals, as well as your in-

vestment personality. It is only when you can clearly define all three that you will ever be able to answer where you are going and why, when you are going to get there and how. Helping you to answer those questions earns financial planners fees ranging from several hundred to several thousand dollars. If it seems like a waste of time, try to think of it as if you were buying your first personal computer. A good salesperson can match you to the best possible machine if that person knows about you and what you want the machine to do. Similarly, I can help match you to the most appropriate investment choices once I know more about you and what you want your investments to do for you.

FIVE TYPES OF INVESTORS

Over a number of years I have come to recognize that there are five distinct investor personality types. Most successful stockbrokers can identify your personality after talking with you for just a few minutes. In fact, a good broker may understand you as an investor better than you know yourself. That is why he or she is so successful. They know what you will buy and then they spend their time selling it to you. The good ones won't waste that time trying to talk you into something you don't want. Later on in this chapter I will show you how good stockbrokers get to know you in their first conversation. It may better help you understand yourself. For now, consider which of these personality types a successful stockbroker would label you.

1. Financial Basket-Cases

The history of these investors has been a race between a little knowledge and catastrophe. They are characterized by a stubborn unwillingness to learn or even to consider anything different. They possess an unreasonable fear of change. They are victims of habit. They trust no one and nothing, least of all their own instincts. They display indecision whenever confronted with an investment decision. A financial basket-case is the sort of person who can be given a dozen irrefutable reasons for doing something differently than he or she is doing it now—and will still refuse to do it. W. Somerset Maugham described a financial basket-case well when he said, "Like all weak men, he laid an exaggerated stress on not changing one's mind."

2. The Nervous Nellie

Nervous Nellies are toe-dippers. They are cautious, generally conservative, but usually willing to try small investments in new areas. As a result many own hodgepodge portfolios that lack any semblance of direction. They are not very confident about their knowledge and as a result are constantly searching for the "right" person to help them. Nervous Nellies tend to spend half their lives looking out of rearview mirrors. They tend to catch on to ideas too late and always seem to be a step behind the right one.

3. Wild Bill Hickock

Wild Bill has acquired enough knowledge of the investing world to be dangerous to himself. He tends to confuse skill with being mistaken at the top of his voice. Bill tends to act impulsively rather than to make well thought-out moves. He or she is an emotional investor likely to be easily influenced by rumors or tall tales. Subscriptions to more than one market letter and a tendency to follow the advice of them all are telltale signs. As a consequence Wild Bill tends to overmanage his or her investments. If he lasts long enough, Wild Bill is generally taught by experience to be a better investor, but the lessons can be expensive. Failed Wild Bills are recognized by their cynicism, a product of having their confidence ravaged by the pattern bombing of disappointment.

4. Captain America

The Captain is a person who decides. Sometimes he makes the wrong decision, but he always decides. As a result he runs his investment life with a high level of confidence. Captain

America is usually a successful businessperson used to decision making and to relying on his or her common sense. The Captain makes quick but thoughtful decisions. He or she is able to comfortably live with those decisions or to reverse them should circumstances warrant. This person is able to tolerate a high level of risk, has a sense of direction, and is quite pragmatic. The Captain seems to know how to invest up to the limit of his or her understanding but not beyond. His response to a lack of understanding is an undertaking to learn.

5. The Financial Junkie

As a sophisticated student of the market, the financial junkie knows exactly what he or she wants to do. If the junkie didn't have another job he or she would probably be a professional investor. Confidence and independence are hallmarks. He or she is usually cost-conscious, demanding, and willing and able to invest the time and energy it takes to run an active investment program.

It should be apparent that as investors we tend to be mixes of all of these personality types rather than solid citizens of any one category. And the best news is that every investor has the potential of getting to be a better investor.

FINANCIAL PLANNING SELF-TAUGHT

If you hire a financial planner to help you organize your financial life, it will quickly become apparent that you have hired someone to help you answer three basic questions. Once you find the answers to these important queries there is no doubt but that you will be a better investor. The questions are these:

I. Where Am I?
II. Where Do I Want to Go?
III. How Am I Going to Get There?

I. WHERE AM I?

The first step is to assess your situation. When you sit down with a financial planner your first task will be to fill out a comprehensive questionnaire. The planner will want to see your:

income tax returns
brokerage, mutual fund, limited partnership statements
bank account information
retirement account information
employee benefit statements
mortgage documents
will, trust agreements
all insurance policies
divorce decree papers
checkbook and other records of spending habits
charge account statements

You will be amazed at what you will learn about yourself if you take the time to gather together all of this information. One of the incidental benefits of the search is that you will discover where all of these documents are. Most of us have them scattered all over the lot. Even if you pursue financial planning no further than this initial step, you will probably think it has been worth the effort simply because you have located and can now centralize your critical papers.

To find out where you are you need to answer the following basic questions.

1. Do You Have a Money-Market Fund?

This is an essential first step. It is your cash reserve for emergencies, for the trip you may want to take, and for your month-to-month expenses. The amount varies based on your spending habits, the amount of money you earn, and how much money it takes for you to feel comfortable as a cushion against the immediate unknown. For someone who earns

$25,000 a year that amount might be $5000. For someone who earns $100,000 it might be $20,000. For the lady with $14,000,000 it will probably be close to $70,000 or $80,000. You can gather from these examples that the amount is not some fixed percentage. It is only what it takes for you to feel comfortable.

Until you have this cash reserve it is silly to think about investing. *Investment money is money that should be insulated from day-do-day requirements and from all but the most acute emergencies.* The main reason I advise that is that you want to be in the position to make investment decisions about investment money. If you need to sell an investment to buy a new refrigerator, for example, rather than because it is the *right time* to sell that investment, you are operating at a great disadvantage. Don't put yourself in that position.

Your cash reserve can be in a tax-free or a taxable money-market fund depending on your tax bracket. Both funds offer equal liquidity, check-writing features, and the day-to-day accumulation of interest. Higher-tax-bracket investors will almost always fare better in a tax-free money-market fund. Investing in the wrong type of money-market fund is the most common mistake made by high-tax-bracket individuals, and it is the most easily remedied. Keep in mind in every investment you make that your *real return* is your *after-tax* return. If you are unclear about how to find the right money-market fund, see page 75.

2. Have You Bought a Home?

On its face, this seems like a throwaway question. Yet it is quite important. A home is going to be one of your biggest, most successful, and probably most enjoyable investments. The tax laws favor home ownership, as does inflation. In every year but seven since the turn of the century the prices of single-family homes have appreciated. That is not a bad performance record. Until you own a home it is premature to develop any long-range investment program. Until you own a home every investment should be designed to accumulate enough money to be able to make the down payment.

3. Have You Funded to the Maximum Extent Possible Every One of Your Retirement Programs?

Those plans include individual-retirement accounts (IRAs), Keogh accounts for the self-employed, employee-sponsored stock-purchase programs, deferred-compensation opportunities, and employer-matching savings accounts. Many of these retirement programs offer terrific tax advantages and a real opportunity to accumulate wealth. Most are made palatable by periodic but regular payroll deductions rather than requiring lump-sum investments. Until you take advantage of these opportunities, other long-range investment commitments are also premature.

The question of how to invest our IRA contributions is rapidly becoming the most important investment decision that most Americans will ever make. Many of the investments that you can use in your Individual Retirement Accounts are the types of investments covered in this book. Matching the right ones to your IRA is critically important. That is why I have devoted a section to that subject; it begins on page 164.

4. What Are You Doing With That Money Now?

Unless the money has just been won in some lotto game, chances are it is already invested. It is also likely that it is in some investment that makes the investor happy—or at least comfortable—or it wouldn't be there. The easiest recommendation is for more of the same. You must guard against falling into a routine just because it is familiar. Force yourself to ask questions about alternatives. Learn what is good and bad about each. Play with some different investments on paper to see how you react. Work to expand your knowledge. Information after all is power.

5. What Is Your Tax Bracket?

Most people don't want to pay the IRS any more than they have to, and most are convinced that everyone else is paying less than they are. Tax-advantaged investments are easily sold for these reasons.

Always remember that the IRS has a continuing interest in your money. It wants some after you earn it (income tax), it wants some more while it is invested (tax on interest and dividends), some more still when you take it out of any successful investment (capital gains), some more if you give it away (gift taxes), and even some when you die (estate taxes). As a prudent investor it is your responsibility to minimize the tax bite every opportunity that you get. It is also your responsibility never to choose an investment based on its tax benefits alone. More stupid investments have been made in recent times to save taxes than for any other single reason. There are scores of people ready to sell you products that appeal to your lack of affection for the IRS. Make sure that is not the primary reason for your choice of investments.

6. What Do You Want This Investment to Do for You?

Some people want income. Some want the money to grow. Some can't tolerate the thought of losing any. Some are quite willing to take the chance of hitting home runs at the risk of striking out. What is it that motivates you?

Not every investment is for every investor. *How much money a person has to invest has nothing to do with investment choice, nor has a person's education or occupation.* More likely, those are also a reflection of his or her basic personality. How do you know what sort of investment personality you have? Answers to the questions in the two exercises at the end of this chapter should help us find out. Keep in mind that there are no right or wrong answers. Each of these questionnaires is designed only to help determine what types of investments might be best suited for you. Don't feel bad if you don't know what many of these investments are. Part of determining what sort of investor you are is recognizing the limits of your investment knowledge.

When you finish this book you will know these investments.

II: WHERE DO I WANT TO GO?

If you don't know where you are going, any road will take you there. That is certainly true about career planning. People who set career goals for themselves almost always outperform their fellow workers who haven't. Since we all have specific ideas about where we want to be with our money, we really needn't concern ourselves with financial goal setting, right?

Wrong! My experience with the thousands of investors whom I've worked with over the span of my financial career suggests otherwise. My experience convinces me that most investors fail to set any investment goals. And most of those who do have goals that are too general.

Let me give you an example of a meaningful investment goal. This one happens to be a goal of Steven Norwitz, the brilliant public relations director for the T. Rowe Price organization. Steve and his wife want to be able to buy a college education for their three-year-old daughter when she reaches college age. In order to do that, he figures he will need to accumulate $136,852. Quite obviously that is not a number that Steve pulled out of the air. It is his estimate of the cost of a college education today ($38,296), adjusted for eighteen years of inflation at an 8 percent inflation rate.

Knowing that he would need $136,852 in eighteen years from his daughter's birth, Steve and his wife began saving $3000 a year, or $250 a month. By their calculations Steve has figured that they need to earn 11 percent interest on that money every year in order to reach their goal. He knows that 11 percent can be earned from a variety of conservative investments, including U.S. Treasury bonds. As a result he has selected a variety of safe investments for his daughter's education account. But what if Steve needed to earn 15 percent a year in order to reach his goal? His choices would necessarily be different. He might choose to become a more aggressive investor, or he would need to save more money each month, or build a smaller college fund.

The point is that a specific financial goal can help each of us do a better job of designing a specific investment program.

Once we know what we *need* to do we can choose from a narrower list of financial tools. We can do this because we know how to eliminate those tools that don't fit. As a result, choices will become much easier to make.

Given that the greater the risk the greater the reward, the concept of investment risk will be easier to handle. Since we know precisely how much reward is necessary, we will understand how much risk we must take. If that amount of risk makes us uncomfortable, we can either change our goal, or, if we are able, raise the amount of our investment.

III: HOW AM I GOING TO GET THERE?

The third financial-planning question is the purpose of this book. It is to help you choose the investments that will allow you to satisfy your investment goals and are appropriate to your investment personality at this stage of your life. With as many choices as are available to you, that task is not an easy one. Part of it is accomplished by taking the mystery out of the money world. Believe me, it is not as challenging as it seems! Follow me, I'll show you what I mean.

It is much easier if you keep your planning and your investment mix simple. One of the dread diseases of the investment world is what Jim Riepe, president of T. Rowe Price Mutual Funds, calls "analysis paralysis." It manifests itself when a person confronts so many options that he drives himself into a complete state of indecision. As Mr. Reapey told me, "It is unrealistic to try to evaluate everything. As a result of trying to consider too much information, many people are unable to deal with any." I'm not going to let that happen to you.

1. SET VERY SPECIFIC INVESTMENT GOALS

When I advocate setting specific investment goals, I mean *long-range specific goals*. Don't get involved with a microscope when you need a telescope to look down the road. It is not enough to say that you are saving for retirement, or to buy a boat, or to take a trip around the world. Retirement planning should include goals on income, standard of living, location, and spending habits. I have yet to meet anyone who doesn't want to enjoy a financially comfortable retirement. But what does that mean to you? Quantify and qualify it! Get as specific as you can. Where will you retire? What type of house? How much will it cost? How will you be able to afford to build it? At what age will you retire? How much income will you want a month? Charts 2-1, 2-2, and 2-3 may help.

2. PLAN A RETIREMENT FUND

These figures assume an annual inflation rate of 8 percent and 10 percent annual return on your invested dollars.

CHART 2-1

If your monthly retirement income goal is	You will need this size fund to pay that amount over		
	10 years	15 years	20 years
$5000	$316,400	$615,000	$819,000
$10,000	757,000	931,000	1,036,000
$15,000	1,135,000	1,396,000	1,554,000
$20,000	1,513,000	1,861,000	2,072,000
$25,000	1,892,000	2,326,000	2,591,000

If these amounts seem staggering, keep in mind that an 8 percent annual inflation rate means that:

CHART 2-2

At Today's Value	To Be Equal Must Be Worth		
	10 years	15 years	20 years
$5000	$10,795	$15,861	$23,305
$10,000	21,589	31,722	46,610

With this in mind, how much should you put away *each year?*

CHART 2-3

If you will be retiring in	Divide the amount from the chart by
5 years	6.105
10 years	15.937
15 years	31.772
20 years	57.275
25 years	98.347
30 years	164.494

For example, if you plan to retire in ten years and want to have $100,000 at that time, you must save $13,546.46 each year (10 × $21,589 ÷ 15.937).

3. VISUALIZE YOUR INVESTMENT PROGRAM

I like to think of an investment program as a thermometer. The base of the bulb in Chart 2-4 is your personal residence. The level above it is your cash reserve. The vial itself must be protected by an adequate insurance program. Only after your assets exceed the "freezing level" should you concern yourself with other investments. The first choices should be our various retirement-account opportunities. And then you can invest to achieve financial independence.

CHART 2-4

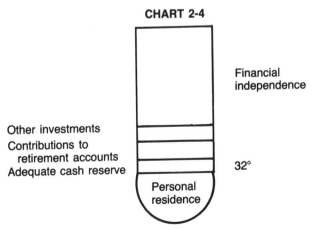

Other investments
Contributions to
  retirement accounts
Adequate cash reserve

Financial
independence

32°

Personal
residence

Only when you lay out a financial blueprint of your life can you understand what it will take to reach your financial goals. That blueprint might begin to shape up something like this:

CHART 2-5

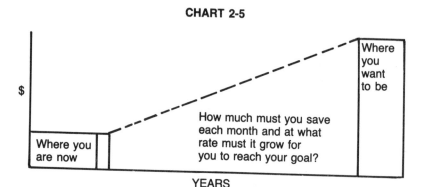

It is an accomplishment for most people just to be able to put aside enough money to own a house, have an adequate cash reserve, and take full advantage of our retirement-account opportunities. If you haven't yet done that you now know where you should concentrate your investment effort. This book can be a help.

WHAT TYPE INVESTOR ARE YOU?

Exercise One

The following is a list of investments. Your task is to rank them by the level of risk that you associate with each. Write the number corresponding to the description in each blank on the left of the investment.

1. Very speculative
2. Involves some risk
3. Solid
4. I'm not familiar with the investment

_____ FSLIC-insured bank savings accounts
_____ Brokerage-firm-sponsored money-market funds
_____ Real-estate investment trusts

_____ Ginnie Mae pass-throughs
_____ Treasury bills
_____ Tax-anticipation notes,
            bond-anticipation notes, revenue-anticipation notes
_____ Tax-deferred annuities
_____ Research and development limited partnerships
_____ Common stocks
_____ Common-stock mutual funds
_____ Tax-free unit trusts
_____ Municipal-bond funds
_____ WOOPS (Washington Public Power System)
            municipal bonds
_____ Corporate bonds
_____ Limited partnerships (real estate)
_____ Oil and gas exploratory programs
_____ Preferred stock
_____ Put and call buying
_____ Option writing
_____ Using margin

If you understand 16 or more of the 20 investments listed in Exercise One enough to explain them to someone else, you are a very savvy investor. If you understand 12 to 16, you have a good working knowledge of the financial world. If you understand 8 to 12, you have an average knowledge. Fewer than 8 indicates that you need to do some more studying before you do any more investing. That is because you should have a better working knowledge of your alternatives.

As far as how you ranked the investments: If you thought of 5 or more as solid, you have a good understanding of investment risk. Fewer than 5 indicates that you may be too cautious an investor or that you need to work on expanding your investment knowledge. That is also true if you thought more than 5 of the investments to be very speculative.

Exercise Two

This questionnaire is designed to determine how you react to investment disappointments.

The following are six hypothetical situations. Place a checkmark next to the answer that most closely reflects your response.

1. I bought a stock at $10 a share. A week later it dropped to $8. There is no fundamental reason why the price dropped. The company has in fact reported higher earnings than expected.

_____ This couldn't have happened to me—I never would have bought a common stock.

_____ I would buy more.

_____ I would wait until I got even and then sell.

_____ I would sell now. I obviously made a mistake.

_____ I would watch the stock closely. If it dropped any more, I would sell.

2. My stockbroker phoned to tell me that the oil and gas partnership in which I invested $10,000 has folded. All my money is lost. My reaction?

_____ I would never again invest in oil and gas partnerships.

_____ I would be more careful about my choice next time.

_____ It happens! I knew it was a risky investment when I invested.

_____ This couldn't have happened to me. I would never have invested in an oil and gas partnership.

3. I have money in a tax-deferred annuity. I've just read that several insurance companies that sell annuities are in serious financial trouble. In fact, one has gone bankrupt, costing thousands of people their life's savings.

_____ I would withdraw all of my money from the annuity and put it into something safe.

_____ I would check the financial strength of the insurance company that issued my annuity. If there were a problem I would transfer to a stronger company.

_____ I would never have invested in an annuity.

4. I might decide to put my savings into a tax-free fund.

_____ Because I realize I am paying too much tax on the interest my savings account earns.

_____ I would never take such a risk with my savings account.

_____ I might put part of my savings in such an investment, but I would still keep a savings account for the larger portion.

5. I've heard from a very reliable source that the Orange Computer Company is about to be bought by IBM. As a result the stock price will likely double. I've been cautioned that I am to tell absolutely no one.

_____ I would buy as many shares of Orange Computer as I could.

_____ I would ignore the rumor.

_____ I would call my broker to ask her to check the rumor. If she said it was possible, I would buy a small amount.

_____ I would spend hours investigating the rumor. I would check a wide range of sources and then act accordingly.

6. A new type of mutual fund is described in _The Wall Street Journal_. The article claims it is ideal for a person in my circumstances.

_____ I probably wouldn't have read the article since I don't read the _Journal_.

_____ I wouldn't have fully understood the investment, but since the _Journal_ so strongly recommended it, I would buy some.

_____ I would call my stockbroker to ask whether she thinks I should buy the fund.

_____ I would call the fund to get a copy of the prospectus so that I could study it further.

And how did you answer the questionnaire?

Question 1 was designed to measure your tolerance for investment disappointment. If you can't stand the idea of losing some money, investments that fluctuate in price are not for you.

Question 2 is a test of your knowledge of tax shelters. Uncle Sam allows generous deductions to entice investors to undertake greater than normal risks with their money. If you don't ever want to put your money in a position to be wiped out, avoid tax shelters.

Question 3 is a subtle reminder that *every* investment involves risk. You must constantly balance risk against reward and make judgments that the trade-offs are fair. Simply because an investment similar to yours goes bad is not a reason to panic out of your investment. It is a reminder to check on its condition, however.

Question 4 is about your willingness to make a change in the way you lead your investment life when all the good reasons in the world tell you that you should. A halfhearted response is not good enough. To be a successful investor you must be willing to make changes.

Question 5: It is your money, no one else's. *Before you invest, investigate*. I assure you that unless the person who passed the rumor on to you mortgaged his home and ransomed his children to raise every dime he could to buy every share he could, there is a good chance that the rumor is worth every penny you paid to hear it. Invest if you must, accordingly. This question was designed to test how impulsive an investor you are. Keep in mind that impulsive investors are usually Wall Street's biggest losers.

And the final question has to do with how you make investment decisions. Wiser investors *study, think*, and then *act*. They almost never rely on one source only for their ideas, and they always check their sources.

The idea behind these exercises is to force you to think about where you belong as an investor. Frequently our greatest obstacle to financial success is ourself. Know yourself, the limits of your knowledge, the financial habits you most would like to change, and the shortcomings you see in the way you respond to change, and you can't help but be a much smarter investor.

3

Mutual Funds

HOW TO WIN ON WALL STREET

IT IS NOT EASY to consistently make money in the stock and bond markets. It is especially difficult for people who lack the time to devote to that endeavor. Many investors quite understandably feel like holiday gamblers when it comes to picking investments. They are well aware that the professionals at the table, given enough time, will wipe them out.

Truly wealthy people understand that feeling and have learned to cope with it. I maintain that you can learn a great deal about managing your money by watching how the truly wealthy do it. Unless "making money" is their business, you will find that most let others do for them what others can do better. They surround themselves with topnotch people and let those people do their job. Good professional money-managers can be unemotional when we might feel frantic, can be patient when we might be hurried, and the best possess an uncanny ability to make decisions based on imperfect information—while the amateurs are running with the crowd.

Money managers who spend all of their time at their craft, who understand the markets and the tools of the markets, who read the right publications, who talk to the right people, who can take the time to do careful research, will usually outperform those of us without the time to do this. There is also something intangible that top-quality professional money-managers bring to the funds. It's a "feel," an "intuition," or an "instinct" for the markets that most of us will never possess. Just as most of us will never play professional golf, become stunt pilots or tournament bridge players. Investing well is a unique skill.

Very wealthy people hire professional money-managers to invest their money. Many others who understand that they don't need or want the social, psychological, or emotional gratification of being directly involved in the stock market have turned their money-management choices over to professionals. Let's face it. Many people simply don't care to learn the difference between a stock's P/E and their children's gym class or the Fed's M-2 and James Bond's boss. Let someone else, they argue, lose sleep about the supply of money, the size of deficits, and the direction of interest rates. Their own deficits—i.e., mortgage, car, and credit card payments—are enough day-to-day monetary worries. Let someone else worry about stocks, bonds, and money markets.

Any of us can do the same by using mutual funds. Mutual funds are nothing more than professionally *managed* securities portfolios. They are extremely easy to use. We can invest in most with modest sums. Dividends are paid quarterly or they can be automatically reinvested. Because they exist, we can combine our money with the money of thousands of other people to be invested by experts in our choice of financial markets. The concept is identical to that of the popular money-market funds that allow us access to the multibillion-dollar money market—a financial marketplace dominated by institutions able to make multimillion-dollar investments. Until 1972, when money-market funds came into existence, individuals without millions of dollars to invest were locked out of that market.

By pooling our money with the money of thousands of other investors, we can now earn the same interest rates that were until recently available only to the very, very wealthy. Other types of mutual funds exist that allow us access to every type of financial market. They allow us to hire the best money managers there are, and allow us the further benefit of *diversifica-*

tion. Diversification is the ability of a fund to spread our money over a number of investments. Diversification protects against having too many eggs in the wrong basket and allows the opportunity to be in a number of different baskets. We can even diversify among mutual funds to include some high-flyers, where the largest opportunities for gains are possible, in our investment portfolio.

Mutual funds allow us to custom-tailor an investment program that is best suited to our goals and personality. They are ideal investments for everyone from the Financial Basket-Case to the Financial Junkie.

BUT WHAT IN THE WORLD ARE THEY?

Mutual funds can seem like strange and mysterious money packages if a person doesn't entirely understand the securities of which they are composed. For those who need a quick review, this story should help.

Let's pretend that you and I form a company to manufacture a marvelous cigarette-smoke-eating machine. The machine is terrific. It turns cigarette smoke into a very discreet scent of flowers. For example, Winstons no longer just taste good—they now smell like roses, Camels smell like petunias, Lucky Strikes like lilies, and the Marlboro man has a slight but unmistakable odor of a bed of tulips. Our invention is so effective that it has caused the tail ends of airplanes to smell like English gardens and has lent to some restaurants the sweet fragrance of flower stands. Smokers love it because nonsmokers no longer find cigarette odor offensive. Smokers aren't forced any longer to put up with the constant griping and complaining of nonsmokers. Our machine proves that nonsmokers never really cared about the physical well-being of their smoking friends. All their warnings about charcoaled lungs, yellowing teeth, wrinkled skin, graveled voices, and "death by cancer" were a subterfuge. It turned out that nonsmokers simply couldn't stand cigarette odor or cigarette smoke. Once those nasties were removed, they stopped griping. Cigars are welcome after dinner because our machine turns cigar smoke into the scent of carnations. Pipes are welcome on airplanes because Sir Walter Raleigh smells something like a pansy.

Our smoke-eating machine is such a huge success that we can't build them fast enough to meet the demand. We need to build a factory for our company, which we modestly named "The Sweet Smell of Success." Factories cost lots of money to build. There are several ways to raise the money.

1. We could borrow it. To do that we might issue bonds. Bonds are IOUs. They are promises to repay those who have lent us the money when the bonds come due and to periodically pay interest on the money we have borrowed. The due date is called maturity. Normally, interest is paid twice a year. The bondholder is due interest payments and to be repaid for the amount of the original loan. Bondholders don't share in the success of our company. They are simply persons to whom we owe money. There are mutual funds that invest in bonds. People buy them to receive income. Since these funds own many different bonds, most will pay interest to the bond-fund holders monthly. The manager of a bond mutual-fund buys and sells bonds to take advantage of changing interest rates and to protect the quality of the portfolio. For example, if The Sweet Smell of Success Company began to have some financial difficulty, the mutual-fund manager might choose to sell our bonds out of his portfolio. An average investor may not be paying attention to the financial condition of our company and continue to hold our bonds to his or her detriment.

2. Another way to raise the money to build our factory would be to sell part of our company to others. We would do that by selling common stock. When we sell bonds we incur a debt that we must repay. We also incur the liability of having to make regular interest payments. Common stocks, on the other hand, require no such payments. The value of the shares of common stock rises and falls with the fate of the company. If the company does well, the price of its common stock should rise. If it does poorly, the price should fall. A common-stock investor buys the stock not because he is promised the return of his money plus interest, but because he expects the stock's price to go up. If it does, he can sell it to take his profit.

Common-stock owners may also be paid dividends. These

are a share of the profits that the Bo...
company may decide to pay. Usually
quarterly. Some companies pay them,
Since ours is a new company we will p
our profits back into the company to h...
pay dividends. An older, better establis...
need for capital will usually pay a dividen...
owners. There are mutual funds that inves...
companies like ours, others that invest in olde...,
companies, and others that invest in a combination of both
types, as well as those that invest in both bonds and stocks.
Other mutual funds invest in specific types of companies, and
there are those that invest in companies located in specific
geographical regions. What all of these funds have in common
is that their value will rise and fall with the value of the securities in their portfolios. When you invest in mutual funds
you are hiring professionals to choose and manage those securities.

A shrewd portfolio manager might have spotted our company just as it was beginning to enjoy success. Investors in his
or her fund would have done well even though most would not
even know our company stock was included in their fund. That
is the beauty of using a mutual fund. It takes you out of the day-
to-day process of making investment decisions. Not all fund
managers are equal. Some might have missed our company
entirely. Some might have bought our stock too late or sold too
soon. Mutual funds are no better or worse than their people.
As you evaluate funds always keep in mind that when you
remove all the trappings, all a mutual fund is, is someone who
picks investments with your money. Let's talk about how to
find the right someone.

"T. Rowe Price . . . Leslie Smith speaking," the confident
voice at the other end of the phone answered. I was already
impressed. The phone had been picked up after the first ring.

"Ms. Smith, this is Wayne Nelson calling. I'm interested in
receiving some information about the T. Rowe Price New
Horizons Fund."

"Certainly," she said. "Can I have your mailing address?"

had given it she said, "Let me just repeat that."

training, I thought. She is making sure that she has
t information. That is smart because when people are a
le nervous (as we might be when making a phone call to a
stranger about investments), they can transpose numbers,
even those in their own address.

"I'll be sending out a prospectus on our New Horizons
Fund to you. May I ask where you heard about the New Horizons Fund?"

"In a *Money* magazine mutual-fund survey." That should
impress her, I thought.

She thanked me and said, "If you have any further questions please be sure to call."

That was easy! Less than two minutes had passed. I had
overcome my anxiety about making that first call to an investment firm and had actually made contact with the famous T.
Rowe Price mutual-fund organization in Baltimore. The
founder of the firm that bears his name was a pioneer of
growth-stock investing in the 1930s. It was also his idea to
begin investing in the early 1960s in what are now called
emerging growth stocks. It was T. Rowe Price's "mystical fore-
sight," according to *Forbes* Magazine, that led to his creating
the New Horizons Fund with a charter to invest exclusively in
those stocks. T. Rowe Price won the reputation as one who
could see "meaningful patterns where others saw only uncon-
nected events." He was a legendary investor who created an
investment firm that is now one of the best known in America.
My conversation with Leslie Smith turned out to be a non-
threatening, even pleasant experience. Leslie Smith sounded
like the sort of person I would ask for again if I ever had a
question.

Ms. Smith had been carefully selected and thoroughly
trained to make me feel comfortable and secure. She is one of a
new breed of specialists whom all of the no-load (that is, no
sales commission) mutual funds employ. At T. Rowe Price the
shareholder service representatives are usually part-time grad-
uate students or well-educated housewives returning to the
work force. Most have attended the same colleges as stock-

brokers at brokerage firms. The only difference is that the housewives got better grades—then went off to have babies.

Ms. Smith is not a salesperson and is not allowed to talk potential investors into buying a fund. Her job is to answer questions, to provide information and service. But every good fund organization knows that how well Ms. Smith and others like her do their job directly affects sales. The authors of *In Search of Excellence* remind us that the values of an organization are set by the leader. Every employee with whom you will deal as a customer is a reflection of what the person running the organization thinks of the organization, and of you. The kind of service you get on your first call is a good indication of the response you might get later when you have a service problem or administrative question.

Just as Ms. Smith promised, a New Horizons Fund prospectus, a brochure about the fund, and an application arrived a few days later.

After I read the material I decided to invest $5000 in the fund. I completed the application and mailed the check. The investment was made the day my check arrived at the State Street Bank and Trust. I received a confirmation indicating my purchase price and date as well as a letter from Ed Mathias, the fund's president. I was a shareholder.

Each day, Mr. Mathias and mutual-fund managers throughout the country get a computer printout indicating how much money was deposited in the fund and how much was withdrawn. At T. Rowe Price amounts over $50,000 are listed separately, and it is not uncommon for Mr. Mathias to pick up the phone to call investors who are withdrawing large amounts to ask why. Good money managers show that sort of concern, and Ed Mathias is one of the country's best.

Fund managers tend to keep a certain amount of cash in money-market instruments to meet liquidations. The rest is available for investment in stocks identified by the firm's analysts as good candidates. While the research specialists identify good stocks, always remember that a mutual fund can be no better than its manager, who is ultimately responsible for each investment choice. For the New Horizons Fund, Ed Mathias picks the stocks and decides how much of each stock the fund will own. Once he has made his choices, the T. Rowe Price stock traders go into action. They execute Mr. Mathias's buy-and-sell instruction. When they buy a large number of shares of a small growth company, it must be done carefully and over time. If not, their own buying could drive the price up artificially. Just as selling a large position could shatter that stock's market price.

As the value of the portfolio of stocks held by the fund goes up and down, so will the value of your shares of the New Horizons Fund. The price is quoted every day in the newspaper. Each share price is the total value of the portfolio divided by the number of shares of the fund. That is also referred to as the fund's net asset value. When you see two prices quoted for a fund, the first price is called the *bid* and the other the *ask* price. The ask price differs from the bid price for load funds. It is the net asset value plus the maximum sales fee the fund charges. The more money you invest in a load fund, the less that fee will be. Usually the sales fee begins to decline for orders of $10,000 or greater. I've included an entire section about mutual-fund fees. It begins on page 60.

HOW TO READ A PROSPECTUS

The idea was to protect the investing public. To do that mutual funds were to provide potential investors with something called a prospectus. But like many good ideas that have been turned over to government lawyers to implement, the results of their efforts are almost incomprehensible. As you read a prospectus it becomes clear that clarity has been sacrificed for complexity. Whenever six simple words could have been used, twelve nonsensical ones have been substituted. Fortunately, you don't need to read the entire prospectus. Your task is simply to discover the answers to these three fundamental questions. If the answers are not in the prospectus, ask the fund to send a copy of its Statement of Additional Information—or call the fund to ask.

1. What Does the Fund Want to Do and How Will It Do It?

This section tells you how aggressive or conservative the fund's manager will be and what types of investments that manager may use to achieve his or her objectives. Sometimes the types of investments the fund is prohibited from making can give an even clearer idea about itself than its list of current investments. Make sure your objectives and those of the fund are in agreement. A fund that can move into cash when the manager thinks it is time can save you some market tumbles. Some funds aren't allowed.

My radio program is broadcast from three to five every Sunday afternoon in Washington, D.C., on WRC radio. I do it during beautiful summer days as well as those gray, dreary, winter days when there is little better going on. I've also done it during two Redskin Super Bowls. Many mutual funds work exactly that way. Their charter may call for them to be *fully invested* in oil stocks while the world suffers the greatest oil glut it has ever known and Texas oilmen make their living pumping oil back into the ground. If being fully invested in oil stocks, for example, happens to be the fund strategy, you should know so that you can sit out the glut in some other investment rather than hope the fund manager will. Like Wayne Nelson broadcasting about money questions during the Super Bowl, he may not have a choice.

2. What Are Its Holdings?

By carefully reading a restaurant's menu you can get a good idea whether the chef specializes in fish or lamb. Count the number of dishes of each. A fund's investment list can similarly give you an excellent idea of the manager's investment philosophy. What type of companies does he or she like? How diversified are his investments? Since this list needn't be updated more than once every sixteen months, don't settle for this list alone. Pick up the phone and call the fund to get a current list of its ten largest holdings. They can give it to you over the phone. Look for a pattern of investing or clues to the fund's personality from the types of investments in the portfolio. Low price-earnings ratios tend to indicate a conservative fund manager. A large number of stocks indicates a desire to be well diversified. Higher dividends tend to point to more established companies in a common-stock portfolio.

3. Are They Writing to You?

The quality of a mutual-fund organization, or lack of it, the concern for you as a customer, and the respect for your intelligence are demonstrated in a variety of ways. How clearly do they explain what they do? Is their literature honest? When mutual funds write about their performance record, Reg Green, the director of information for the Investment Company Institute, the largest trade association for mutual funds, says that we should ask: "Do they say how well they did in relation to others? Did they give *good* reasons for their performance? How much did they disclose? How well do you understand what they write?" You can safely ignore the performance chart. Keep in mind that it is the work of a talented artist whose job is to make the best drawing of whatever the fund's performance has been. Since different time periods are used by different funds, you won't be able to compare one chart with another for performance ratings. Refer to the widely respected Lipper Analytical Survey in *Barron's* quarterly issue, or the annual rankings reported in the August issue of *Forbes*, the November issue of *Money*, or the October issue of *Changing Times*. Good libraries and most stockbrokerage branch offices will have a current copy of *The Weisenberger Investment Company Services*, the *Johnson Chart* book, or *The United Mutual Fund Selector*.

Forbes Magazine also publishes an annual mutual-fund honor roll. To be a member of the honor role, a fund must do well in both up and down markets. This is *Forbes's* most recent list.

The officers and directors can also be ignored. Unless they are notably inexperienced, the qualifications of the board will tell you nothing. Every mutual fund adds "name" players to its board. Few have any impact on their investment policy or performance.

CHART 3-1. At the Head of the Class

These 25 funds excel in both up and down return since Sept. 30, 1974, at least three markets and have a compound annual points above that of the S&P's 500.

Name (years on honor roll)	Type	Market ratings UP	DOWN	Annual return	Assets (mil)	Lead Manager (years)
Acorn	no load	B	B	24.0%	$171.5	Ralph Wanger (14)
Amcap (6)	load	B	B	24.7	924.1	Fund has 3 managers
American Capital Comstock (4)	load	A	B	27.8	538.9	George Adler (1)
American Capital Convert Sec*	closed end	A+	A	23.3	67.4	Fund has 3 managers
American Capital Pace (3)	load	A	B	29.7	1,125.2	John Doney (5)
American Capital Venture (2)	load	A	B	30.8	371.2	Steve Hayward (1)
Baker, Fentress & Co	closed end	A	B	26.9	301.3	George H. Smith (14)‡
Central Securities	closed end	A+	B	27.7	89.7	Wilmot Kidd (11)
Claremont Capital	closed end	A	A	35.2	41.3	Erik Bergstrom (8)
Fidelity Density (2)	load	A	B	26.9	533.2	George Vanderheiden (4)
Fidelity Equity-Income	load	B	B	24.3	841.6	Bruce Johnstone (13)
Fidelity Magellan (3)	load	A+	B	34.7	1,613.7	Peter Lynch (7)
General American Investors (5)	closed end	B	B	22.3	223.2	Malcolm Smith (23)
Growth Fund of America (2)	load	B	A	22.2	434.6	Fund has 3 managers
Janus (3)	no load	B	B	19.7	281.7	Thomas Bailey (15)
The Japan Fund (7)	closed end	B	B	23.2	264.7	Timothy Schilt (1)†
Mutual Shares (9)	no load	B	A	25.4	370.3	Max Heine (9)‡
Nicholas (3)	no load	B	B	25.7	157.1	Albet Nicholas (15)
Over-The-Counter Securities (3)	load	B	B	23.5	77.8	Binkley Shorts (3)
Pennsylvania Mutual	no load	A	A	30.9	145.6	Charles Royce (11)
Phoenix Convertible Fund Series*	load	B	B	19.4	58.6	John Martin (3)
Pioneer II (3)	load	B	B	25.1	1,231.4	David Tripple (10)
Source Capital	closed end	B	A+	38.2	239.9	George Michaelis (6)
Templeton Growth (11)	load	B	B	20.9	842.9	John Templeton (30)
Windsor (6)	no load	B	A	22.8	1,887.3	John Neff (20)

*Balanced fund.   †Founder of fund still acts as chairman.   ‡Fund has two managers.

4

How to Pick
a Mutual Fund

MOST INVESTORS DON'T KNOW HOW to pick the right mutual funds. They inevitably turn to the most recent annual performance rating and pick last year's hot fund. That is almost always a mistake for at least four good reasons.

1. *Anyone can have one good year in a row.* George Russel, president of Frank Russel and Co., advises thirty-seven different corporate pension funds about selecting money managers. *The Wall Street Journal* calls him the most powerful person in the multibillion-dollar money-management business. He says that you are more likely to make money picking last year's losers than the winners. The reason—different strategies work in different market environments—and the market environment is almost certain to be different this year than it was last.

2. *Last year's hot fund tends to attract more capital than most managers can successfully handle.* As a result of the sudden inflow of new money, the hot hands become hand-holders forced to cope with new administrative duties, to supervise a larger staff, while at the same time finding even more hot stocks in which to invest the additional new money. Most studies show that funds *under* $100 million in size regularly outperform their larger brothers.

3. *Last year's hot-stock fund manager suddenly believes that he is a genius.* Magazines write articles about him. The PBS television program "Wall Street Week" praises him, newspapers call him whenever the market goes up or down for his brilliant observations, seminars all over the world feature him as a speaker, and guess what? He doesn't have much time to manage his fund. Worse yet, he may even begin to believe it himself.

4. *One-year performance records are especially vulnerable if the fund is a specialty or niche fund.* The shelf life of a fad fund is about as long as the popularity of the Hula-Hoops and Nehru jackets. Single industries often become overvalued. After flashing into our consciousness like a meteor they simply disappear from the radar screen. Nobody talks about them. Gradually they sink into the oblivion we reserve for our friends.

If you use past performance to help make your fund selection, the experts who run mutual funds say that you should base your judgment on a fund's performance *over the last five years* or even a full market cycle. Judge performance, they say, based on both a good and bad market. I learned that from a questionnaire I sent to the president of every mutual-fund organization in America. There are other answers from the survey that should help you make your mutual fund selection. This is a copy of the letter and questionnaire that I sent.

MUTUAL-FUND SURVEY FOR PRESIDENTS OF MUTUAL-FUND ORGANIZATIONS

I am writing an investment book about how to evaluate and choose money packages—mutual funds, limited partnerships, and unit trusts. It will be published by Putnam in 1985.

This letter has been sent to the president of every mutual-fund organization. Its purpose is to ask for a couple of minutes of your time to complete and return the attached questionnaire. The results of this survey will be included in my book. I will send you a copy from the first printing.

Thank you for taking your time to hopefully help investors who struggle with so many challenging choices.

MUTUAL-FUND QUESTIONNAIRE

In your opinion, which five mutual-fund organizations do you admire most? (Please rank from highest to lowest.)

1._____
2._____
3._____
4._____
5._____

Which do you admire least?

1._____
2._____
3._____
4._____
5._____

If investors give up on your fund, is it because of its (rank 1, 2, 3)
_____ Performance
_____ Service
_____ Communication
_____ A different reason (Explain)
_____
_____

Regarding investment performance over different lengths of time, how long is a long enough performance record on which to base an investment decision?

_____ One year
_____ Two years
_____ Three years
_____ Four years
_____ Five years
_____ Number of years is not an important determinant

How many years should you give a fund to perform before you decide you've made a mistake and sell?

_____ One year
_____ Two years
_____ Three years
_____ Four years
_____ Number of years is not an important determinant

You would advise an investor to choose a mutual fund based on:

1._____   4._____
2._____   5._____
3._____   6._____

HOW MANY YEARS SHOULD YOU GIVE A FUND TO PERFORM BEFORE YOU DECIDE YOU'VE MADE A MISTAKE AND SELL?

Again, the experts either checked three to five years or wrote, "a full market cycle." I believe the lesson in this is that the fund managers would like you to give your mutual fund time to work. Many of the managers mentioned the market-timing services. They called them a nuisance. From the fund manager's perspective it is hard enough to manage money without having waves of it coming and going with each perceived blip in the market. *In Search of Excellence* used the term "simultaneous loose tight properties" as one of the eight reasons certain American corporations are better managed than others. Applied to supervising your money in a mutual fund, that characteristic may be interpreted as meaning "get out of the kitchen." Let the managers run the fund. Monitor its performance no more than quarterly—certainly not weekly or monthly—and forget the timing services. *No one can call market turns. Absolutely no one!* By trading your funds you are probably overmanaging your account, and according to many fund managers may even be contributing to its poor performance.

YOU WOULD ADVISE AN INVESTOR TO CHOOSE A MUTUAL FUND BASED ON:

1. How well it serves personal investment goals: Make sure the philosophy of the fund matches your own.
2. The performance of the fund over time.
3. The quality of the fund's management.
4. How well the fund provides services and communication.
5. Its belonging to a family of funds.

This is the advice about how to pick a mutual fund from the presidents of those funds. It is ranked in order of importance. Only two respondents even mentioned fees or commissions.

And yet, from nearly everything you read about mutual funds you would think that whether a fund is a load or no-load is the most important criterion on which to base your selection. Wrong!

What Is a Load Fund?

Load is not one of "those" four-letter words. It simply means sales commission, or fee that a stockbrokerage firm, financial planner, or investment salesperson receives for selling you a mutual fund. A large number of funds such as T. Rowe Price can be bought directly from the mutual-fund organization. Because they don't charge a sales commission, these funds are called "no-load." It is not much of a challenge to find reading material about no-load funds. So many financial publications, newsletters, and books have emerged to provide information about them that the no-load periodical business is, hands down, the biggest cottage industry in the investment world.

Even though it is trendy for financial writers to recommend no-load funds only, I must tell you that such advice is wrong. "Load" has nothing to do with performance and never has. Interestingly, that is the central argument of those who recommend only no-load funds. They say that since load and no-load funds as a group have equivalent performance records, why pay a commission for performance that you can get without paying one? Since that is so, the other side of the argument must be—if the performance records are equal, why should you limit your choices to only half of the funds available to you? By so doing you eliminate too many excellent choices, and that is not in your best interest.

When you look at mutual-fund performance results, keep in mind that the result for each fund *is after all the fees have been subtracted*. Keep in mind also that all funds charge some type of fees. As much fun as it might be to work for T. Rowe Price or manage money at Fidelity, as far as I know there is not a single person at those organizations who is working for free. It also costs to do the fancy printing, to keep the electricity going, and to purchase ads in major newspapers throughout the United

States. And even no-load funds need to pay bright (expensive) people to encourage you to buy their funds. That is, unless you believe that only investment houses like Merrill Lynch and Shearson/American Express attract people who like to make money.

More confusing yet is that the distinction between full loads and no-loads is becoming blurred. Many of the so-called no-load funds pay their expenses by charging investors hidden loads, back-end loads, contingent deferred sales charges, redemption or switching fees. So that you will know what they are, I am going to explain each. *My bottom-line advice is, however, that fees should not be the determining factor when it comes to picking your mutual fund.*

Hidden loads come disguised as account start-up fees, annual maintenance fees, or management fees. A contingent deferred sales charge is a fee that is levied if you sell a fund before a certain amount of time has elapsed. For example, a fund may be offered to you without a front-end load, and in this example no load will ever be charged if you hold the fund for at least four years. If you sell early, a load will be subtracted from the amount of your withdrawal. Some of these funds have a descending scale of charges for early sale. The first year's penalty might be 4 percent, the second year 3 percent, and so on. Some funds assess the charge only on the amount of the original investment. Let us say that you invested $10,000 and in two years the fund grew to $15,000. At the time you withdraw the entire $15,000, your penalty would be 4 percent of $10,000. Other funds will charge the penalty against the entire $15,000.

When mutual funds charge a penalty for withdrawal that never disappears, that fee is called a back-end load. If the fund charges to switch from one of the funds in their family of funds to another it is a redemption, or switching fee. Some funds permit a limited number of switches without a fee. Some will charge a fee if the number of switches becomes excessive. If you are planning to aggressively manage your funds, a fee of this sort is obviously a detriment.

There are over two hundred no-load funds now established as 12b-1 plans. Such an arrangement allows them to deduct promotion and marketing expenses from the fund's assets.

Some of those expenses could be sales commissions to brokers. And of course there are the low loads. These are funds that charge less than the highest commissions charged by the majority of funds sold by stockbrokers and financial planners, but more than the no-loads. Typical up-front sales commissions for low loads are in the 2 to 4 percent range, versus 7 to 8½ percent for full-load funds. It is only a matter of time before you will be able to negotiate the sales charge for mutual-fund purchases. Different brokerage firms are certain to have different policies about discounting, but the result should be a considerable savings to individuals who make mutual-fund purchases.

What You Should Expect for a Sales Commission

If you accept the notion that a person who is being paid a commission to sell you a mutual fund can't be entirely objective about his or her recommendation, you can be a much more demanding mutual-fund purchaser.

Presumably you pay someone for recommendations because you don't enjoy the "hunt!" According to Edward A. Taber, III, vice president of T. Rowe Price, for many people the choice of a mutual fund is a result of a combination of fatigue and indifference. Many investors are happy to pay someone else to go through the selection struggle for them. That someone should be very familiar with the mutual-fund industry. He or she should be able to talk about performance, fees, and the fund's investment strategy off the top of his or her head. Be careful of those who tell you that they need to check on answers to your most basic questions. There are salespeople who specialize in mutual funds and know the industry well. Others deal with funds only casually, and may base their advice on something they heard at lunch from another stockbroker. To help you find the right broker, call the office manager and ask for recommendations for the top mutual-fund salesperson in the office.

Make certain from the beginning that the salesperson will help you monitor the performance of the fund. Be sure to let that person know that you want to be advised, if in his or her judgment, it is an appropriate time to switch. You need to do this for two reasons: (1) Since the sales fee is paid up front, some brokers lose interest in their investors once the purchase has been made. (2) Others, conscious of the high sales fee they received, are reluctant to advise investors to switch, thus generating another fee and perhaps being accused of "churning" your account. Churning is an offense that can bring stiff penalties. Switching out of one fund into another is looked on with such disfavor that a broker's office manager must usually approve such a recommendation.

You can avoid those fees and this problem by selecting a mutual fund that belongs to a family of funds offering several choices. Be certain that before you make your purchase you tell the salesperson that you want advice about switching, and expect a call at least once a year about the fund's performance, about whether or not there have been any key management changes, and whether to discuss if the fund's objectives continue to match your own.

Your salesperson is also there to help you with any administrative problems, to interpret any confusing communication from the fund, to do your legwork, and to stimulate you to stick with your investment program. Payment of a commission *entitles* you to prompt and knowledgeable service. From a good salesperson all of this is worth every penny you pay to get it.

There is one plan that is definitely too expensive. That is a contractual plan.

Contractual Plans

To belong to a contractual program you must sign a contract agreeing to make fixed, regular payments to the fund. In this respect they are something like a forced savings plan. Investors who might not otherwise have the discipline to set aside money regularly use them for the incentive they provide, but it is a costly mistake. The sales commission is *very* high. In some cases it is over 50 percent of your first year's investment. That is at least four times higher than the highest-load funds, most of which can be bought in relatively modest increments as regularly as you want. To make matters worse there are sometimes account-maintenance fees in addition to the normal management expenses. Contractual plans make little sense and should be avoided. Unfortunately they are being sold to the sort of people who don't take the time to read investment articles that would warn them about that. They are true financial basketcases.

IN YOUR OPINION, WHICH FIVE MUTUAL-FUND ORGANIZATIONS DO YOU ADMIRE MOST? (PLEASE RANK FROM HIGHEST TO LOWEST.)

Good organizations hire good people, and when it comes right down to the most basic issue, your choice of a mutual fund is a choice of people. *Fortune* told the story of a Honda factory worker who on his way home from the factory each evening straightens up the windshield wiper blades on all of the Hondas he passes. He does this because he just can't stand to see a flaw in a Honda. We all know companies that have similar pride in their products. As investors you will learn about mutual funds that exhibit a genuine concern for their people, their customers, and their products. By listening to what other customers and competitors are saying about an organization, you will be able to make some very intelligent investment decisions.

The most admired fund groups are:

1. T. Rowe Price
2. Fidelity
3. Massachusetts Financial
4. (tied) Pioneer, Putnam, and Vanguard

Honorable mentions include Twentieth Century, Kemper, and Capital Research.

There was no consensus on which to base a ranking of least-admired funds.

IF INVESTORS GIVE UP ON YOUR FUND, IT IS BECAUSE OF ITS (RANK 1, 2, 3)

1. Performance
2. Service
3. Communication
4. Timing services
5.. Need for cash

YOUR WIDE RANGE OF CHOICES AMONG MUTUAL FUNDS

Mutual funds are generally separated into categories. The most conservative are the income funds. The most speculative are aggressive-growth funds. Chart 4-1 illustrates your range of choices, from conservative to speculative: I am going to describe each type of fund for you in this chapter.

CHART 4-1

Most Conservative Mutual Funds to Most Speculative →

Major Categories:	Income	Balanced	Growth & Income	Growth	Aggressive Growth
Tax status of income from each type	Taxable and tax-free	Taxable only	Taxable only	Taxable only	Taxable only
Other characteristics	Can be bonds of short-, medium-, and long-term maturities		Can include option/income funds		Can be called capital-appreciation funds and option growth funds

A group of specialty funds also exists. They may invest in gold or natural resources or stocks of foreign companies or even stocks of companies located in specific geographic regions. In this section I will explain the purpose for each of these fund categories and list funds that belong to each. This should enable you to match your objectives to the funds that are available to you.

Keep in mind that different types of funds perform better in different markets. In a roaring bull-market, aggressive-growth funds generally excel. When interest rates are on the decline, income funds can do much better than provide a high level of income, and when particular market sectors are on the move the right specialty trend can be a spectacular performer. No one fund is an investment for all seasons. That is why diversifying among a number of good funds makes sense. Also keep your objectives, concerns, feelings, needs, and tax status in mind. Make your choices based on those rather than on how appealing the fund sounds. And keep your investment mix simple. John Templeton, one of the most successful mutual-fund managers of all time, constantly reminds people to keep their investment decisions, in his words, "simpleminded." It is a mistake to make your investment life any more complicated than it need be.

If you plan to use specialty funds I don't believe that it is wise to invest more than 10 percent of your assets in any one area. Special segments of the markets are generally more volatile than the market as a whole. The next chapter is about specialty funds. The more money you have to invest, the larger the number of fund managers you should use. AT&T has many more managers for its pension funds than does U.S. Air. The

CHART 4-2

Amount of Money to Invest	Number of Different Funds
$1,000–$10,000	2–3
$10,000–$25,000	4–5
$25,000–$100,000	5–6
$100,000–$500,000	6–10
$500,000 plus	10

amount of money involved is vastly different. This does not include money-market funds, where there is little purpose in having more than one.

Many mutual funds belong to families. Each member of the family is a different type of fund. The largest mutual-fund families in order of size are:

Merrill Lynch
Federated Research
Fidelity
Dreyfus
Shearson/American Express

Kemper
Dean Witter Reynolds
IDS (Investors Diversified Services)

A complete listing of mutual funds, with their addresses and phone numbers, may be found in the appendix.

MUTUAL FUNDS VERSUS INFLATION

Common stock and even some of the new, aggressively managed bond funds have historically proven to be an effective hedge against inflation. Chart 4-3 is a vivid demonstration of that fact.

As you look at the chart, keep in mind that the zero (0) at the bottom of each chart indiicates when the return on stocks or bonds was equal to the inflation rate. Those years to the right of zero are those in which either stocks or bonds beat inflation. The years to the left of the zero are those in which the inflation rate beat the performance of either stocks or bonds.

NICHEMANSHIP: THE ART OF BEING IN THE RIGHT NICHE

The traditional advantage of investing with a mutual fund rather than slugging it out in the stock market on your own is that a fund allows you to protect yourself by being well-diversified in a large number of stocks. Market swings will almost certainly affect you less in a fund than in any portfolio you put together yourself.

CHART 4-3
Common Stocks

Real Returns on Stocks
All 10-year periods 1926 to 1984, ending in years shown

Number of Periods (histogram of 10-year periods by real return bin):

Level	−4	−2	0	2	4	6	8	10	12	14	16
11							1942				
10							1944				
9							1945				
8						1941	1950				
7						1943	1951				
6				1937		1947	1952	1935			
5			1974	1938		1949	1954	1936			
4			1975	1946	1939	1953	1955	1957	1956		1961
3			1977	1973	1940	1969	1966	1960	1959	1958	1963
2			1978	1976	1948	1970	1968	1965	1964	1962	1982
1		1979	1981	1980	1971	1984	1972	1983	1967		

Annualized 10-year Rates of Return Minus Annualized 10-year Inflation as Measured by the Consumer Price Index, %

Real Returns on Bonds
All 10-year periods 1926 to 1984, ending in years shown

Number
of
Periods

Periods	-6	-5	-4	-3	-2	-1	0	1	2	3	4	5	6	7	8	9	10
12																	
11							1946										
10							1958										
9							1960										
8				1947	1950		1969										
7				1948	1951		1970		1944								
6				1949	1954		1971		1945								
5				1952	1956		1972	1957	1961								
4				1953	1959		1976	1965	1962								
3				1955	1973		1977	1967	1963								1935
2				1974	1975		1978	1968	1964	1943						1937	1936
1	1981			1980	1979		1983	1984	1966	1982	1942			1941	1940	1938	1939

Annualized 10-year-Rates of Return Minus Annualized 10-year Inflation as Measured by the Consumer Price Index, %.

Source: Peat, Marwick Mitchell & Co.

And now there is another advantage. It is the ability to use a fund to invest in a particular sector or niche of the financial market. For example, if you think gold is a good place to have some money, there are a number of gold funds from which you can pick. If you like energy stocks, you can pick an energy fund. If you like foreign stocks, pick an international or global mutual fund. The listings provided in the appendix should make picking a fund with a particular specialty easy for you to do. Remember while you are being a nicheman that you shouldn't be chasing last year's best idea with this year's money. The bubble of enthusiasm will eventually burst, leaving a crowd of mourners at the graveside of yet another investment that has lived its full, albeit short life. In general, there is not much to be said after the water has gone over the dam. The best advice might be to buy a sector fund when it is out of favor rather than when everyone including the hatcheck girl at the local McDonald's restaurant thinks it is a good idea.

INCOME FUNDS

This is a very general description of a wide variety of mutual-fund types, all of which are designed to provide some income to their shareholders. The amount of income varies considerably from one type of fund to another. Some funds invest in bonds only. Others invest in a combination of common stocks and bonds. Some invest in particular types of "debt" securities such as preferred stocks or convertible bonds. Some are managed aggressively. Others are almost unmanaged. The investment philosophy of the fund is described in the prospectus. Look at it because income funds *are* managed differently.

Investors use income funds to take advantage of professional management, professional portfolio selection, and to take advantage of turns in the marketplace that can make the investments worth more. They also use them to protect against having investments in their portfolio turn sour without their knowledge. Income funds offer the protection of diversification, which by its very nature minimizes risk. They also minimize price fluctuation. The size of your investment can be as little as $1000 and in some cases even less.

A more recent development that makes professional management even more advantageous is a fund manager's ability to use futures trading to hedge against unforeseen interest-rate turns. Hedging is a concept not usually understood or employed by most individual investors. It can be used to protect the value of a bond portfolio. If, for example, a bond-fund manager thinks interest rates will go up, he or she could sell Treasury-bond futures, agreeing to deliver bonds on some specified future date at a specific price—one he or she believes will be higher than the market price at the time. This can act as an insurance policy against significant price declines. If the fund's manager's guess is wrong and the price decline doesn't occur, the fund is out only the price of the option.

The most basic type of income fund is the one with which people are most familiar. It is the money-market fund or money-market account.

Money-Market Fund or Money-Market Account: What Is the Difference?

Banks and other savings institutions are permitted to offer money-market *accounts*. They do not offer money-market *funds*. The accounts are federally insured either by FDIC or FSLIC. The interest rate is arbitrarily set by the offering institution, and it is usually guaranteed for some fixed time period. As an investor in such a fund, government regulations allow you to write no more than three checks a month, limiting you to three fund transfers. An example of a transfer is switching money from the money-market account to your checking account. Some financial institutions charge transfer and check-writing fees as well. Federal law requires all institutions to set a minimum account balance of at least $2500, but each is free to set its own higher limit. If your balance drops below the limit, you will get a lesser rate of interest. Some banks and S&Ls pay passbook rates when that happens, while others pay no interest at all. Be sure to find out how the bank computes your balance. While at some you will lose the higher rate of interest only for those days when your balance dips below the minimum, others will penalize you for the entire month. Also ask about *all* the fees. In some cases there are fees for both opening and closing an account. These accounts are certainly better places to store funds than in your bank's passbook savings plan, but are less attractive than central-asset accounts.

CENTRAL-ASSET ACCOUNTS

Everyone should have one! I believe so strongly in them that I think people who don't have one are jeopardizing their financial future. These are the magic accounts that consolidate a wide range of financial services under one personal money-management plan. They are also the accounts through which nearly every new financial innovation will be delivered to you in the future. Today, central-asset accounts allow you to:

- Purchase securities and savings certificates.
- Automatically invest money that comes into the account—either checks you deposit or dividends from securities held in the account.
- Most central-asset accounts offer a choice of money-market funds, including the traditional money-market fund, a tax-free fund, one that invests in short-term U.S. Government securities only, and a banklike money-market account that is federally insured. (High-tax-bracket individuals should almost always use the tax-exempt fund—and almost always don't. This is an easily remedied investment mistake since you can move the funds from one fund to another by making a phone call.
- Draw cash from the account from virtually anywhere in the world, using the account's credit or debit card. Depending on the brokerage firm, the card could be VISA, Mastercard, or American Express.
- Enjoy a line of credit—either secured by securities held in the account or unsecured based on your creditworthiness.
- Enjoy a comprehensive monthly statement detailing all account activity. This is priceless at tax-preparation time.
- Write checks for any amount, usually without any check-writing fee.

Unfortunately, not all of these accounts are alike, so choosing one is not as easy as visiting the nearest brokerage firm or bank. Below is the checklist offered by Bill Donoghue, author of two best-selling books and the editor of *Donoghue's Money Letter*.* This checklist is quite useful in evaluating the various choices. Some of these services may not matter to you. They are on the checklist only to let you know that some firms offer them and others don't.

To find the highest money-market fund rates available and most competitive bank money-market fund rates, see Bill Donoghue's book called *The National Consumers Money Market Fund Directory*. It is available for only $10 by writing the Donoghue Organization, P. O. Box 411, Holliston, MA 01746.

CAA Checklist

If you're in the market for this kind of personal money-management plan, be sure to scrutinize all sales information and legal agreements. Here's a checklist of important points to consider when looking at a CAA:

- What is the minimum-balance requirement, and will they accept marketable securities as well as cash?
- How do the loan rates compare with the rates charged to non-CAA holders?
- Is the interest rate on your MMDA, NOW, or Super NOW account compounded daily, weekly, or monthly? Daily compounding means your earnings get back to work sooner.
- How much is the annual service fee, and is free checking included?
- Will you get a personal account representative?
- Are there additional services like estate, investment, and tax planning available?
- Will your checks be returned to you? Some brokerage houses do not return canceled checks to their CAA customers.
- What is used as your central account? Some CAAs let you choose from an MMDA, a money fund, or a tax-free money fund.
- Do you get a credit or debit card? A debit-card purchase deducts money from your account right away. A credit card can give you free credit for up to thirty days or more.

* $87 a year, The Donoghue Organization, PO Box 411, Holliston, MA 01746, (617) 429-5930.

- Will idle funds be swept into an interest-earning account daily, or will your money sit in a non-interest-bearing checking account for a period before it is put to work earning interest?
- What is the institution's reputation for service? If an account is being offered by a bank that is notorious for its poor service in your community, then it is best to steer clear of its CAA.
- What does the monthly statement look like? They vary in simplicity and clarity. Remember, the purpose of a CAA is to simplify your financial life.

TRADITIONAL MONEY-MARKET FUNDS

In the middle to late 1970s Americans woke up to the notion that they could make their money work extra hard for them by investing in money-market funds. By combining your money with that of thousands of other investors, many market-fund managers had enough to buy the same large-denomination money-market instruments that institutions bought. These instruments include bank certificates of deposit, short-term loans to corporations (called commercial paper) and government notes. All of these securities are short-term. Some last just overnight. Some over the weekend. Some for several days. Because they are short-term, their price fluctuates only slightly. That means that the money market is a very stable place to invest your savings dollars.

There are over three hundred different money-market funds from which to choose. Most mutual-fund families have a money fund as a member head of the family. Since there are so many choices, the best advice about picking one is to choose a money fund that is convenient to use, that is lenient about the minimum size of deposits and withdrawals, and that credits your deposits quickly. Old-fashioned money funds are like horse and buggies compared to the CAAs, which are like race cars. Money funds are better than passbook bank accounts, but most investors would be better served by upgrading to a CAA.

Rating Money-Market Funds

If you were the manager of a money-market fund invested

in the mix of money-market instruments that happened to meet the specifications established by the Standard and Poor's organization, you could pay $5000 to $15,000 to receive an AAA rating. If you managed a money fund with a different investment mix, or if you didn't care, you wouldn't spend the money to get the rating. I wouldn't spend the money. I think rating a money-market fund is frivolous—and the principal benefactor of such an exercise is the rating service that earns the fee. Money-market funds have proven themselves to be safe investments. I can't imagine why any fund manager would spend the money to buy the rating for any purpose other than to stimulate sales. And I can't imagine any investor other than the financial basket-case who would care whether the money-market fund he or she bought had a rating.

OTHER INCOME FUNDS

U.S. Government Bond Funds

These are funds that invest only in bonds issued by Uncle Sam. Some government funds invest only in direct U.S. obligations—such as Treasury bonds. Others invest in indirectly backed government bonds, such as those issued by various U.S. agencies including the Federal National Mortgage Association (Fannie Mae) or the U.S. Postal Service.

General Corporate Bond Funds

Invest in bonds issued by American corporations. Usually the bonds are of good quality—and the risk of losing money from a corporate default is minimal. The goal of these funds is to provide high income rather than growth for your investment.

The gap between bond yields and inflation is at historical peaks, with the Consumer Price Index up about 3 percent and AA utilities yielding 12½ percent. The real return is almost 10 percent, compared to 3 to 5 percent, which was typical in earlier periods of economic expansion.

Chart 4-4 illustrates the potential for a significant rally in

CHART 4-4   Long-Term Bond Rate Versus the Rate of Inflation

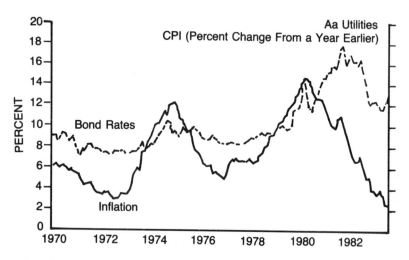

bond prices. But the mix of fiscal and monetary policies is expected to keep real bond rates much higher than they have been historically.

Junque-Bond Funds

John Maynard Keynes said that "nine out of ten times the extremes of misfortune do not occur." Junque-bond-fund buyers bet their money that Keynes is right. These are portfolios of high-risk bonds. Many of the companies represented in the portfolios are either in or near bankruptcy. According to Bill Grace, Jr., author of *The Phoenix Approach,* a best-selling book about investing in distressed companies, junque-bond funds have historically done well. Mr. Grace writes:

"Junk bonds, over the years, have proven to yield a total return that is 50% greater than investment-grade bonds as a group, even after figuring losses resulting from default. The default rate is amazingly low, only slightly higher with the lower-grade bonds than the higher-grade bonds: far fewer than 1% of all low-grade bonds have defaulted during the entire 20th century. When the default does occur, the investment potential for most bonds is anything but finished. Debt se-

JUNK-BOND FUNDS

	Minimum Initial Investment	Minimum Subsequent Investment
American General High Yield Investments 2777 Allen Parkway Houston, TX 77701 (713) 522-1111	$500	$50
American Investors Income Fund PO Box 2500 88 Field Point Rd. Greenwich, CT 06836 (800) 243-5353	$400	$20
Colonial High Yield Securities 75 Federal St. Boston, MA 02110 (800) 225-2364	$250	$25
Federated High Income Securities 421 Seventh Ave. Pittsburgh, PA 15219 (800) 245-2423	$1500	$100
First Investors Bond Appreciation Fund 120 Wall St. New York, NY 10005 (212) 825-7905	$1000	$100
Kemper High Yield Fund 120 S. LaSalle St. Chicago, IL 60603 (312) 781-1121	$1000	$100
Keystone B-4 Fund 99 High St. Boston, MA 02110 (800) 225-8720	$250	none
Lord Abbett Bond Debenture Fund 63 Wall St. New York, NY 10005 (212) 425-8720	$1000	none
Massachusetts Financial High Income Trust 200 Berkeley St. Boston, MA 02116 (616) 423-3500	none	none
Oppenheimer High Yield Fund 3600 South Yosemite St. Denver, CO 80237 (303) 770-2345	$2500	$25
Pioneer Bond Fund 60 State St. Boston, MA 02109 (800) 225-6292	$1000	$100

	Minimum Initial Investment	Minimum Subsequent Investment
United High Income Fund PO Box 1343 One Crown Center Kansas City, MO 64101 (816) 283-4000	$500	$50
Vanguard Fixed Income Securities Fund- High Yield Portfolio PO Box 876 Valley Forge, PA 19482 (800) 523-7910	$3000	$50
Venture Income Plus 309 Johnson St. PO Box 1688 Santa Fe, NM 85701 (505) 983-4335	$1000	$25

curities of bankrupt companies provide all sorts of opportunities. As a group junk bonds are not really as risky as their high returns would imply."

For those willing to put a portion of their money into this type of security, the preceding is a list of funds that specialize in just that.

Convertible-Securities Funds

Certain preferred stocks and bonds are convertible into shares of the common stocks of the same company. Investors buy them because they usually pay a higher income than the common stock of that company. Yet, because they can be converted into a certain number of its common shares, they can go up if the company does well. They will go down if the company does poorly, but the higher-than-common-stock dividend protects them from sharp declines. Mutual funds that invest in convertible bonds or in shares of convertible preferred stocks are called convertible-securities funds.

Preferred-Stock Funds

If a company gets into financial difficulty, bondholders have first claim on its assets. Preferred-stock owners are next, and what is left belongs to the common-stock owners. Preferred stocks are a form of debt security. They go up and down in value like bond prices, based on prevailing market interest rates rather than on how well the company is doing. Mutual funds that own these stocks are called preferred-stock funds.

Tax-Free vs. Taxable Bond Funds

Tax-free funds invest in municipal, or tax-exempt bonds. The words are used interchangeably. Taxable bond funds invest in corporate or government bonds, all of which are federally taxable.

Untaxed income can grow at a remarkable pace. Chart 4-5 shows what will happen if it is reinvested to earn and compound interest.

CHART 4-5

Each Dollar Invested at	Will Double in	Will Multiply by 5 in	Will Multiply by 10 in
8%	8.7 years	20.4 years	29.1 years
9%	7.8 years	18.1 years	25.9 years
10%	7.0 years	16.3 years	23.3 years
11%	6.4 years	14.8 years	21.3 years
12%	5.9 years	13.6 years	19.5 years

General Municipal-Bond Funds

These funds invest in a broad range of tax-exempt bonds. The tax-free interest is passed on to the shareholders.

High-Yield Municipal-Bond Funds

These funds strive for a higher yield by including some bonds in the portfolio of lesser quality in order to generate a higher return than those provided by a general municipal-bond fund. In the last few years this hasn't happened. General municipal-bond funds have yielded as much as those designed to be "high yield"—and in many cases are portfolios of better-quality bonds.

Insured Municipal-Bond Funds

The bonds are insured by private insurance companies so that if any bond in the portfolio misses an interest payment or fails to pay off at maturity, the insurance company will make the payment. Since the insurance company decides which bonds it will allow the fund to buy, the portfolios usually include good-quality bonds that really don't need to be insured. Those bonds most in need of insurance are never insured. For this reason you can be relatively certain that if you invest in an insured-bond fund you have made a secure investment.

Short/Intermediate-Term Municipal-Bond Funds

Bond prices are subject to fluctuation based on two things—quality and maturity. Changing interest rates can dra-

CHART 4-6

These are some of the largest municipal-bond mutual funds that are free of federal, state, and local taxes in the states concerned. For residents of other states, they are free only of federal tax.

Fund	Minimum	Fee	Yield
DMC Tax-Free Income Trust—Pennsylvania (800) 523-4640	$1000	4.50%	8.55%
Dreyfus (800) 645-6561; in New York (212) 895-1206			
New York Tax-Exempt Bond Fund	2500	none	8.62
California Tax-Exempt Bond Fund	2500	none	9.05
Franklin (800) 227-6781; in California (800) 632-2350			
California Tax-Free Income Fund	100	4.00	9.26
New York Tax-Free Income Fund	100	4.00	9.35
Hutton (contact a broker)			
New York Municipal Fund	1000	4.00	8.92
California Municipal Fund	1000	4.00	8.82
Kemper California Tax-Free Income Fund (800) 621-1048	1000	4.75	8.58
National Securities California Tax-Exempt Bonds, Inc. (800) 223-7757; in New York (212) 661-3000	1000	5.25	8.60
New York MuniFund (800) 528-6050; in New York (212) 747-9215	1000	none	8.45
Putnam (800) 225-1581; in Mass. (617) 292-1000			
California Tax-Exempt Income Fund	500	4.75	8.90
New York Tax-Exempt Income Fund	500	4.75	8.49
Scudder (800) 225-2470			
New York Tax-Free Fund	1000	none	8.90
California Tax-Free Fund	1000	none	8.22

matically affect the market value of bonds with long-term maturity dates. The price fluctuation is much less in bonds of shorter maturities. The trade-off is that short- and intermediate-term bond funds will typically pay less interest than a long-term bond fund in exchange for less price fluctuation. Some of the short- and intermediate-managed funds are: Federated Short-Intermediate Municipal Trust (1¼ years), Merrill Lynch's Limited Maturity Portfolio (2 years), Vanguard's Short-Term Portfolio (2½ years), T. Rowe Price's Tax-Free Short-Intermediate Fund (5 years), Fidelity's Limited-Term Municipal (10 years), and Dreyfus's Intermediate Tax-Exempt Bond Fund (10 years).

Funds That Deal with Bonds of Only One State

WHAT'S YOUR BRACKET?

You can determine your federal income tax bracket by using Charts 4-7, 4-8, and 4-9. Bear in mind that your taxable income is not your gross income. It is your gross income less any deductions you may have such as individual retirement account contributions and state and local taxes.

HOW TO USE CHARTS 4-7 AND 4-8

First, using Chart 4-8, find your effective state tax rate. Then, using Chart 4-7, locate in the left-hand column the yield of the out-of-state bond you might buy. Read across to the appropriate effective state tax column to find the equivalent yield on an in-state bond.

Example: Using Chart 4-8, a Connecticut investor in the 50 percent federal tax bracket would have an effective rate of 6.5 percent. Applying this effective tax rate to Chart 4-7, we find that a Connecticut investor would have to earn at least a 9.35 percent yield on an in-state bond to match a 10 percent yield on an out-of-state bond.

The formula for determining the after-state-tax yield figures was computed as follows:

Current yield on out-of-state bond × (1 − effective rate). In the above example, 10 percent × (1 − 6.5%) = 9.35% yield.

CHART 4-7. After-Tax Yields on Out-of-State Bonds

Out-of-State Yield	Effective Tax (50% Federal Bracket)													
	1½	2½	3	3½	4	4½	5	5½	6	6½	7	8	9¼	12
6.00	5.91	5.85	5.82	5.79	5.76	5.73	5.70	5.67	5.64	5.61	5.58	5.52	5.43	5.28
7.00	6.89	6.82	6.79	6.75	6.72	6.68	6.65	6.61	6.58	6.54	6.51	6.44	6.35	6.15
7.50	7.39	7.31	7.27	7.24	7.20	7.16	7.12	7.08	7.05	7.01	6.97	6.89	6.81	6.60
8.00	7.88	7.80	7.76	7.72	7.68	7.64	7.60	7.56	7.52	7.48	7.44	7.36	7.26	7.04
8.50	8.37	8.29	8.24	8.20	8.16	8.12	8.07	8.03	7.99	7.95	7.90	7.82	7.71	7.48
9.00	8.87	8.78	8.73	8.68	8.64	8.60	8.55	8.51	8.46	8.42	8.37	8.28	8.17	7.92
9.50	9.36	9.26	9.22	9.17	9.12	9.07	9.03	8.98	8.93	8.88	8.84	8.74	8.62	8.36
10.00	9.85	9.75	9.70	9.65	9.60	9.55	9.50	9.45	9.40	9.35	9.30	9.20	9.08	8.80
10.50	10.34	10.24	10.19	10.13	10.08	10.03	9.98	9.92	9.87	9.82	9.76	9.66	9.53	9.24
11.00	10.84	10.73	10.67	10.62	10.56	10.50	10.45	10.40	10.34	10.29	10.23	10.12	9.98	9.68
11.50	11.33	11.22	11.16	11.10	11.04	10.98	10.93	10.87	10.81	10.75	10.70	10.58	10.44	10.12
12.00	11.82	11.70	11.64	11.58	11.52	11.46	11.40	11.34	11.28	11.22	11.16	11.04	10.89	10.58

CHART 4-8. State Taxes on Out-of-State Bonds

State*	Nominal Tax Personal Property	Top Income Tax Rate	Effective Tax Rate (50% Federal Bracket)
Alabama	.25%	5.00%	4.0%
Arizona	none	8.00	4.2
Arkansas	none	7.00	3.5
California	none	11.00	5.5
Colorado	none	8.00	4.7
Connecticut	none	13.00	6.5
Delaware	none	13.50	6.8
Florida	.10%	none	6.0
Georgia	.10%	6.00	3.5
Hawaii	none	11.00	4.9
Idaho	none	7.50	3.8
Illinois	none	2.50	1.3
Indiana	.25%	NA	1.4
Iowa	none	13.00	6.9
Kansas	3.00%	9.00	6.8
Kentucky	.25%	6.00	4.5
Louisiana	none	6.00	3.1
Maine	none	10.00	5.0
Maryland	none	7.50	3.8
Massachusetts	none	10.75	5.4
Michigan	3.50%	4.60	4.1
Minnesota	none	17.00	11.9
Mississippi	none	5.00	2.5
Missouri	none	6.00	3.3
Montana	none	12.10	6.4
New Hampshire	none	5.00	2.5
New Jersey	none	3.50	1.8
New York	none	14.00	7.0
New York City	none	18.30	9.2
North Carolina	.25%	7.00	4.8
North Dakota	none	7.50	4.2
Ohio	.80%	5.00	3.3
Oklahoma	none	6.00	3.0
Oregon	none	10.00	5.0
Pennsylvania	.40%	2.00	3.2
Allegheny County	1.20%	2.00	7.8
Rhode Island	none	19.00	4.3
South Carolina	none	7.00	3.5
Tennessee	none	6.00	3.0
Virginia	none	5.75	2.9
West Virginia	.76%	7.90	7.9
Wisconsin	none	10.00	5.0

*No taxes applied to municipals of Nevada, South Dakota, Texas, Washington, Wyoming, District of Columbia, Nebraska, New Mexico, Utah, Vermont, or Alaska.

CHART 4-9

	25%	26%	28%	30%	33%	34%	38%	42%	45%	48%	49%	50%
Single Return	$24.6-29.9	$18.2-23.5	$29.9-35.2	$23.5-28.8	$35.2-45.8	$28.8-34.1	$34.1-41.5	$41.5-55.3	$55.3-81.8	over $81.8		
Joint Return	$29.9-35.2		$35.2-45.8		$45.8-60.0		$60.0-85.6		$85.6-109.4	$109.4-162.4		over $162.4

% Tax Bracket — Tax-Exempt Yield

Yield	25%	26%	28%	30%	33%	34%	38%	42%	45%	48%	49%	50%
5	6.67	6.76	6.94	7.14	7.46	7.58	8.06	8.62	9.09	9.62	9.80	10.00
6	8.00	8.11	8.33	8.57	8.96	9.09	9.68	10.34	10.91	11.54	11.76	12.00
7	9.33	9.46	9.72	10.00	10.45	10.61	11.29	12.07	12.73	13.46	13.73	14.00
8	10.67	10.81	11.11	11.43	11.94	12.12	12.90	13.79	14.55	15.38	15.69	16.00
9	12.00	12.16	12.50	12.86	13.43	13.64	14.52	15.52	16.36	17.31	17.65	18.00
10	13.33	13.51	13.89	14.29	14.93	15.15	16.13	17.24	18.18	19.23	19.61	20.00
11	14.67	14.86	15.28	15.71	16.42	16.67	17.74	18.97	20.00	21.15	21.57	22.00
12	16.00	16.22	16.67	17.14	17.91	18.18	19.35	20.69	21.82	23.08	23.53	24.00
13	17.33	17.57	18.06	18.57	19.40	19.70	20.97	22.41	23.64	25.00	25.49	26.00
14	18.67	18.42	19.44	20.00	20.90	21.21	22.58	24.14	25.45	26.92	27.45	28.00

THE TAX-EXEMPT EDGE OF MUNICIPAL BONDS

To see what a taxable-interest bond would have to yield to equal your take-home yield in a tax-exempt municipal bond, find your taxable income bracket. Then find the yield in the left-hand column of a tax-exempt bond you might buy and read across until you find what percentage interest you would have to receive from a taxable security to equal that yield (taxable income in thousands of dollars). Based on tax tables in effect as of January 1982.

Common-Stock Income Funds

The stocks you will find in these funds are frequently referred to as "total return" stocks. They pay an attractive dividend as well as offer a reasonable chance for appreciation. They are relatively stable in both up and down markets. The companies in the portfolio are generally seasoned and well established.

Balanced Funds

These funds will invest in both fixed-income securities— bonds, convertible bonds, and various types of preferred stocks, as well as common stocks.

Growth Funds

These funds try to concentrate their investments in stocks of high quality but that still offer good opportunities for appreciation. Most would select mature, successful companies with large numbers of shares on the market, such as IBM, Merck, and General Electric. These kinds of companies tend to grow in value with the economy. They are less volatile than emerging growth companies. They tend to move up and down with the Dow Jones Industrial Average or the Standard and Poor 500-stock average. In fact, most of the growth-stock fund managers attempt to beat those averages by selecting DJII-caliber stocks they believe will outperform the averages.

Aggressive Growth

If you will allow me to use a baseball analogy, think of these funds as "home run funds." Long-ball hitters swing for the fences. When they hit, it's magic. When they miss they tend to strike out. That is precisely the strategy of an aggressive-growth fund. It offers high risk and high potential reward. Some funds can use speculative trading techniques (such as

CHART 4-10

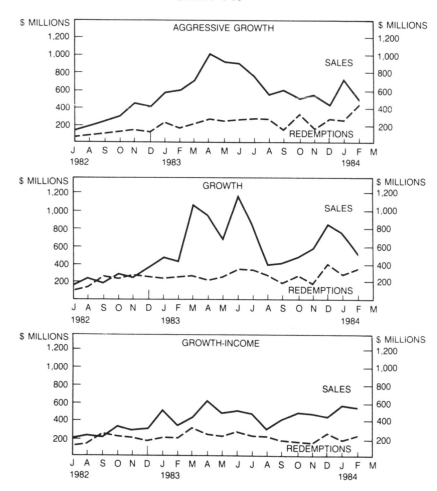

short selling) and speculative trading vehicles (such as options). Generally these funds will own stocks that pay little or no dividends. They do best in up markets and poorly in down markets. They tend to lead the bulls and are the first to be mauled by the bears. You shouldn't buy and forget this sort of fund. My advice is to set a mental stop-loss and sell when you reach that point to protect your capital. These funds tend to be so volatile that 25- to 75-percent swings in value are possible in the shortest time periods.

Index Funds

Some people make a lot of money managing other people's money. But there is a school of thought that says these wheeling and dealing money managers are spinning their wheels. They argue that it is an illusion that active money managers can regularly beat the market. If that is right, it certainly would be a great deal smarter to save the money-management fees and invest money in an index fund. In other words, if you can't beat the market join it. An index fund invests in a portfolio of stocks that is as close to a mirror image of the market's composition as possible. It is designed to equal rather than outperform the market averages.

The estimate is that $50 billion of the $1.76 trillion in U.S. mutual funds is indexed. These funds become very popular when stock pickings get a bit knotty. They lose their luster when various stocks or industry groups outperform the market by wide margins as they do periodically. In the 1970s the Standard and Poor index outperformed 87 percent of the fund managers. In the bull market of the eighties over 90 percent of the fund managers outperformed the index.

Should you wish to invest in an index fund, contact: Vanguard Index Trust, (800) 523-7025. Vanguard invests in all the stocks of the S&P 500 stocks.

Gold Funds

Put some ore in your investment core is the advice of the International Investors Fund, the number-one-performing gold fund over the last decade. And one of the easiest ways to do that would be to buy the shares of mutual funds that invest in stocks of gold-mining companies and in some cases in gold bullion. The ones with the best records over a long time period are those whose managers know when to be in gold and when it is more prudent to be in cash. That is because the price of gold can be extremely volatile, and money-market rates can be quite attractive. In gold funds, more than in any other type, it is vital to have fund managers with a demonstrated record as market timers.

Fidelity Precious Metals	(800) 225-6190
Fidelity Select Port.—Precious Metals	(800) 225-6190
Golconda Investors	(800) 847-4200
International Investors Fund	(800) 221-2220
Lexington Gold Fund	(800) 526-4791
Oppenheimer Gold & Special Minerals	(800) 525-7048
Precious Metals Holdings	
bullion as well as shares	(800) 251-4653
Research Capital Fund	(800) 227-6781
Sherman Dean Fund	(212) 577-3850
Strategic Investments Fund	(800) 527-5027
United Services Gold Shares	(800) 531-5777
United Services Prospector	
no South African mining stocks—mainly	
Canadian, U.S., and Australian gold mining	
companies	(800) 531-5777

CLOSED END

ASA Ltd. (NYSE)
South African gold shares

The Good Stuff

Bill Donoghue refers to the socially conscious or humanistic funds as those that invest in the "good stuff." *Business Week* refers to them as "investments for capitalists with a social conscience." They are mutual funds that screen their investments for social as well as investment merit. The fund managers attempt to invest in only those companies that contribute positively to society with their services, products, and method of doing business. Since every fund has a different definition of the good stuff, an investor should read the prospectus to make sure his or her ideas concur with those of the fund manager. Some will stay away from nukes, others from South Africa, others from tobacco, liquor, or companies involved in gambling.

Calvert Social Investments Managed Growth Fund	(800) 368-2745
Calvert Social Investments Money-Market Fund	(800) 368-2745
Dreyfus Third Century Fund	(800) 645-6561
Foursquare (Eaton and Howard)	(800) 225-6265
Pax World Fund	(301) 229-2647

The Good Stuff Funds—Newsletters

These are market letters that specialize in socially conscious investments:

Good Money, Center for Economic Revitalization, 21 Main St., Montpelier, VT 05602
Insight, Franklin Research and Development, 222 Lewis Wharf, Boston, MA 02110
Market Conscience, Box 81, Burlington, PA 18814

Commodity Funds

Everyone calls them "funds" but they are not. They are professionally managed commodity portfolios usually organized as limited partnerships. As an investor you put up the money and the fund manager buys and sells commodity futures contracts. (A futures contract is a commitment to buy or sell a specified amount of a commodity at a fixed price some months away.) Any dealer in a good who is worried about price fluctuations can lock in a future price by using the futures markets. In the early 1970s, when interest rates began their wild ride, financial futures were spawned. Suddenly, institutions involved in currencies and government bonds and mortgages were able to buy futures contracts that cut their risks by specifying future values for their investments. The markets became far broader in reach, and the industry embarked on a period of frenetic growth. More recently, stock-index contracts were born. Whereas in the past a typical hedger might have been a grain elevator company that would use the markets to guard against a precipitous decline in wheat prices three or four months down the road, now a pension fund that owns a wide array of stocks might hedge with a stock-index contract that rises or falls according to the price movement of a broad batch of stocks. The principal benefit of using a fund over investing in commodities on your own is that your liability is limited to the amount of your investment. You can lose even more than that trading commodity contracts on your own.

Successful commodity investing is very tricky. The commodity markets are often volatile. Even most of the sixty or so professionally managed funds lost money in the difficult 1983 market. Fund managers are quick to point out that a commodity fund should be thought of as a long-term investment that deals in a short-term medium. These people typically invest in a diversified portfolio of commodities—pork bellies, currency futures, grains, lumber, etc. The sponsoring brokerage firms love them because the fees are high, the commissions are high, and the firm usually earns a percentage of the profits if there are any.

For those stout-hearted gamblers willing to speculate in this high-risk, high-reward investment area, the best advice is to look for a manager with a good reputation and a good *audited* track record. Fund managers employ different trading systems. Some are purely technical, some are computerized, and some are based on fundamental analysis of the markets.

Jay Klopfrenstein, president of Norwood Securities in Chicago, the capital of the commodities markets, has been following publicly traded commodity funds since October 1978. He is the editor of *The Norwood Index*, a commodity newsletter that is published monthly. It is the best guide available to the performance of these funds. Subscriptions are $50 a year and can be had by writing: 6134 N. Milwaukee Ave., Chicago, IL 60646, (312) 763-1540.

Chart 4-11 shows the number of dollars invested in public commodity funds and how investors have done in those funds.

CHART 4-11

Monthly performance of all public commodity funds combined. Percentage performance figures show gains or losses based on monthly trading. Asset figures include only gains or losses, but also new funds and money withdrawn from established funds.

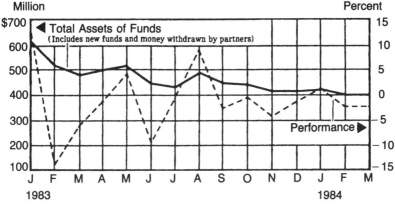

Source: the Norwood Index, compiled by Norwood Securities.

Option Income Funds

An option is the right to buy or sell one hundred shares of stock at a specified price within a certain period of time. The right to buy is called a call option. The right to sell is called a put option. If you are a gambler, options offer you the chance to place a small bet on stock prices and make a bundle or lose only the amount of the bet. If you are a conservative investor and own some stocks, options can be a hedge against sharp moves in those stocks. Options can produce some additional income for stock owners. Mutual funds that specialize in buying stocks and selling options on them are called option income funds.

The most common option strategy is to write (sell) call options on stocks the fund already owns. That is called covered writing. The money the fund receives by selling calls gives it some additional income. Option selling also gives the fund some downside price protection. For example, let's say it bought 100 shares of a stock at $25 and sold an April 30 call. For selling the call the fund received $3 per share. That means that the fund reduced its true cost from $25 to $22.

The call buyer is betting that the price of the stock will go up before the expiration date in April. If it does, the option price will go up. If it goes down, the price will go down. Why buy an option? The option buyer can double his or her money overnight, but he could as easily lose his entire investment. Option buying is as close to gambling as you can come on Wall Street.

Another strategy is buying puts, which can provide a hedge against a stock price collapse. The put buyer has the right to sell the stock at the agreed-upon strike price. So, if the stock declines in value, you have the right to sell it at the higher agreed-upon price. If the stock price rises and you sell it, your profit is reduced by the amount you paid to buy the put.

Puts and calls are only two types of options, and these strategies are only a few of the ones available. As you see, the world of options is far from basic investing. The fund managers can use an array of stock-related instruments such as stock-index-futures contracts and options on stock-index futures. The fund hopes its ability to hedge and purchase puts in a market decline will help protect the portfolio value in a market decline. It is an investment form best used by someone who considers himself a knowledgeable investor. That is why many investors choose to do it through mutual funds.

The following are companies dealing in options:

Analytic Option Equity Fund	(714) 833-0294
Colonial Option Income Fund	(617) 426-3750
First Investors Option Fund	(212) 825-7900
Gateway Option Income Fund	(513) 621-7774
Kemper Option Income Fund	(312) 781-1121
Money Market/Options Investments	(612) 338-3200
Oppenheimer Option Income Fund	(303) 671-3200
Putnam Option Income Trust	(612) 292-1000

Penny Stock Mutual Fund

The world of penny stocks is a volatile, fast-paced one that has been treacherous for many individual investors. That is because the spreads between bid and ask prices are generally large, it's tough for individuals to get the good new issues, and information about these small companies is scarce. A closed-end mutual fund was started in 1984 to overcome those difficulties for individual investors. Combined Penny Stock Fund, Inc. (symbol PENY), trades over the counter and specializes in stocks selling for under $5 a share. Because of the success of this fund, the management has created a similar fund—the Penny Fund of North America. This fund intends to be 80 percent invested in stocks under $10, including some issues not traded publicly.

Tax-Managed Funds

These funds use all of the tax laws to shelter almost all of their income from taxes. Because they reinvest all dividends and capital gains, they qualify as corporations rather than as mutual funds for tax purposes. These funds make no distributions to shareholders. When you sell, all of your gains are treated as long term.

American Birthright Trust	(800) 327-4508
Colonial Tax-Managed Trust	(800) 225-2365
Eaton Vance Tax-Managed Trust	(800) 225-6265
Tax-Managed Fund for Utility Shares	(800) 327-4508

Funds Investing in Energy Stocks

Eberstadt Energy Resources	(800) 221-5233
Energy Fund	(212) 850-8300
Energy & Utility Shares, Inc.	(215) 542-8025
Fidelity Select Portfolio—Energy	(617) 726-0200
	(800) 225-6190
SteinRoe & Farnham Capital Opportunities Fund	(312) 368-7800
United Science & Energy Fund	(316) 283-4000

Funds Investing in Utilities

Chancellor Tax-Managed Utility Fund	(212) 791-1000
Colonial Tax-Managed Trust	(800) 225-2365
Eaton Vance Tax-Managed Trust	(800) 225-6265
Energy Fund Inc.	(212) 850-8300
Energy & Utility Shares	(215) 542-8025
Franklin Utilities Series	(800) 227-6781
Fidelity Qualified Dividend Fund	(800) 225-6190
(corporations only)	
Tax-Managed Fund for Utility Shares	(800) 327-4508

Funds Investing in the Health Care Industry

Fidelity Select Health Care Portfolio
82 Devonshire St.
Boston, MA 02109
(617) 726-0200
(800) 225-6190

Putnam Health Sciences Trust
One Post Office Sq.
Boston, MA 02109
(617) 292-1000
(800) 225-1581

Medical Technology Fund
1107 Bethlehem Pike
Flourtown, PA 19031
(215) 836-1300

Mutual Funds Investing in Technology Stocks

Alliance Technology Fund
140 Broadway
New York, NY 10005
(212) 902-4126, (800) 221-5672

The Constellation Growth Fund
331 Madison Ave.
New York, NY 10017
(212) 557-8787

Fidelity Select Portfolios
Technology Portfolio
82 Devonshire St.
Boston, MA 02109
(617) 726-0200, (800) 225-6190
(800) 343-0867

Medical Technology Fund
1107 Bethlehem Pike
Flourtown, PA 19031
(215) 836-1300, (800) 523-0864
except PA)

National Aviation & Technology Corp.
50 Broad St.
New York, NY 10004
(212) 482-8100

T. Rowe Price New Horizons Fund
100 East Pratt St.
Baltimore, MD 21202
(301) 547-2308
(800) 638-1527

Security Ultra Fund
700 Harrison St.
Topeka, KS 66636
(913) 295-3127, (800) 432-3536 (KC only)
(800) 255-3509

Technology Fund
120 S. LaSalle St.
Chicago, IL 60603
(312) 781-1121
(800) 621-1048

Twentieth Century Growth
Investors
PO Box 200
605 W. 47th St.
Kansas City, MO 64141
(816) 531-5575

Regional Funds

When you share the same backyard you tend to be more familiar with the companies, the managements of those companies, and the economy of the region. A regional fund's managers can offer highly specialized and intense analysis of the companies in their regions. That is because there are a finite number of corporations in any region of the country. Keep in mind that to do well in this sort of fund it helps to pick the right backyard.

	MINIMUM INVESTMENT
Fund of the Southwest PO Box 2511 Houston, TX 77001 (713) 757-2131	no minimum
North Star Regional Fund P.O. Box 1160 Minneapolis, MN 55440 (612) 371-7772	$2500
Sunbelt Growth Fund 333 Clay St. Suite 4300 Houston, TX 77007 (713) 751-2400	$100
USAA Sunbelt Era Fund 9800 Fredricksburg Rd. San Antonio, TX 78288 (512) 690-3390 (800) 531-8181	$1000

Foreign-Stock Funds

There are stock markets other than the New York and American exchanges, and there are stocks of companies other than those of U.S. corporations. There are also companies that you cannot buy in the U.S. that are outperforming their American counterparts. If you ignore them you are missing one half of the world's investment opportunities. To invest in them, or even to take advantage of currency fluctuations, foreign mutual funds make excellent sense. There are three types of foreign mutual funds. Those that invest in foreign firms only are called *international* funds. *Global* funds are allowed to invest in U.S. companies as well. *Regional* funds invest in specific areas of the world such as Canada, Mexico, or Japan. Lynn Asinof of *The Wall Street Journal* advises: "You can pick one of these mutual funds by looking at its portfolio, but it is also important to understand its investment philosophy. Some funds pick stocks using the 'top down' approach—starting with the broad political and economic issues affecting a country and working slowly toward the individual companies. Other funds work from the bottom up, looking primarily at individual companies." Providing income is not an objective of the foreign funds now available. These funds should be bought for their growth potential. A currency play works like this. If the dollar is strong you will be able to buy a greater number of shares than if it is weak against foreign currencies. When the dollar declines against the other currency, you can sell the stock, which will then buy more dollars. Most funds constantly work to improve their total return by holding a number of different currencies, including Australian dollars, Deutschemarks, Hong Kong dollars, Japanese yen, U.K. sterling, and Singapore dollars. If the stocks go up, so much the better.

Foreign stocks also often outperform U.S. stocks, but knowing which to buy from thousands of miles away is almost an impossible task. Also a challenge is coping with foreign taxes, commissions, and information sources. Foreign mutual funds are the easiest way to add exotic flavor to your investment mix.

Chart 4-12 indicates why that flavor may be just what your total investment program needs. Six major stock markets outperformed the U.S. markets over the period indicated.

CHART 4-12. Total Stock Market Return 1970–82 Compound % Per Year (U.S. $ Returns)

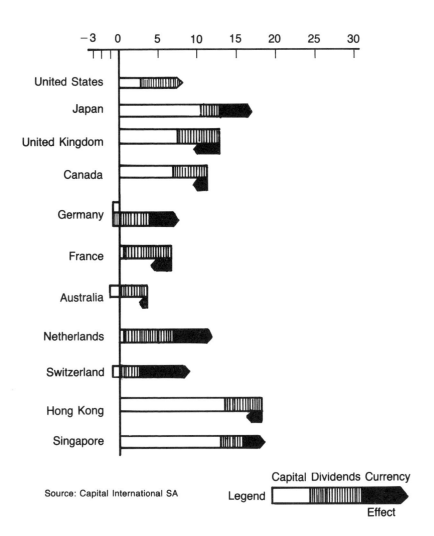

Source: Capital International SA

Canadian Fund (Calvin Bullock)	Canadian	(800) 221-5757
First Investors International Securities Fund	International	(800) 825-7900
G.T. Pacific Fund	Far East	(800) 824-1580
Kemper International Fund	International	(800) 225-1587
Keystone International Fund	Global	(800) 621-1048
Merrill Lynch International Holdings	International	any Merrill Lynch office
Merrill Lynch Pacific Fund	Far East	any Merrill Lynch office
New Perspective Fund	Global	(800) 421-0180
Oppenheimer A.I.M. Fund	Global	(800) 221-9839
T. Rowe Price International Fund	International	(800) 638-1527
Putnam International Equities Fund	International	(800) 225-1581
Scudder International Fund	International	(800) 225-2470
Templeton Foreign Fund	International	(800) 237-0738
Templeton Growth Fund	Global	(800) 237-0738
Templeton World Fund	Global	(800) 237-0738
Transatlantic Fund (Kleinwort, Benson)	International	(212)747-0440
Trustees Commingled Equity Fund (Vanguard)	International (index fund)	(800) 523-7025
United International Growth Fund	International	(800) 821-5664

Closed-End Funds Defined

The primary difference between open- and closed-end funds is how you can buy and sell their shares. Closed-end funds are publicly traded like common stocks, either on a stock exchange or in the over-the-counter market. There is a specified number of shares on the market. When you buy any of those shares you must buy them through a broker from someone else who is selling. Open-end funds will usually offer an unlimited number of shares. They issue new shares whenever you want to buy some and redeem the old ones at "net asset value" whenever you want to sell. Remember, net asset value is the market value of the fund's holdings divided by the number of shares. For example, if the value of all of the shares owned by a mutual fund is $10,000,000, and the number of shares outstanding is 1,000,000, the net asset value would be $10 a share. Because closed-end-fund shares are traded at whatever price the buyer will pay, the price and the net asset value will be different than the "net asset value." For a number of reasons it is usually less. The best time to buy a closed-end fund is when the difference in price is the greatest. The share prices tend to move in a narrow range because the gains are passed on to the shareholders as capital distributions. A growing number of closed-end funds permit the automatic reinvestment of both dividends and gains. There are both closed-end bond and stock funds. As with open-end funds, many specialize in the stocks of particular industries and geographic areas. The most definitive guide to these funds is *High-Return, Low Risk Investment: Combining Market Timing, Stock Selection, and Closed-End Funds*, by Thomas Herzfeld and Robert Drach. G. P. Putnam's Sons.

The following is a list of all closed-end funds along with the funds' objectives as described in Standard and Poor's stock reports. Updated copies of these reports are available at branch offices of most stockbrokerage firms and in good libraries.

Diversified Common-Stock Funds

Adams Express Co. The company has net assets of over $345 million. A large part of its investments are in shares of well-established companies, with some emphasis on oil and natural gas issues.

General American Investors. Resources of this company are largely in a diversified list of well-known common stocks, with important positions in health care (including instrumentation),

retail and wholesale trade, electronics, and data handling.
Lehman Corporation. This is one of the largest investment
companies, with net assets of over $672 million. The primary
investment objectives are conservation and growth of capital,
which are sought principally through a diversified portfolio of
common stocks.

Niagara Share Corporation. The company keeps its funds
essentially fully invested in U.S. and foreign common stocks of
industries with above-average growth potential. The company
has generally outperformed the stock market; for the first nine
months of 1983 net asset values rose 28.4 percent, versus an
18.1 percent advance in the Standard & Poor's 500 Stock
Index.

Overseas Securities. This small company has agreed to
make a tender offer for all of the common shares of Farrah
Resources Ltd., a Canadian energy company that owns 48 percent of Overseas Securities capital stock. Upon completion of
the transaction, subject to SEC approval, Overseas would be
converted to an operating company in the energy development
business.

Source Capital. This company seeks to maximize total return from income and appreciation for its common shareholders while providing income for preferred shareholders.
SOR's portfolio puts primary emphasis on common stocks.

Specialized Equity and Convertible Funds

American General Convertible Securities. On September
9, 1983, American Can Co. completed the acquisition of the
mutual-fund operations of American General Corporation, con-
sisting of American General Capital Corporation and its sub-
sidiaries, which currently had approximately $4.5 billion of
assets under management. The acquired businesses would be
operated under the name American Capital Comstock, a subsidiary of American Can. The name of American General Convertible Securities has thus been changed to American Capital
Convertible Securities.

Bancroft Convertible Fund. This company seeks income
and capital appreciation through investments primarily in con-

vertible securities. In 1982–83, it repurchased approximately 38 percent of its shares through a tender offer, reducing total assets by $18.8 million, but increasing net asset value per share slightly.

Castle Convertible Fund. This company seeks income and possible long-term appreciation by investing in a portfolio of convertible and other securities.

Central Securities Corporation. This company seeks capital appreciation, concentrating a large portion of its portfolio in a relatively small number of investments.

Claremont Capital. This company seeks long-term capital appreciation; it has reduced its holdings of restricted and venture securities in recent years. Marketable equity securities now account for more than 60 percent of the company's investments, with marketable debt securities and short-term notes accounting for most of the balance.

Madison Fund. This nondiversified management company is in the process of converting to an operating company, with interests primarily in the natural resources area. In July 1983 MAD agreed to acquire a 25 percent interest in Conquest Exploration Co., an oil and gas explorer, producer, and developer. Earlier in 1983 a private investor purchased $10 million in MAD convertible preferred stock and agreed to purchase $40 million of MAD common from the company or in the open market.

Petroleum & Resources Corporation. This company has a diversified portfolio of leading oil stocks and also holds interests in oil and gas producers and oil service firms. Adams Express owns about 12 percent of the common stock.

Bond Funds

Bunker Hill. This company, managed by Security Pacific National Bank, invests its assets primarily in a diversified portfolio of high-quality marketable debt securities. Its objective is to seek a high level of current income, consistent with prudent investment risk. In March 1983, BHL sold publicly $15 million of senior convertible notes.

CNA Income Shares. This company invests its assets primarily in investment-grade debt securities. A high level of current income is the primary investment objective, and capital appreciation is a secondary objective.

Drexel Bond-Debenture Trading Fund. This bond-debenture trading fund is a diversified-management investment fund which seeks a high rate of return, primarily from interest income and trading activity. Recently, the company restructured its investment portfolio to increase current income.

Excelsior Inc. Shares. This company invests primarily in fixed-income securities. Its primary investment objective is to provide shareholders with as high a level of current income as is consistent with prudent risk; capital appreciation is a secondary objective.

Fort Dearborn Income Securities. This company, managed by the trust department of the First National Bank of Chicago, invests primarily in fixed-income debt securities. Its primary investment objective is to generate current income for distribution to shareholders; capital appreciation is a secondary objective.

Hatteras Income Securities. This company, managed by North Carolina National Bank, invests primarily in fixed-income debt securities. Its primary objective is to seek as high a level of current income as is consistent with prudent investment risk; capital appreciation is a secondary objective. Dividends are declared and paid monthly.

INA Investment Securities. This company invests principally in debt securities. The fund's primary investment objective is to generate a high level of income, with capital appreciation a secondary consideration. Dividends are paid monthly.

Inter Capital Income Securities. This fund invests principally in fixed-income securities. The primary investment objective of the fund is to provide as high a level of current income to shareholders as is consistent with prudent investment risk; capital appreciation is a secondary objective. Dividends are declared quarterly and paid monthly.

John Hancock Income Securities. The investment objective of this company is to generate a high level of current income consistent with prudent investment risk for distribution to its shareholders. The fund's portfolio consists mainly of a diversified list of debt securities.

John Hancock Investors. This bond fund, advised by a subsidiary of John Hancock Mutual Life Insurance, seeks to generate income for distribution to stockholders as its primary goal. Although the major portion of its assets is invested in readily marketable debt securities, substantial amounts of privately placed debt issues are also held.

Pacific American Income Shares. This company keeps at least 75 percent of its total assets in high-quality, straight-debt securities, government securities, and commercial paper. Its primary investment objective is to provide shareholders with a high level of current income; capital appreciation is secondary.

St. Paul Securities. This company maintains most of its assets in investment-grade debt securities. Lower-grade obligations and securities with equity features may also be held. The primary objective of the fund is to generate a high level of current income, with capital appreciation a secondary consideration. Dividends are declared and paid monthly.

State Mutual Securities. The company has most of its assets in long-term securities, a few of which have equity features or are restricted. The primary objective is the generation of a high level of current income; capital appreciation is a secondary objective.

Transamerica Income Shares. This company invests principally in fixed-income debt securities. Its primary investment objective is to generate as high a level of current income as is consistent with prudent investment; capital appreciation is a secondary objective. Dividends are paid monthly.

Mass Mutual Corporate Investors. This company invests primarily in long-term obligations which have certain equity features and are purchased directly from the issuer. The primary objective of the fund is to provide a fixed yield and an opportunity for capital gains. The shares tend to sell at a discount from net asset value.

Montgomery Street Income Securities. This company, managed by a subsidiary of BankAmerica, is substantially invested in quality corporate and government debt securities. The primary investment objective is to provide shareholders with as high a level of current income as is consistent with prudent risk; capital appreciation is a secondary objective. Dividends are declared and paid monthly.

Mutual of Omaha Interest Shares. This company, managed by a subsidiary of BankAmerica, is substantially invested in quality corporate and government debt securities. The primary investment objective is to provide shareholders with as high a level of current income as is consistent with prudent risk; capital appreciation is a secondary objective. Dividends are declared and paid monthly.

Dual-Purpose Funds

The unique feature of these closed-end funds is that they are a package of two distinct types of shares. One type is designed for income, the other for growth. Shareholders who own the income shares receive all of the income earned by all of the stocks in the fund's portfolio. Those who own the growth shares benefit or suffer from the fund's change in value.

It works this way. Let's say that the fund begins with $1,000,000 with which it buys stocks in various companies just like every other common-stock mutual fund. The fund has 100,000 shares, all of which are initially priced at $10. Fifty thousand of those shares are income shares. The other 50,000 are growth shares. If the fund earns $50,000 of dividends they are all split among the 50,000 income-share owners. In this example each income-share owner would receive $1 in dividends. The growth shareholders would earn no dividends. On the other hand let's say the total value of the fund increased from $1,000,000 to $1,250,000. In that case the value of each of the growth shares would have increased from $10 a share to $15 (the original value of the 50,000 growth shares is $500,000. The new value is $500,000 plus the profit $250,000 divided by 50,000 shares equals $15 per share).

The great advantage of being a dual-fund shareholder is the leverage you get from the money that belongs to the other class of shareholders. The disadvantage is that if you are an income-share owner and the fund grows nicely, you won't benefit. If you are a growth shareholder and the fund does poorly you lose two ways. You receive neither growth nor income.

The income shares pay a stated minimum dividend that is cumulative. That means that if for some reason the fund skips a dividend payment it must eventually make it up.

There are two dual-purpose funds:

CHART 4-13

Name of Fund	Income share	Where traded
Hemisphere Fund	6-30-85 at $11.44	NYSE
Gemini Fund	12-31-84 at $11.00	NYSE

5

Important Facts for Mutual-Fund Investors

THERE ARE SOME VERY FERTILE MINDS at work continually creating new money packages. The tax laws change, as do investment opportunities. To keep up with these changes I find the following periodicals quite useful:

1. *Forbes:* the Funds section.
2. *Money:* the Fund Watch section.
3. *Personal Wealth Digest:* A valuable summary of articles from financial magazines and newsletters about stocks, bonds, mutual funds, hard assets, real estate, tax shelters, money management, retirement, and estate planning. 10076 Boca Entrada Blvd., Boca Raton, FL 33433 (305) 483-2600.
4. *Weisenberger Investment Companies Service:* Management results. There are a lot of numbers about how the funds stack up. Published by Warren, Gorham & Lamont, Inc., 1633 Broadway, 33rd Fl., New York, NY 10019.

MARKET-TIMING SERVICES

Clearly there are times when it is smarter to be in the market than out of it. Predicting those times has become the work of several market-timing services, each of which produces a newsletter to which you can subscribe. Each service attempts to call "technical" turns in the market. Some recommend specific funds. Most deal with no-load funds only.

Old-time investment professionals will tell you that anticipating and reacting to broad economic turns is useful and profitable. They will also tell you that no one can accurately and consistently call short-term market movements. Trying to respond to each market blip is as fruitless as the frequent changing of lanes in the supermarket. Over the long run it has *never* been shown to be profitable. Charles H. Dow, the first editor of *The Wall Street Journal* and creator of the Dow Theory, said that major stock-market movements are like tides in the ocean. You should pay attention to them. Short-term fluctuations, on the other hand, are like ripples. They have no meaning. However, if you would like to try, one or more of these newsletters might be useful to you. To test the suitability of any of these letters, ask for a free sample issue. Most will be happy to send one to you. My feeling about newsletters and investment periodicals is that if you get one idea from the letter that earns for you more than the cost of the tax-deductible subscription, it was worth the price.

Donoghue's Moneyletter	$87	Box 540
(Semimonthly)		Holliston, MA 01746
Fundline	$87	Box 663
(Monthly with updates)		Woodland Hills, CA 91365
Growth Fund Guide	$79	Box 6600
(Monthly)		Rapid City, SD 57709
Mutual Fund Specialist	$48	Box 1025
(Monthly)		Eau Claire, WI 54701
No Load Fund Investor	$45	Box 283
(Quarterly)		Hastings-on-Hudson, NY 20706
No Load Fund X	$77	DAL Investment Co.
(Monthly)		235 Montgomery St.
		San Francisco, CA 94104
Switch Fund Advisory	$125	8943 Shady Grove Ct.
(Monthly)		Gaithersburg, MD 20877
Systems and Forecasts	$140	185 Great Neck Rd.
(Semimonthly)		Great Neck, NY 11021
Telephone Switch Newsletter	$97	Box 2538
(Monthly)		Huntington Beach, CA 92647
United Mutual Fund Selector	$105	210 Newbury St.
(Semimonthly)		Boston, MA 02116

A TIME TO BUY AND A TIME TO SELL

The most difficult decision an investor ever makes is not which fund to buy, but when to sell it. But the decision to sell becomes easier if you recognize from the beginning that you will probably pick more poor investments over your investment life than great ones. Your task, then, becomes one of constantly replacing the poor choices with better ones. Think of it not as selling but constantly upgrading. Also realize that when the price of your mutual fund shares drop *you have lost money*. There is no such thing as a paper loss. The only difference between what some people consider a paper and real loss is that the IRS won't let you write off paper losses. So they are even worse than "real ones." I believe in selling losers. I don't believe in selling winners. That is easy to say. What I mean is that I don't believe in selling shares that have appreciated to some preset price objective. You will hear many advisers tell you to sell when you "double" your investment, or when it has reached some other predetermined price objective. Just because the fund shares have reached that price doesn't mean they are through—any more than John Riggins or Marcus Allen are through for the day after they have gained 100 yards. You should stay with your successful players as a coach, and with your successful investments as an investor. Many funds have doubled and doubled again. Keep your good investments. Sell only when they have stopped appreciating or when they have turned and a downtrend has been established.

TIMING FUND PURCHASES

Since mutual funds must distribute all net realized capital gains to their shareholders, it makes sense to pay attention to their capital-gains-distribution dates. Even though these distributions won't make you any wealthier, because the value of the fund will be adjusted by the amount of the gain, the IRS says that you must pay tax on the gain. For example, let's say you purchase a fund for $20 a share the day before its ex-dividend date. In our example, we will also say that the capital-gains distribution is $5 a share, which you can receive in cash or reinvest. According to the IRS, you must pay tax on the $5 even though the shares have been adjusted in value so that they are now worth only $15 each. Your real wealth has stayed the same, $15 per share + $5 dividend per share. Even though that is so, you owe the tax anyway.

Mutual funds tend to distribute those gains after the end of their fiscal year. There is little point in making a purchase right before that happens and incurring an unnecessary tax liability.

Robert McGough, of *Forbes*, offers some advice about how to predict whether a fund will make a meaningful capital-gains payment. "Semiannual fund reports show net realized gains for the first six months of the fund's year. Toward the end of the year, by checking the net asset value of the fund you can estimate whether its year-end distribution will be sizable or not. Another indicator is the portfolio turnover rate. A portfolio manager selling off stocks as they advance is, all other things being equal, going to have more realized gains to distribute than a manager who would simply buy and hold."

HOW TO SHARE THE LOAD WITH THE IRS

Suppose you want to invest in a mutual fund that charges a front-end load but are troubled by the load. This may help. Instead of buying the fund you want, buy another fund that belongs to the same mutual-fund family and charges the same entrance fee. After thirty days switch from the fund you bought to the one you want. Assuming that the price of neither fund moved, you will be switching out of the first fund at a loss. That is because the sale price will be the net asset value. The purchase price was the net asset value plus the sales fee. The difference in price is counted as a short-term capital loss. It can be applied against capital gains or against ordinary income up to $3000 in any one year. Any excess can be carried forward into subsequent tax years. By doing this you have cut your commission by the amount of the tax savings.

ABOUT NEW MUTUAL FUNDS

Barbara Rudolph, writing for *Forbes*, said, "Mutual-fund managers create new products not because of new research ideas or sophisticated market strategies. They gear up to sell what they think the public will buy." Indeed, the fact that a brokerage firm is marketing a brand-new mutual fund in a specific investment area might be the clearest warning you get that the market is about to top out in that area. History shows again and again that to be the case. Ms. Rudolph advises that "fads fade and money that follows fads is notoriously fickle." In the *Handbook for No-Load Investors*, by Sheldon Jacobs, the editors point out two other disadvantages. The first is that the new fund has no performance record on which to base an intelligent decision. "Don't get excited because a firm with four funds starts a fifth. That's no guarantee of success. Every fund group wants a complete product line. The fact they have an outstanding growth fund doesn't guarantee a superior government securities or other type of fund." The second disadvantage is that, unlike a new common-stock offering of a limited number of new shares, "open-end funds can create an unlimited number of new shares as public demand increases. Buying early provides no advantage whatsoever." In fact, a fund that raises a massive amount of money may find it difficult to invest in enough attractively priced issues. The best advice is to wait. Watch the fund after it has traded several months. If you still like the idea you will probably be able to buy it cheaper.

HOW TO BORROW TO BUY

You don't need to have cash to pay for your entire mutual-fund purchase. Several brokerage firms will allow you to *margin* your purchases, just as you have always been able to use margin (money borrowed from the broker), to buy other stocks and bonds. The amount that you are permitted to borrow is set by the federal government. At this time it is equal to

50 percent of the value of the security. For example, you would need to come up with $10,000 in cash to pay for a $20,000 mutual-fund purchase. You will be borrowing the other $10,000 from the brokerage firm and paying interest to do it. The rate of interest fluctuates daily, just like the rate of interest that you are paid on your money-market fund. It will be ½ to 1½ percent above the rate the broker pays to borrow the money. That is called the "broker call" rate. By the way, that rate is usually negotiable, and will almost always be lower for larger loans.

Most brokerage firms require investors to maintain a 30 percent margin, and the government steps in if the margin falls to 25 percent. When that happens you will get a "T" call asking you to deposit more cash in your account ("T" stands for Federal Reserve Regulation T). What this means is that if the value of your securities falls, you will need to add more cash to your account. It works this way. The market has declined and your $20,000 investment is now worth only $14,000. As a result you have lost $6000 of your original $10,000 investment. The $4000 remaining is called your equity and it now represents less than 29 percent of the market value of the investment ($4000 ÷ 14,000 = 28.5 percent). You now must add enough cash or sell enough of your mutual fund to raise your equity to 34 percent.

Therein lies the danger of using someone else's money to buy securities. You can lose that money as well as your own, and you will be required to pay back every penny you borrowed plus interest.

Investors use margin because it gives their money leverage. With $10,000 you can buy $20,000 of stock. If that doubles, the $10,000 has quadrupled ($40,000 less interest charges), whereas without margin a doubling would put the value of the investment at only $20,000. Margin interest is tax deductible, and often it is cheaper than the interest rates offered for other types of loans. Since the money borrowed from the margin account can be used for any purpose, it might be a lower-cost loan than otherwise available to purchase a car or pay college expenses. And it might be preferable to selling securities to pay those expenses.

6

What Is a Unit Trust?

IN NORMAN SCHVEY WALL STREET "TRUSTS"

He works in a corner office on the twenty-first floor of the Merrill Lynch building in the heart of America's financial district. The corner location is about the only mistake Norman Schvey has made as the undisputed guru of the multibillion-dollar unit-trust business. It seems to me that his office would be better placed in the middle of the floor so that his one hundred and ten staffers who constantly flow through it seeking advice, quick decisions, or even fatherly praise wouldn't have to walk quite so far to get it. How he can think in an office that is only slightly less trafficked than the terminal at Chicago's O'Hare Airport is hard to understand. But think he does. The *New York Times* calls him the leading innovator in the unit-trust industry. He is a creative genius who has not only survived but mastered the toughest street in America for over forty years. And during that time he has dreamed up more new investment products than any person before him and probably anyone who will follow.

Norman Schvey is responsible for bringing more unit trusts to the investing public than anyone in America. It is a responsibility that he takes so seriously that he is involved with every aspect of the creation and distribution of every unit trust his organization brings to market. That accounts for the Grand Central-like atmosphere of his bustling office. And while his employer is Merrill Lynch, with its vast resources, Norman Schvey's unit-trust department operates independently with its own research and trading staffs. Merrill Lynch has an army of product-development people. Mr. Schvey is his own product-development staff.

As a Wall Street visionary with a wonderful sense of securities history, he sees his task as one of matching what investors want or need with the raw material (i.e., stocks and bonds) available from Wall Street. As a mark of corporate wisdom, Merrill Lynch leaves him alone to do it.

UNIT TRUSTS DEFINED

The unit trust is an old Scottish investment concept. It was modified slightly and first offered to American investors by the investment firm of Ira Haupt and Company in 1951. Norman Schvey was part of the team that developed that product, and has been working exclusively with unit trusts ever since. The investment firm of John Nuveen is also a major force in the unit-trust business, and virtually all securities firms have their own unit-trust departments. This is a major Wall Street business indeed.

Unit trusts are unmanaged but professionally assembled and supervised portfolios. The granddaddy of the unit-trust family is the long-term-maturity municipal-bond trust. But the family is rapidly growing. There are now unit trusts composed of every type of stock and bond. They have grown in popularity because they are convenient for people to use, simple to understand, and reasonably safe. For as little as $1000 an investor can buy a unit or piece of a multimillion-dollar investment portfolio. Just as with mutual funds, a large portfolio provides the protection that comes from diversification. There is a ready market to sell the units, and the price fluctuates with the value of the underlying securities. The difference between a fund and a unit trust is that a unit trust is not managed. No management means no management fees—and that can translate into a higher return for investors. Another advantage is that the return is fixed. It won't fluctuate like the income from a managed fund. I mentioned that while unit trusts are *unmanaged,* they are *monitored.* By that I mean that unit-trust sponsors have the authority to sell securities to protect the investor.

Unit trusts are packages of the *same type* of securities. For example, a unit trust of three-year tax-exempt bonds would be made up of twenty or twenty-five different three-year tax-exempt bonds. An investor would receive his or her proportional share of the tax-free interest, usually monthly. Some trusts pay quarterly, some semiannually, and most will allow you to accumulate the interest payments rather than receive them—if you choose.

For the services provided by the unit-trust sponsor the investor would pay an initial sales charge of 2 to 5 percent, depending on the trust,* but no fee to sell. And when he sells, just as if he owned the bonds themselves, he would receive interest to the day of settlement.

There are both taxable unit trusts composed of corporate or government bonds and tax-free trusts made up of municipal bonds. You can choose trusts with different maturities: short term (1–3 years), intermediate term (10–12 years), and long term (20–30 years).

There is a wide variety of choices available to you now, and new varieties seem to be limited only to Norman Schvey's active imagination. These are among the most widely held:

Individual State Municipal-Bond Trusts

There are twenty different state tax-free bond trusts. Since most states charge an income tax on the interest from out-of-

---

*Take, as an example, a trust selling at a public offering price of $1003.37 per unit including a sales charge of 3.9 percent. The sales charge is calculated by taking 3.9 percent of the public offering price (3.9 percent of $1003.37 equals $39.13). The offering price net of the sales charge is, once again, the value of the underlying bonds, which in the example is $964.24 ($1003.37 minus $39.13 equals $964.24). Expressed as a percentage of the $964.24 aggregate offering price of the underlying bonds, $39.13 is a sales charge of 4.058 percent.

The impact of this sales charge is significant if the investor holds the unit for a short time. For this reason, long-term unit investment trusts are not good short-term investments.

state municipal bonds, there is an advantage to owning only tax-exempt bonds of your own state. These trusts allow you to enjoy the unit-trust advantage with a diversified portfolio of bonds from one state only.

Put Trusts

These trusts give investors the right to "put" or sell the units back to the sponsor at par. This feature eliminates the risk of price fluctuation due to changing market rates.

Insured-Bond Trusts

Both the interest payments and principal are fully guaranteed by private insurance companies. If any of the bonds in the portfolio default, the insurance company makes up the loss.

Preferred-Stock Trusts

Corporations like to invest in preferred stock because the dividends are high and 85 percent tax-free to corporate investors. The trust offers the corporate buyer the additional benefits of diversification and regular monthly payments. These are really not the best choice for individual investors.

Utility Common-Stock Trusts

This is a portfolio of utility common stocks. Since well-managed utility companies have historically raised their dividends over time, this trust provides some hedge against inflation. It is also eligible for the 85 percent corporate-dividend-tax exclusion.

Humpty-Dumpty Trusts

These are units made up of the eight companies that resulted from the breakup of the old American Telephone and Telegraph (AT&T) company. Each unit is identical to a share of the old Telephone stock, as if the company had never been divided.

Floating-Rate Unit Trusts

This is another trust in which the value is designed to remain stable. The interest rate adjusts or "floats" with changing interest rates. That should minimize the fluctuation of the principal. Most of these trusts are pegged to the prime rate. Some have floors and ceilings. That is, they won't pay less than a certain amount (6½ percent, for example) or more than a certain amount (20 percent, for example).

The Americus Trust

The original trust was created when the old AT&T went out of existence. Shareholders were allowed to exchange their old AT&T shares for AT&T Americus Trust Units. The units can be separated into two patented parts that the trust calls *Prime* and *Score*. The *Prime* part entitles the owner to all the dividend income, the voting rights, and any price appreciation up to the equivalent of $75 to each old AT&T share. *Score* holders get any appreciation above $75 when the trust is dissolved in 1989. In the meantime the units and the parts can be traded on the NYSE.

There are now Americus trust units in many stocks with similar features.

Bank LOC-Backed Trusts

Some unit trusts are backed by letters of credit from one or more banks. These letters guarantee interest payments when due and the payment of principal at the scheduled maturity date. The trust pays a fee to the banks to get the letter of credit, which is really a form of insurance for the investor. If the added protection of the LOC helps you sleep better, you should buy trusts that have it.

Unit Trusts of Mortgage-Backed Securities

Ginnie Mae, Fannie Mae, and Freddie Mac are not two daughters and a son of a genteel Southern family. They are acronyms for different types of securities that allow you as an investor to own homeowner mortgages. And while these three were the first, you can expect the number and variety of mortgage-backed securities to grow exponentially in the next several years. That is because Wall Street is finding a new way to finance home ownership in America by designing investments that will offer investors an attractive combination of safety and return. There are also mutual funds that buy mortgage-backed securities and unmanaged unit trusts.

Mortgage-backed unit trusts are like bond trusts. They are a pool of a large number of debt securities. As an investor you are lending your money to earn interest, and receive your money back when the loan comes due. Unlike traditional bonds, mortgages pay monthly. So as an investor you will receive a monthly interest check. Also, unlike traditional bonds that repay your loans at the end of the term, part of each mortgage payment is a repayment of the loan. At first the amount is quite small, but it grows over time. Think of your own mortgage payments. At first it seems that nearly every dime of your monthly payment is interest, but as the years roll along, your debt is gradually reduced as more of your monthly payment is used to pay off the basic home loan. From your standpoint as the investor, as the principal repayments are made, you receive part of the money you lent back each month along with the interest. Principal and interest are clearly labeled—so that you can keep track. Homeowners also have the right to sell their homes and repay their loans, in which case all of the principal would be returned. They can also refinance their loans, which many do when interest rates fall. Refinancing would also cause you to receive your principal early. For these reasons your monthly payments, as an investor, can be uneven.

It was once standard procedure to tell investors that the typical life of a mortgage pool was twelve years. That was because most homeowners in America used to turn over their mortgages in an average of twelve years. Those were the days when interest rates were stable and mortgages were 6 to 9 percent. Now people with an 8 percent mortgage are crazy to pay it off. As a result, old mortgages turn over very infrequently and the life of a GNMA turn can go well beyond twelve years.

Despite this, the reason investors like mortgage-backed securities is that the interest rate on these quality investments is much higher than on other similar investments and because the monthly cash flow can provide monthly income or the opportunity to reinvest the cash flow each month. Remember, most bonds pay interest only once every six months.

The best advice about investing in the mortgage-backed pools is to buy the units at par value ($1 a share) or less. The reason for that is homeowners can repay their mortgages at par value. If as an investor you buy a unit at $1.05 because it offers a higher rate of return than one selling at $.93 a unit, you can be hurt in two ways. The first is if the home buyer refinances his or her mortgage. When that happens the mortgage is repaid at $1 a unit. You lose $.05 a unit. The second is that presumably one of the higher-yielding mortgages in the portfolio has been removed. The overall yield of the mortgage pool will decline. If, on the other hand, a mortgage in the pool you bought at $.93 is repaid, you will gain $.07 a unit. Your yield shouldn't be adversely affected by the payback either.

Collateralized Mortgage Obligations (CMOs)

These were invented to overcome some investor's objection to the dribbling back of irregular and unpredictable principal paybacks. Instead of making monthly interest payments, these mortgage-backed bonds pay semiannually. The bonds have a maturity date. Some are short term, some intermediate term and some very long term. They are often referred to as PATs, (programmed amortization, term securities). Principal payments begin immediately if you own the short-term bond. The intermediate-term holders won't get any principal payback until all the short-term holders have been repaid; principal is then directed to the holders on the next-shortest maturities, and so on. This allows investors who don't want early principal paybacks the opportunity of investing in the longer-term bonds where their principal paybacks would come only after the shorter-term bond owners have been repaid, probably a number of years down the road.

Builder Bonds

These are issued by such private home-builders as Ryan Homes, Centex Corporation, or Pulte Homes. They can be bought in varying maturities. They come about after these home builders have lent money to their home buyers. The mortgages are guaranteed either by Ginnie or Freddie Mac or by private insurance companies.

Reinvestment Programs

Most unit trusts will allow investors to have either or both their interest and principal payments reinvested in more units of shares of the same. For those who don't want monthly checks, this is an ideal method of compounding their earnings without the headache of worrying about how to reinvest the distributions. For those investors who want to receive the interest but reinvest the principal so they won't spend it, a reinvestment program is especially ideal.

Mortgage-Backed Securities Go Up and Down

The variety of mortgage-backed unit trusts and mutual funds will multiply over time. Keep in mind when you evaluate them that their value will fluctuate with changing interest rates. A unit that you buy at $1 a share can drop to $.90 if interest rates rise.

I advised you earlier to buy units at a discount or at face value rather than at a premium so as to avoid the loss that would result from the early payoff of mortgages in your pool. The second half of that advice is this: *Check the price per unit against the current par value per unit*. As the mortgages in your pool are paid off, you will no longer have $1 worth of mortgages per unit. You may have only $.80 worth of mortgages. This is what I mean. When your pool was new it was worth $100,000,000. It bought $100,000,000 of mortgages and issued 100,000,000 units at $1 a unit. Since then $20,000,000 of mortgages have been repaid, but there are still 100,000,000 units outstanding. Each person who owned a unit has already received $.20 for each unit he or she owned as the mortgages were repaid. As a result, if all the mortgages remaining in the pool were repaid today, unit holders would receive $.80. Therefore, the par value per unit is $.80.

As a result of the current level of interest rates, the market value could be more or less than $.80 per unit. For example, if the interest rate that pool is paying is 13 percent, and the interest rate on newly assembled pools (presumably the "current" or "going" interest rate is 14 percent), the old pool will sell at a discount. It will sell under $.80 a unit. Let's say $.76. If the going interest rate is 12 percent, the old pool will sell at a premium to its face value. Let's say $.84. According to what I have just advised you, the pool is a good buy at $.76 but a bad one at $.84.

You can see from this example that it is not enough to check the current price per unit. You must check that price against the par value per unit.

CHART 6-1. Choices Among Mortgage-Backed Securities

Security	Guarantor	Underlying Assets
Ginnie Mae	Government National Mortgage Assoc. (full faith of credit of U.S.)	FHA Farm HA VA Mortgages
Freddie Mac PCs (participation certificates)	Federal Home Loan Mortgage Corp.	Private FHA and VA mortgages
Fannie Mae	Federal National Mortgage Assoc.	Private FHA and VA mortgages
Private Issues by banks, savings institutions, home builders (i.e., Sears, GE Credit, Merrill Lynch)	usually private mortgage insurers	Private mortgages

7

How to Find Legitimate Tax Shelters

FEW INVESTMENT PROGRAMS ARE more appealing, or even more potentially rewarding, than those popularly described as tax shelters. Most are also high risk, difficult to evaluate, and almost impossible to unload. All but a few are for aggressive investors who realize from the moment they commit themselves to a deal that some bad ones are going to find them. That is what characterizes high-risk, high-reward investment.

Tax shelters aren't for everyone. Financial basket-cases, nervous Nellies, and Wild Bill Hickocks are not psychologically attuned to be tax-shelter investors. And many people who have the temperament lack the need. *Make certain you take all the easy steps to reduce your taxes before you turn to tax shelters.* Those easy steps include maximizing the use of every retirement program to which you are eligible, and using tax-exempt bonds and deferred-compensation programs. And then, if you invest, your strategy should be to diversify among a number of programs and to understand as much as you can about the good and bad of each before you invest.

If the United States Government didn't want to encourage you to put money into oil wells, venture-capital deals, and real estate projects, you wouldn't have such tax benefits as depletion allowances, investment-tax credits, and accelerated depreciation. But the tax benefits alone are never enough justification to invest in a so-called tax shelter. *Every investment should be made because it appeals to you as an opportunity to build your personal wealth.* Part of the appeal of a tax shelter is the tax savings it offers. You should determine exactly what the amount of that savings will be, add it to what you expect will be the return on your investment, and then make the decision whether the investment is one that you want to make and is worth the risk. Because there will indeed be risk in a tax-advantaged investment. Notice how many times I've told you that. It is with good reason! Just recently *Money* published a story about a young nurse who invested most of her savings in tax shelters. According to *Money*, she "never clearly understood the nature of these ventures and how they might affect her financial security." The conclusion of the article: "Middle-income people are just starting to get into limited partnerships. Many of them don't understand these deals." They do it for the tax benefits, the appeal of which is almost blinding. The government attempts to make the risk of investing in these deals more tolerable by allowing some tax breaks. In the process I'm afraid that it has mistakenly created the impression that the primary attraction of a tax-advantaged investment is the tax advantage.

Wise investors know that the primary reason to put money in any investment is because the investment *as an investment* is attractive. The tax advantage may make it more attractive, but tax savings should never be the reason you put money in anything. Every tax expert you listen to will counsel you to make your investments for economic rather than tax reasons, and every year thousands of investors will do exactly the opposite.

I've watched scores of people purchase all varieties of tax-advantaged investments. Those investments ranged from oil wells to box cars, and I have yet to meet the investor who on April 16, the day after the tax season ends, hasn't already forgotten the tax savings and is now looking for the first distribution check. Every tax-advantaged investment must have economic merit. That is the first test the IRS uses to determine whether a deal should be audited. If the economic merit is in doubt in any particular program that you are evaluating, answer these questions about the deal:

- Is the purpose of the investment to make money? Some investments aren't even designed with that motive in mind. They are almost certainly abusive.
- Does the investment serve the *intent* of whatever law the Congress wrote to authorize it? Watch out for the ones designed to squeeze through the tax loopholes.
- Would you really put money in the program if there were no tax advantages? Come on—*really?*

The second problem involved with tax shelters is the risk of running into scoundrels. Along with all the legitimate ways to use the tax laws, there are plenty of promoters who put together schemes that range from questionable to downright dishonest. Most of these surface during the silly season, which begins around Thanksgiving, when the talk inevitably turns to turkeys and tax shelters, and when the difference between the two becomes difficult to distinguish. It is during this season that people looking for tax breaks will jump at almost any investment that promises one. Every expert in the business will advise you not to even bother responding to the newspaper ads that promise 3 to 1, 5 to 1, or even 8 to 1 tax write-offs. They are gimmicks. Truly good deals are not likely to be found in newspaper ads at year-end. Remember also that IRS agents also read newspapers and answer ads. You can bet that the ad itself will cause the IRS to examine the deal and to program the agency's powerful computers to track down those foolish enough to put money in them. Those deals practically beg for a tax audit, which, I assure you, is as certain as gravity.

And then there are the rascals who sell deals that don't even exist—the movie that is never made, the coal mine that is not mined, the herd of cattle that is never fed. They continue to exist because people continue to buy them. Not just ordinary people. The November 28, 1983, issue of *Barron's* gave a complete list of limited partners by name and amount of "alleged net false deduction" for a deal that reportedly involved bogus securities trades. Among the luminaries were producer Norman Lear, who according to *Barron's* invested $450,000 and deducted $1,800,000; weatherman Storm Field, $75,000 investment, $294,375 deduction; and composer Henry Mancini, $100,000 investment, $392,000 deduction. *The Wall Street Journal* reported in December 1983 that another major tax-shelter operation collapsed because the managing partner allegedly looted the partnership of millions of dollars. Those involved were "many wealthy and prominent members of the financial community, whose companies offer financial advice to governments and major corporations."

This leads to another suggestion about evaluating limited partnerships. It's not mine actually. It comes from financial writer Andrew Tobias, but I like it enough to borrow it and share it with you. "If the deal sounds too good to be true, it probably is." Simply because those who are rich and those who should know better are involved in some deal doesn't mean that it is a good one.

All investments should be subjected to your own sniff test. Some deals stink! Certain parts of the prospectus should be read with your nose to the paper as if you were smelling the words—and if they smell, don't get involved.

If you plan to invest in a deal that is offered by someone whose reputation you don't know, be certain your certified public accountant (CPA) reads the prospectus. The accountant is not an investment expert, so don't expect him or her to vouch for its investment merit. In fact, it would be wise to tell your accountant when you hand him or her the prospectus that you don't expect advice about its investment merit. I say that because asking an accountant for advice of that nature will almost always result in a recommendation against the investment. Why? You put the accountant in a "no-win" position. If the investment turns out to be a bummer, he or she is blamed for recommending it. If it turns out to be a winner, you will have long since forgotten the CPA's advice. You see, we all have a tendency to praise ourselves for picking winners and to blame others for suggesting losers. Worst of all, the CPA gains not a dime from the sales commission. For these reasons it is always easier for the CPA to be negative.

Use your accountant to check the tax aspects. A CPA who is

experienced with tax-advantaged investments should also be able to help you make certain it passes the sniff test, anticipate IRS challenges, and warn you of any potential adverse tax consequences—such as triggering the Alternative Minimum Tax (see page 152). Richard H. Lager, the national director of tax practice for the certified public accounting firm Alexander Grant, says that a good accountant "will help an investor understand the tax aspect of a tax-advantaged investment. He or she can show what it is about the investment that generates the shelter as well as to make certain those techniques are likely to be accepted by the IRS." Even more important, according to Mr. Lager, "is the process an accountant will go through to see how the investment impacts your tax liabilities on a *multiyear* basis—rather than just the here and now that so many investors are paranoid about. A number of different factors may negate some of the tax benefits, including the possibility of a giant tax bill when the shelter program comes to an end. In America these taxes that work to offset past tax benefits are referred to as 'recapture.' The English have a more descriptive term; it is 'claw back.' English accountants say it has to do with the amount of screaming and yelling that goes on when the tax bill for the long-since-forgotten tax shelter arrives. A CPA will be able to evaluate the program's effect on you not only on the basis of the tax savings but on the projected income in the years to come. CPAs see more deals in one tax season than most of us see in our lifetimes."

LIMITED PARTNERSHIPS—THE BASICS OF WHAT THEY ARE

I've used a few terms that might need some definition, and there are others that I would like you to understand so that you can feel comfortable when working with tax shelters. For instance, a partnership form of organization is used because unlike a corporation it is not a taxable entity. The tax gains or losses flow through the partnership to the partners. These gains and losses can be allocated disproportionately to the different classes of partners—limited and general, according to the partnership agreement. In that way the limited partners can enjoy the bulk of the tax benefits. Limited partners are not expected to become involved in the management of the venture. That task belongs to the general partner. The limited partner is involved only to the extent of his investment. Any exposure to monetary risk beyond that amount belongs to the general partner. In higher-risk ventures this is particularly advantageous to the limited partner.

Public and Private Deals

Public limited partnerships are those that have been registered with the Securities and Exchange Commission. They are sold to large numbers of people for amounts as low as $3000 to $5000. Private deals are usually not registered with the SEC. Whereas public programs can be offered to an unlimited number of investors, private programs can be shown to only a limited number. Private programs usually call for a substantially larger investment. For these reasons the SEC says that they are to be offered to only those investors who are considered to be "sophisticated." (The government defines a "sophisticated" person as someone with a boat full of money.) Each program has qualification "net worth" and "income" minimums for the prospective participants. The higher the requirements, the more risky the program. That is always a good point to keep in mind when you look at a prospectus.

Some partnerships allow investors to phase in their investment over a number of years. Other programs issue "warrants." The warrant is usually a *right*, not an *obligation*, to continue to stage-in contributions. If the outlook dims, the investor can stop investing. This type of payment schedule makes it easier for many investors to participate in larger deals.

I strongly urge anyone in a financial position to invest in limited partnerships to add a CPA to his or her financial team. The tax law is challenging even to someone who spends his or her career working with it. Trying to do it part-time is foolhardy. It is impossible to keep up with the intricacies, interpretations, and applications of the tax code part-time. You need an expert to help, someone who can provide professional, unbiased, unemotional evaluations for you. The key words are *professional, unbiased,* and *unemotional.* The person attempting to sell you the limited partnership, no matter how much a saint, will be hard pressed to be any of those. If your tax adviser is also the person offering you the limited partnership, you had better find a new tax adviser, at least for the deal under consideration. That is not to say CPAs don't offer good tax shelters. In fact, they may offer the best deals you will ever see. But you need impartiality when it comes to evaluating these programs. Salesmen aren't impartial. The IRS is willing to help. Should you want its opinion of the tax merits of any limited partnership, simply send a copy of the prospectus to:

The Office of the Assistant Commissioner, Technical
Internal Revenue Service
Washington, DC 20224

How to Evaluate Limited Partnership

Limited partnerships are a "trust me" business. As the investor you turn over money to someone else, the general partner, who is supposed to provide knowledge, skill, experience, and judgment. Obviously, those qualities vary from one general partner to the next. I'm going to show you how the experts go about judging them. I will also show you how to evaluate each of the major types of limited partnerships by giving you keys to review them. However, there are some general guidelines that apply to all. Here are some good general rules.

- If you don't understand it, don't buy it. You wouldn't invest in a store down the street whose method of operation was a mystery to you. Why should you act any differently about a tax shelter?
- Read the prospectus with these tests in mind:
  Conflict-of-interest section. Look for related-party transactions. Is there potential for a general partner's private interests to conflict with your interests as a limited partner?
  Compensation section. In a good deal, most compensation to the general partner should be based on the success of the project rather than on the fees to set it up.

Is there any significant caveat in the legal opinion about the program's tax status?

Who performed the "due diligence," that is, investigated the statements made in the prospectus for accuracy? The bigger and better the law and accounting firms, the bigger the reputations that are on the line.

- Who is the general partner? Remember, the chief executive manages the *values* of the organization.
- What are the potential rewards? What is the upside? How are the partners to share the gain?

What projections do the sellers make about the upside potential—do they seem reasonable?

- Record of success. What is the track record; how many years in the business? Let the newcomers learn the business with someone else's money. You want someone with a successful and extensive record of accomplishment.
- Ability to work with this amount of money. Is this the first deal she/he has managed of this size? How have the previous partnerships done? How long has the general partner been in this business?
- Reputation in the industry. Integrity is key. Pick up the phone and ask others in the business. A call to some local businessmen, newspapers, and even the general partner's accountant could tell you if she/he is well thought of.
- What are, and how high are, the fees?

They include the front-end fees (the ongoing or management fees) and the back-end fees (split of profits with the general partner fees). The best deals provide that there be modest front-end fees and no general-partner back-end fees until after the limited gets back his or her original investment plus some return on the money (usually that is the equivalent of 6 to 10 percent annual interest).

- What are the investor qualifications for net worth and tax bracket? The higher they are the more risky they are.

Do you really have to spend the time it takes to evaluate each and every deal that you are offered? Heavens no! The real key is to find investment counselors (salespeople) who will do it for you. Use my questions to test them. Make certain you understand what it is that makes one deal better than another, but it shouldn't be your task to grind out the answers. In every walk of life good managers make management decisions based on the information supplied by their subordinates. As an investor you must either train your investment advisers to find the answers that you need or find advisers who know enough about limited partnerships to hunt for those answers on their own.

If you plan to invest in more than a couple of these programs, it will pay you to subscribe to a good tax-shelter newsletter. Is it worth it? Absolutely! A few hundred tax-deductible dollars spent on up-to-date advice from the experts' expert is a bargain. I think these are the best:

Brennan Reports
Valley Forge Office Colony
PO Box 882
Valley Forge, PA 19482
$145 a year
(215) 383-0647

This report also evaluates the past performance of shelter sponsors, analyzes new offerings, and makes recommendations.

The Real Estate Tax Shelter Review
PO Box 1357
Concord, NH 03301
$128 a year
(603) 225-7288

The Stanger Report
Box 8
Fair Haven, NJ 07701
$325 a year

Robert Stanger also writes *The Stanger Register* ($179 a year). *The Register* makes sense of every available publicly offered tax shelter, using easy-to-understand tables that compare fees, tax benefits, and risk levels.

Tax Shelter Insider
10076 Boca Entrada Blvd.
Boca Raton, FL 33433
(305) 483-2600

And then, of course, have the deal evaluated by your accountant.

REAL ESTATE PARTNERSHIPS

By far the most popular tax-sheltered investment is real estate. That is probably because it is tangible. You can go out and kick it. Many people have made money with it, even if their only experience has been owning their own home. And you don't have to possess specialized knowledge to make a fair evaluation of its investment worth.

There are limited partnerships that invest in office buildings, apartment complexes, warehouses and mini warehouses, shopping centers, fast-food restaurants, hotels, and almost any other type of real estate that you can think of. As one advertisement for a real estate limited partnership so accurately proclaimed, "Today it is easier for you to invest in a seventy-story office building than in a six-room house."

As a part owner you receive a share of the income paid by the renters, some tax benefits resulting from depreciation, and a share of the profits if the property is sold for more than it was purchased. For many people a limited partnership is the only way they could afford to own a part of a major piece of real estate. Historically those pieces have been very good investments indeed. Therein lies the problem. Because real estate investments have been so successful, vast amounts of money have become available to purchase commercial real estate. It comes not only from limited partnerships but from insurance companies, retirement funds, universities, and cash-rich corporations. This has driven the price up, in some cases to unrealistic levels. It has also brought into the syndication business many whose talents lie elsewhere. And as I've warned before, as an investor you must be especially wary of any investment that everyone agrees is terrific. Real Estate Investment Trusts (REITs) were the darlings of the early 1970s. Many investors who were attracted to them for their high dividends from real estate investments suffered major losses when interest rates skyrocketed. It was then that people learned that it was possible to lose money even in real estate.

What to Look For

There are six standards by which you should judge a real estate limited partnership. A good program won't necessarily score well on each standard. But if in evaluating a program you find that it consistently scores poorly, it probably is a lousy program. Since there are so many other choices, the prudent act would be to avoid it.

1. *Acquisition Talent.* The greatest danger in real estate investing appears to be buying overpriced properties. We like to assume that the price the partnership paid for the property represents the fair market price. That is not always the case. There are so many dollars now chasing "institutional quality" real estate that some prices are tragically out of line. A few phone calls to commercial real estate salespeople in the area can give you an idea if property in the partnership that you are considering has been purchased at a fair price. Ask the realtors about the price of similar properties, or how the cost on a square-foot basis compares to the going market. Acquisition talent also applies to the selection of the right mix of prime properties, geographically dispersed, all with favorable financing. The professionals once said that in real estate success depended on three things—location, location, and location. Now, as E. Stephen White, vice president of Mortgage Guaranty Insurance Corporation, says, the criterion for success these days is financing, financing, financing.

2. *The Price to the Partnership.* Compare the amount the partnership is paying for the property (the adjusted purchase price) to the purchase price paid to the seller. The adjusted purchase price is the purchase price plus any additional liabilities, including debt, to which the property is subject. In a typical deal, according to the tax-shelter expert Robert Stanger, the markup is about 15 percent. In a potentially abusive deal the markup could range from 50 to 200 percent. What you are trying to assess is the fairness of the deal to the partnership. You don't want to pay $20,000,000 for a piece of property that sold only a few months earlier for $10,000,000. And you wouldn't want to own a property that has been changing hands

frequently. That suggests that many other owners haven't been able to make a go of it.

3. *Fees*. In real estate there are front-end fees, including the sales commission, organization expenses, and property-acquisition fees. There are property-management fees and finally liquidation fees. Robert A. Stanger & Company evaluates fees in all publicly registered real estate limited partnerships and assigns each program one of five ratings from Lowest (most favorable to the investor) to Highest. Chart 7-1, compiled by Stanger, ranks leveraged partnerships (those financing more than 50 percent of purchases with mortgage debt) and unleveraged and mortgage loan partnerships based on the level of program fees. You can see that there is a significant variation in fees. So it pays to compare fee structures before investing.

4. *The Split*. The level of the fees will affect your return as will the profit split with the general partner. Usually it is an 85-15 split. That means 85 percent of the profit will go to the limited partners and 15 percent to the general.

It is important that the general partner receive a fair share of the profits so that he will work to sell the property for as high a price as he can get, thereby increasing the amount of his share. But it shouldn't be out of line.

The better deals provide that the limited partners receive some minimal annual return on their investment (6 to 10 percent) before the general partner receives his or her share of the profit. That is called *subordinating* the general partner's share.

5. *Cash Sales vs. More Paper*. It is further to your advantage that the property be sold for as much *cash* as possible, rather than taking back mortgages. You can ascertain if this has been the practice of a general partner by looking at the *cash distributions* made to limited partners of previous partnerships. Many sales but small cash distributions indicate that you may continue to be an owner forever, rather than for the seven to twelve years it should take to be completely out of the partnership. Since most partnership interests are difficult to sell, a high level of cash sales is important.

6. *Do You Like the Partnership?* What is your gut reaction to the property in the program? Is it desirable property? Is it likely to appreciate? As a real estate consumer, would you be

CHART 7-1. Real Estate Promotion Rating Leveraged Programs

LOWEST
(39.9 or lower)

Program	Total Front-End Costs	Adjusted Liquidation Phase Fees	Total Program Fees
Rotan Mosle Realty Fund I, Ltd.	14.2	15.5	29.7
The Naples Fund, Ltd.	15.5	15.0	30.5
Travelers Income Properties - I, LP	15.0	18.5	33.5
Boettcher Western Properties III, Ltd.	10.5	25.0	35.5
National Real Estate Ltd Part-IV	14.0	25.5	39.5

MEDIUM LOW
(40.0 - 46.7)

Program	Total Front-End Costs	Adjusted Liquidation Phase Fees	Total Program Fees
Capital Realty Investors - II, LP	22.0	18.5	40.5
Super 8 Economy Lodging IV, Ltd.	26.0	15.0	41.0
Amshel Apartment Investors, Ltd.	14.5	28.0	42.5
Angeles Partners XI	24.8	18.0	42.8
FMA Realty Investors - I LP	17.3	25.5	42.8
Windsor Properties I	18.0	25.0	43.0
McCombs Pension Investment Fund, Ltd.	17.7	25.5	43.2
American Property Investors - 83	24.2	20.5	44.7
Security Spring & Boe Investors, Ltd. 82	19.5	25.5	45.0
Indepro Property Fund I, L.P.	21.0	25.0	46.0
Paine Webber Growth Properties, LP	27.8	18.5	46.3
Liberty Real Estate LP - II	21.0*	25.5	46.5

MEDIUM
(46.8 - 53.3)

Program	Total Front-End Costs	Adjusted Liquidation Phase Fees	Total Program Fees
John Hancock Real Estate LP	21.8*	25.5	47.3
Prudential/Bache VMS Realty Assoc., LP I	22.0*	25.5	47.5
Super 8 Motels Northwest II	22.6	25.5	48.1
Consolidated Capital Properties 4	24.0	24.5	48.5
American Income Properties Realty Fund	24.3	24.5	48.8
Landsing Diversified Properties - II	28.8	20.0	48.8
Real Estate Associates Limited VI	30.0	18.8	48.8
Winthrop Residential Associates III	18.5	30.5	49.0
Essex Real Estate Partners, Ltd.	24.0*	25.5	49.5
Jacques-Miller Realty Partners	24.0*	25.5	49.5
University High Equity Fund II	24.0*	25.5	49.5
Brauvin Real Estate Fund LP 3	24.5	25.5	50.0
Property Resources Fund VI	24.5	25.5	50.0
Century Properties Fund XVIII	24.7	25.5	50.2
Admiralty General Real Estate Fund	25.0	25.5	50.5
American Republic Realty Fund I	25.0	25.5	50.5
Preferred Properties Fund 82	25.3	25.5	50.8
Equitec 83 Real Estate Investors	30.9	20.0	50.9
McNeil Real Estate Fund XIV, Ltd.	25.8	25.5	51.3
National Property Investors 6	26.8	24.5	51.3
Griffin Real Estate Fund III	26.0	25.5	51.5
Realmark Property Investors LP - II	27.5	24.5	52.0
Nooney Real Property Investors - Five	21.7	30.5	52.2
Jason-Northco Properties LP - I	26.5*	26.4	52.9

MEDIUM HIGH
(53.4 - 59.9)

Program	Total Front-End Costs	Adjusted Liquidation Phase Fees	Total Program Fees
SunWard Properties I, Ltd.	24.8	30.5	55.3
McCombs Properties VII, Ltd.	30.0	25.5	55.5
University Real Estate Fund 12	30.0	25.5	55.5
Phoenix/Murray Realty Investors Ltd. 83	27.8	31.3	59.1

HIGHEST
(60.0 or higher)

Program	Total Front-End Costs	Adjusted Liquidation Phase Fees	Total Program Fees
Equity Investors Ltd.	33.0	31.8	64.8
Centennial Development Fund III	31.6	34.5	66.1
Keyes-Kanter Real Estate Partners, Ltd.	26.0	41.0	67.0

Real Estate Promotion Rating
Unleveraged and Mortgage Loan Programs

LOWEST
(17.9 or lower)

Program	Total Front-End Costs	Adjusted Liquidation Phase Fees	Total Program Fees
Qualified Mortgage Investors I	10.8	4.5	15.3
Balcor Pension Investors - IV	12.8	3.0	15.8
JMB Mortgage Partners, Ltd.	11.0	5.0	16.0
Prime Plus Realty Partners	12.0	4.5	16.5
Equitec 82 Mortgage Investors	10.8	6.6	17.4

MEDIUM LOW
(18.0 - 22.6)

Program	Total Front-End Costs	Adjusted Liquidation Phase Fees	Total Program Fees
Insured Income Properties 1983	11.5*	9.5	21.0
Insured Pension Investors 1983	11.5	9.5	21.0
Hutton/Con Am Realty Investors 3	13.8*	8.0	21.8
New England Life Pension Properties	12.3	9.5	21.8
Paine Webber Qualified Plan Prop Fund Two	16.0*	6.2	22.2
MLH Income Realty Partnership III	13.0	9.5	22.5

MEDIUM
(22.7 - 27.3)

Program	Total Front-End Costs	Adjusted Liquidation Phase Fees	Total Program Fees
Del Taco Restaurant Properties I	14.9	8.3	23.2
Shurgard Income Properties III	17.0	6.6	23.6
Public Storage Properties IX, Ltd.	15.5*	8.3	23.8
Qualified Realty Income Fund '83 L.P.	16.5	7.7	24.2
Consolidated Capital Institutional Prop.	16.1	8.3	24.4

MEDIUM HIGH
(27.4 - 31.9)

Program	Total Front-End Costs	Adjusted Liquidation Phase Fees	Total Program Fees
Dain Real Estate Partners I	17.3	11.1	28.4
Angeles Income Properties, Ltd. II	20.0	9.5	29.5
Doctors Hotel Investment, Ltd.	20.2	11.6	31.8

HIGHEST
(32.0 or higher)

Program	Total Front-End Costs	Adjusted Liquidation Phase Fees	Total Program Fees
Butterfield Preferred Growth Fund 83	22.5	9.5	32.0
Sierra-Pacific Development Fund	24.3	11.1	35.4
Executel Limited Partnership 83	26.3	12.8	39.1
August Properties Fund II	26.2	25.5	51.7

Note: The information necessary to calculate the Promotion Rating for the following programs is not available from the sponsor: Landsing Realty Partners; Sovereign Realty 1982-I.

*Based on general partner's estimate of the use of proceeds.

willing to buy it from the partnership? Chances are that if you don't really like it, others won't either.

How to Sell

One of the traditional problems faced by owners of limited partnerships has been their lack of liquidity. One tax-shelter insider is said to have remarked that "the only way to get out of a program is to die." The industry is making an effort to address this issue. In time I believe you will see some innovations that will provide for an active secondary market in the programs.

There are at least two companies in existence that will buy real estate partnership interests from investors. The largest has reportedly purchased over $20,000,000 in the secondary market already. The Liquidity Fund Investment Corporation is located at 1900 Powell St., Suite 235, Emeryville, CA, (415) 652-1462. Ron Baker, Liquidity Fund's vice president, said that his firm stands ready to bid on over 100 different partnerships. The Liquidity Fund then sells limited-partnership interests to investors who want to own what turns out to be a fund of the partnerships it has purchased. Real Estate Securities Fund (415) 362-1018 will also buy some interests of public programs, while Equity Resources (617) 523-2001 will buy limited-partnership interests in private placements.

It is important for investors to realize that their partnership interest is worth only their share of the *actual equity* of their program. Because of the expenses involved in setting up the program, on day one, a dollar's worth of a new program is probably worth 50 to 70 cents' worth of real estate. The equity in a good program will grow with time.

Most major brokerage firms offer an informal market in which an investor can sell the real estate units purchased through them. Of these only Merrill Lynch makes an effort to return to the investor his or her original investment. While that is better than what an investor can expect from many other brokerage firms, you will probably do better still by selling an older unit to a buyer who will pay something for the equity buildup.

Most general partners also maintain a list of people interested in either buying or selling partnership interests. The best advice seems to be that if you can buy an older unit at or near face value from a distressed seller, do it. Let your broker know that you are interested. Not many investors know that they are available. And when you are offered a unit, check with the Liquidity Fund to see how much it is offering to buy that unit so that you will know whether or not the price is a good one.

Christopher Metzger has inaugurated The Partnership Exchange, a company that publishes *The Partnership Greens,* a list of some three hundred publicly registered limited partnerships. The listing provides historical information about each partnership including tax deductions and income. It also shows the nonbinding bids of interested buyers and their phone numbers.

The Economic Benefits

Over the years good-quality real estate has appreciated faster than the rate of inflation. It can be purchased with sizable loans (mortgages). As long as it appreciates at a greater pace than the amount of interest you are paying on the loan, that will also work to your advantage. There are other real estate programs that shun debt. These limited partnerships purchase or develop properties entirely for cash. The absence of debt means no interest expenses and therefore higher rental income for the partners.

Chart 7-2 demonstrates how a successful $10,000 real estate program is meant to work.

Chart 7-2 shows that tax-sheltered income starts low but increases as rents are increased. Typically, after a few years rents are renegotiated and properties are sold. Many limited partnerships that have been in existence for over five years are returning 15 percent or more of the investor's original investment.

The Tax Benefits

The IRS now allows eighteen-year accelerated depreciation. This means that most of the income received from a real

CHART 7-2

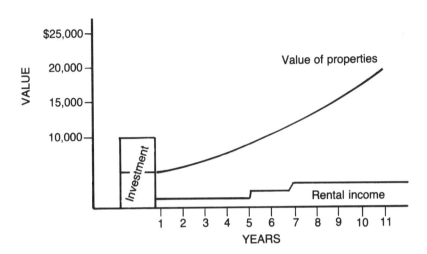

estate limited partnership for the first five to seven years will be sheltered. When the properties are sold, the gain is treated as long term.

Specialized Real Estate Programs
Real Estate Triple Net Lease Programs

The limited partners buy and then lease, on a long-term basis, a building to a corporate tenant. In many of these deals it is a building that the corporation itself built to its own specifications in precisely the location of its choice. The corporation sells the building to the partnership so that its own cash is not tied up in the property. Leasing is usually cheaper to the corporation than the cost of carrying the mortgage on the property. In these deals the corporate tenant agrees to pay all of the operating expenses including taxes, operating expenses, and maintenance. Thus the term "triple" net lease.

The limited partner enjoys the tax benefits coming from depreciation and interest expense. While the income in most of these programs is nominal, the tax benefits can be substantial.

If the tenant is a high-quality one, and the deal is properly structured, this can be an attractive sheltered investment.

Real Estate Mortgage Partnerships

These programs buy Federal Housing Administration (FHA) insured mortgages for properties with rental apartments. If the apartments are converted to condominiums, the mortgages are paid off and the investor could realize a profit. Until any payoff occurs the partners receive income from the mortgage payments.

OIL AND GAS PROGRAMS

One thing on which everyone in the oil business will agree is that in time both the demand and the price of oil and gas will increase. Since Mother Earth stores only a limited amount, finding oil and gas can be quite a profitable venture.

There are four major types of oil and gas tax shelters: exploratory, developmental, balanced, and income. The most risky and therefore the program that offers investors the greatest possibility of significant return is the *exploratory* program. Oil people also call these programs "wildcatting." They involve looking for oil or gas where they are suspected but where nothing has yet been found. *Developmental* programs are less risky because the general partner searches for oil and gas in areas where some have already been discovered. *Balanced* programs are a combination of wildcatting and developmental drilling. All three of these programs drill a number of wells in several different locations to increase their chances of being successful. If and when oil and gas are found, the limited partners get income from its sale. Part of that income is tax free because of the depletion allowance, a kind of depreciation for natural resources.

The fourth type of oil and gas program, the *income* program, usually involves no drilling. Instead, as a limited partner you own an interest in a defined pool of producing wells and receive income from the sale of the oil and gas as they are pumped from these wells.

The Economic Benefit

Oil and gas are valuable commodities. A successful exploratory program can return to you several times your investment. A successful developmental program can return a modest multiple of your investment, but it involves less risk and offers the same tax benefits as an exploratory program. A good income program can provide steady cash flow for a number of years. I have a client, now in his eighties, who has been receiving oil and gas income checks quarter after quarter for over forty years. And as the price of oil and gas has gone up with inflation, so have his quarterly payments.

The Tax Benefits

All of the costs of drilling a well that have no salvage value, such as labor, are referred to as *intangible drilling costs* and are deductible. As a result, most exploratory, developmental, and balanced programs produce a generous 80 to 90 percent first-year write-off. First year means the first twelve calendar months of the program. That may span over two different tax years, so the earlier in the year you invest the better if you want a big deduction the year that you invest. Income programs and drilling programs that turn up enough oil and gas to be sold receive a modest tax break from the depletion allowance which permits some of the income from the sale of oil and gas to be treated as tax free.

What to Look For

Read the Conflicts of Interests section of the prospectus. If the general partner also owns the drilling company, is he or she charging the partnership the going rate to drill?

If the general partner also sells income programs, is he or she permitted to sell successful wells from your program to his or her income funds? That could reduce your income.

Try to make certain that the general partner is drilling in areas he knows. Drilling expertise does not necessarily carry from one section of the country to another.

Don't sign a promissory note.

Don't become involved in a program that is allowed to borrow.

How much general-partner compensation is unrelated to successful drilling?

Read the Allocation of Costs and Revenues section of the prospectus.

How much general-partner money is in the deal? The fee-splitting arrangement—is it fair? Also check the revenue-sharing arrangement. Your chances of a decent return will be higher if the limited and general partners share both the nondeductible capital costs and deductible drilling costs. In this way you share the drilling risk. Read the Use of Proceeds section of the prospectus.

How much of your money ends up in the ground and how much in expenses?

What is the experience of the general partner?

What about his or her track record? There is no reason to believe that an oilman who has consistently proven that he can't find oil will be any better when he gets your money.

Fees—management fee should be under 5 percent. Sales commission should be under 8 percent.

General-partner experience—does he have experience *successfully* working with a large amount of money—if the program is a large one? History shows that partnerships which work with between $5 and $7 million are the most successful, and larger programs are the least successful.

Does the general partner have experienced in-house land men, geologists, engineers? There has been a significant number of new and inexperienced entrants in the business. Their performance has generally been miserable.

Watch out for multiple write-offs. If they are offered, you can bet that you will be on the hook for a note.

Finally, diversify among a number of programs.

Whatever the economic benefits, if it weren't for the tax-savings incentives I'm convinced few people would put money in oil and gas programs. The odds of making money are horrible. The track record is that only 1 in 15 exploratory wells results in a small find; 1 in 1000 results in a large find. According to Robert Stanger, only 1 in 10 investors gets his or her investment back. Developmental and income programs have much better track records.

But the tax incentives are enticing. Oil and gas programs can deliver a sizable write-off for a tax year right up until year end. And many investors would rather take a 10 percent chance of getting their money back than to send a check to the IRS knowing that nothing will ever be returned.

The Zero Coupon and Insurance Gimmick

A number of oil and gas limited partnerships have attempted to spruce up their programs by adding zero-coupon bonds or insurance policies. These additions usually guarantee investors the return of their original investment after a number of years if the programs are otherwise unsuccessful. At best these gimmicks turn your investment into a long-term, interest-free loan. And since the bond and/or insurance cost money, they direct dollars from your program that should be spent for oil or gas. The best advice, if that sort of protection is appealing, is to buy the zero-coupon bonds apart from the program. You can buy zero-coupon, Treasury-backed bonds for a few dollars each that will become worth $1000 each in twenty to thirty years. In the meantime, like U.S. Government Series EE bonds, they make no regular interest payments to you.

EQUIPMENT-LEASING PARTNERSHIPS

Many businesses prefer to lease equipment rather than tie up wads of corporate cash buying it or incur debt financing it. The equipment involved in leasing programs is of every description. It includes airplanes and barges, drilling rigs and railroad box cars, computers and reverse vending machines. The equipment-leasing partnerships exist to raise money from investors to buy the equipment, to lease that equipment to corporate users, to provide the maintenance for the equipment, and then to sell the equipment when the tax benefits run out. The limited partners receive income from the lease payments, some tax savings, and, hopefully, some return from the eventual sale of the used property.

With leasing it is important to select an experienced general partner who has expertise in buying equipment, negotiating favorable lease arrangements, and managing leasing programs. A successful, long-term track record is vital.

The types of leasing programs run from those with high income and modest tax advantages as their central objectives to those with high tax benefits and no income. Those with the biggest tax advantages are highly leveraged. Because they have sizable loans, the high interest charges coupled with the depreciation deductions and investment tax credits can provide some of the highest first-year write-offs in the tax-shelter field.

Other programs use less borrowed money to purchase equipment. Some use none at all. Make certain your CPA reviews the program, especially if high write-offs are promised. The IRS will want to be convinced that the lease is a good one, not simply a disguised installment sale. The term of the lease, including option periods, must be less than half of the expected life of the equipment. If there are loans involved, the investor must be liable for those loans.

Economic Benefits

Cash distribution from equipment rental can be 8 to 10 percent in the programs without much debt. As the level of debt increases, the level of income will drop since part of the rent will be used to pay off the debt. It makes sense to have some debt so that more than a dollar's worth of equipment can be being purchased with each dollar invested. As the debt to buy that equipment is paid, the partnership will own equipment that can be sold when the depreciation runs out. When that happens the partners receive a share of the sales proceeds.

It works like this. A partnership raises $100,000 from ten investors who each put up $10,000. The partnership buys $200,000 of equipment. Each month as the rental income comes to the partnership, part of the rent is used to pay for the $100,000 equipment loan. When the partnership ends, the used equipment is no longer worth $200,000. Let's say it is worth only half of its original cost, $100,000. The partners split the sale proceeds. Each receives $10,000. If no loan had been used, and we made the same assumption about the final value of the equipment, each partner would have received more income during the life of the program but only $5000 when the equipment was sold. Keep in mind that the value of used equipment depends on technological developments as well as wear and tear. That is why it makes sense to invest in equipment-leasing deals that have a diversified mix of low-obsolescence equipment.

Tax Benefits

When the equipment is sold, any gain (the amount received less the depreciated value) will be taxed as ordinary income. Some of the depreciation may also be subject to the Alternative Minimum Tax (see Chart 7-3).

In the end, the best equipment-leasing program you will ever be a part of will probably be the purchase of equipment that you can use in your own business. That is, some piece of equipment that can make your business more successful and one which you have control over. A personal computer or word processor, for example.

RESEARCH AND DEVELOPMENT PARTNERSHIPS

R&D partnerships are used by a growing number of companies to fund research or to pursue specific technological development projects or both without using their own money. Investors put up the cash, and in return they own rights to any products developed as a result of the research they funded. These rights usually entitle the limited partners to receive a

CHART 7-3

Alternative Minimum Tax (AMT)*

This is Congress's idea about how to prevent people from using too many tax shelters to avoid paying taxes at all. It is computed like this:

Take your adjusted gross income   _____
Subtract the following:
    Deductible portion of medical/dental expense   _____
    Contributions   _____
    Deductible portion of casualty and theft loss   _____
    Mortgage interest   _____
    Other interest (but no more than the amount of net
      investment income)   _____
Add the following:
    Many tax-shelter deductions considered tax-prefer-
      ence items. For example, the difference between
      accelerated and straight-line depreciation, excess
      oil-depletion allowances and intangible drilling
      costs, mining exploration and drilling costs   _____
    The $200 dividend exclusion if you are filing a joint
      return ($100 if single)   _____
    The 60 percent portion of the long-term capital gains
      that you excluded before   _____
    The difference between the market price and the price
      you paid for incentive corporate stock options   _____
Subtract $40,000 if you are married filing jointly,
    $30,000 if you are single, or $20,000 if married filing
    separate returns   _____
Multiply this by 20 percent, pay whatever is greater, this
    amount or the amount of regular tax you computed on
    your Form 1040   _____

If you find that you may be subject to the AMT, there are ways to avoid paying this additional tax.

1. Defer deductions until the following year because you do not get any tax benefit from many itemized deductions in the year you are subject to the AMT.
2. Accelerate the receipt of ordinary income. If you can do this, you are effectively only paying tax at a rate of 20 percent due to the impact of the AMT, which is presumably lower than your personal tax bracket.

---

*Reprinted courtesy of Watkins, Meegan, and Drury, Suite 955N, 7315 Wisconsin Avenue, Bethesda, MD 20814.

royalty based on sales, perhaps some common stock in the firm, or both. The limited partners also get some tax write-offs. It can be a good deal for both the companies and the investors. It is certainly one of the sexiest, potentially most rewarding, and in some cases most altruistic investments available.

In return for a share of potential future profits the companies transfer the developmental or research risk to investors who put up the money. Many companies use it to fund projects they might otherwise postpone or forgo. Should the R&D effort fail, the company has lost none of its own money. As an investor you could lose all of yours.

The most notorious R&D partnership is unfortunately one that didn't work, the financing of the DeLorean sports car. Limited partners who each invested $150,000 (reportedly $45,000 in cash, the balance in loans) have nothing but perhaps a used car to show for their investment.

Start-up companies with little more than ideas and dreams stand alongside such major corporations as Emerson Electric, Cummins Engine, and Becton Dickenson with R&D deals for you to evaluate. Gene Amdahl, the creator of the IBM360 computer while at IBM and later the founder of the very successful Amdahl Corporation, used an R&D partnership to raise $55 million to create the Trilogy Corporation. Initial investors put up a minimum of $10,000. In less than two years they had deducted most of their investment and were given the option of converting their partnership interest to common stock.

Other investors have provided capital to drug companies such as Cetus and Syntex to fund the research and development of various diagnostic products. Others still have provided funds to Genetech to develop human growth hormones and blood-clotting agents. And there are other companies raising money for cancer research. I have one client, a former top airline executive, who likes these programs, not only for their tax benefits and potential economic gain, but because he believes his investment in R&D might be doing society some good.

Economic Benefits

R&D partnerships are high risk/high reward ventures. Returns may be several times invested capital and are taxed as capital gains rather than ordinary income.

Tax Benefits

The portion of the money actually spent on R&D can be deducted from an investor's gross income. Administrative and setup expenses don't count. Usual write-offs over a two-year period are 50 to 100 percent of the investment. Major corporations that sponsor such programs might be able to charge the program only relatively small administrative costs. Thus the write-off can be close to 100 percent, while a start-up company with heavier administrative costs might be able to offer only a 50 percent deduction.

What to Look For

In general, experts say that D is better than R. That is because development is usually more reliable than research. It emphasizes bringing products to the market, while research can be nebulous—and go on forever without result.

Since this is a rapidly growing investment area, many bad deals are certain to surface along with the good ones. Be especially wary not to get caught in the inevitable shakeout. As with every other type of investment, you are betting on *people*. Find out whether they are experienced in this field. Look at the track record of the general partner. Evaluate the incentives and risks to the general partner. Does the product to be developed have a potentially strong market? Can the sponsoring organization market the product itself?

R&D investing is not for the faint-hearted. It is high risk minimized only by some luck, good fortune, and good people on your side. Money invested in these deals should be from your high-risk pool—every dollar of which could afford to be lost.

VENTURE-CAPITAL PARTNERSHIPS

The venture-capital business was alive and well long enough before August 1982, when the stock market discovered high-tech companies. This business is one of matching entrepreneurs who have dreams with the people who have money that can turn those dreams into operating companies capable of producing marketable products. A good venture-capital partnership provides more than money. To maximize a start-up company's chance to succeed, an experienced partnership should provide financial savvy, access to bankers, suppliers, and customers. The broader the network of contacts the greater chance the young company has to survive. The Apple Computer Corporation was a venture-capital project. In the process it made its original investors millions of dollars. A major midwestern bank's initial investment of $500,000 is now worth in the order of $40,000,000. In fact, venture-capital partnerships have spawned over 10,000 start-up companies since 1980. Limited partnerships permit individual investors to be involved in a number of professionally selected young companies that have the potential for rapid growth. To the extent any of them are successful, the limited partners benefit.

Economic Benefits

The pooling of capital offers the protection of diversification. In most instances it is the only way individuals with a few thousand dollars to invest can participate in this market of gutsy gambles and long shots. One good venture-capital hit could make the partnership a success and the investors a fortune.

Tax Benefits

The write-offs are generally modest, averaging approximately 50 percent of the investment. There is capital-gains treatment of royalties from the sale of the technology.

What to Look For

There is a vast amount of money being thrown at this market. Everyone from the neighborhood bank to several hundred new funds are chasing venture-capital deals. Quality talent that can evaluate those deals is difficult to find. And these are not short-term commitments. It takes time to cultivate pearls. I have one client who invested $5000 in a deal that became worth $5,000,000, but it took so long that by the time it worked out my client had forgotten he had even made the investment. It took over twenty years. There is a magazine well worth reading to keep up with the field. It is *Venture*, 35 W. 45 St., New York, NY 10036, (212) 840-5580.

RACEHORSE SYNDICATION

For exciting cocktail conversation, a racehorse tax shelter beats hands down a cow-feeding farm or an apartment building about to go condo in Gaithersburg, Maryland. Those sleek and glamorous thoroughbreds have to be the most exciting limited partnership on four legs. Horse racing, after all, is the sport of kings. And watching your horse come thundering down the stretch sure beats watching an apartment house depreciate.

The thoroughbred is the descendant of a cross between purebred Arabian stallions that were imported to England long ago and English mares. The first studbook, published in 1790, caused thoroughbreds to be the first breed of horses to be assigned a history and to be genealogically traced. They are the purebred of horses and in America all are registered with the Jockey Club in New York City.

There are two types of thoroughbred horse deals. One is called a racing partnership, the other a breeding partnership. There are also partnerships for standard breeds (trotters) and even polo ponies. Limited partners share the profits from purses, breeding fees, and from the sale of offspring. The partners pay for the purchase and care of the horses.

Tax Benefits

Expenses, losses, and depreciation are deductible. Horses can be depreciated in three or five years depending on their age and whether they are used for racing or breeding. The total deduction will generally range from 50 to 75 percent of your investment over a several-year period.

Economic Benefits

Astronomical profits are possible if one of your horses becomes a Triple Crown winner. Since that is unlikely, fortunately there is also a good deal of money to be made between this ultimate measure of success and the meatpacking plant. Horse racing appears to be a growth industry in the U.S., and as the number of racetracks increases so does the demand for horses capable of galloping around them. There is money to be made by owning horses that win races, and a steady income stream is possible from a successful brood mare partnership. Brood mares can produce one foal a year, which can be sold. If any do well at the track, the value of the mare increases.

What to Look For

Look for a general partner who knows the business, who has a solid reputation and track record. Try to make sure the value of the horses the partnership buys is not inflated. You can do that by calling around.

This can be a fun investment for someone looking for interesting diversification, a chance for growth of their capital, some cash flow, modest tax benefits, and an opportunity to be part of the prestigious American thoroughbred industry.

But when the sport of kings becomes the investment of the masses, it is usually an indication that the kings need a market for their less impressive stock. Investors should also remember that horses can go lame, get sick, and die. Apart from that, the market for horses could soften. This is not an investment for the meek.

CABLE TV PARTNERSHIPS

Cable television companies have turned to investors to provide the capital to build new cable systems or to buy and expand existing ones. Investors will usually be able to write off their entire investment in three to five years. Investors hope that the general manager will be able to build an operation successful enough to be sold for a profit. Quality, experienced management is one of the keys to a successful business.

Economic Benefits

Successful cable TV operations can be sold for five to ten times their cash flow. Typically it is low or nonexistent when the limited partners become involved. Good management and some luck can change that dramatically.

Tax Benefits

The cost of equipment, such as the cable, amplifiers, and signal processors can be depreciated. It is also eligible for investment-tax-credit tax benefits. Interest payments on the borrowed money is also deductible. All of this usually means that a person's entire investment can be deducted as it is spent.

What to Look For

There are of course some major hurdles to overcome in building a successful cable TV business. Most lose money in the early years. For that reason, as an investor you increase your chances for success by investing in the expansion of existing systems. Competition from other cable companies and from satellite and other technologies could cause your partnership to be less successful than you hoped. There is also the problem of local government interference, which has made cable TV a political football in many communities.

WINDMILL PARTNERSHIPS

Wind power is a technology revived by the oil sheikhs. It is clean, renewable, and fairly inexpensive to harness. A combination of generous state and federal energy-tax credits has made California the wind tax-shelter capital of the world. Wind parks sell electric power to utilities, which by an "it could only happen in California" law *must* purchase it. Limited partners provide the capital to build the wind parks in return for the tax benefits, which include the energy credit and depreciation of the wind-harnessing equipment.

Economic Benefits

Wind parks generate more tax benefits than electricity. Unless the cost of producing electricity from conventional sources quintuples, the wind generators can't compete. At the moment electricity can be generated less expensively by burning used dollar bills. Without the tax benefits there is no economic reason to invest in them.

Tax Benefits

Windmill investors get a 25 percent tax credit in California. On top of that Uncle Sam allows a special 15 percent special federal energy-property investment-tax credit to be added to the standard 10 percent investment-tax credit. According to *Forbes* writer Ellen Paris, "That means if you build a windmill in California, and are in the top tax bracket, you can reduce state and federal taxes by 37.5% of the windmill's cost (only half California's 25% credit is allowed on federal returns). The state and federal credits, in effect, can reduce the cost of wind power to around 6 to 8 cents per kilowatt-hour, almost competitive with oil."

What to Look For

The programs generate such a high tax loss that many observers have dubbed them "tax farms" rather than "wind farms." Therein lies the risk in this investment. Should good sense ever win the day in the congressional hearing rooms where tax legislation is drafted, windmill farms will go the way of Hula-Hoops and cabbage-patch dolls. The technology is suspect. The economic incentive is not there. Windmill farms seem to be an environmentalist dream funded by a notorious lack of congressional business sense.

MOVIE PARTNERSHIPS

Other than that they were box office smashes, what do *Flashdance, Staying Alive, Tootsie, Blue Thunder,* and *Annie* have in common? If you answered that they were all at least partially funded by limited partnerships you are right. Movie partnerships allow investors to pay part of the costs of bringing movies to the silver screen. The idea is that to the extent the films are box office winners the investors benefit. Because the partnerships invest in a number of films, there is the further advantage of diversification.

Economic Benefits

If some movies in the partnership are successful and the costs are recovered, investors should benefit by sharing the profits proportionately to the extent of their investment.

Some deals provide for a guaranteed return after a number of years of your entire investment. While that has been hyped as a great advantage to investors, it at best makes your investment simply a non-interest-bearing loan.

Tax Benefits

Some deals provide first-year deductions in the 50 to 70 percent range. Others offer no tax advantage.

What to Look For

The standard rule about investing is that if you put money

in speculative ventures that fail you will never see that money again. In the movie business that can happen to you even if the venture is successful. It happens because much of the entertainment world chooses to reward limited partners with a share of "net" profits. *The Wall Street Journal* says that in the entertainment field "net" almost always means "no." In movie deals the search for net profits has a lot in common with the search for Amelia Earhart. James Garner, star of the successful TV series *The Rockford Files*, was to be paid 37½ percent of the net profits. According to Mr. Garner, the studio told him there were never any net profits. The Hollywood method of accounting is reportedly so bad that even reaching break-even is a spectacular achievement. Part of that is because for many studios the real profits aren't made in the production of a movie but in its distribution. The cost of distribution is subtracted before net profits are arrived at, as are the astronomical salaries of the "talent," business-related expenses that would make non-Hollywood accountants blanch, an arbitrary overhead fee regardless of the actual cost, and interest on all costs until the break-even point is reached. The definition of when a film has reached break-even, by the way, is always up for negotiation.

The worst of these deals are dying out, I think of embarrassment, the embarrassment at taking up space on the planet. For most movie deals there hasn't been a flicker of hope in them from the moment they were created. It may be fun to tell your friends at the neighborhood cookout that you have money in the movies, but unless you count that as sufficient investment return, most investors should probably confine their movie money to the dollars spent on tickets at the box office.

THERE ARE OTHER WAYS

Tax-Shelter Alternatives

If you like the idea of putting some of your money into real estate, oil and gas, or research and development programs, or the movies, but the tax-shelter business is a bit overwhelming to you, consider buying the *common stocks* of many of the same companies. For example, most of the companies that offer limited partnerships are publicly traded. That means you can buy an interest in them without becoming involved in their tax deals. True, you won't engineer a tax break for yourself by buying the common stock rather than the limited partnership, but as a stockholder you will profit from many of the economic benefits that result from the partnership program while preserving your liquidity.

As a shareholder you can get out by simply selling your stock. It is never that easy as a limited partner. Another important benefit is that you can avoid the high partnership setup and sales charges. For example, let's say the Optimistic Pharmaceutical firm is a medium-size drug company. It's offering investors limited-partnership interests in a program designed to find a cancer cure. Investors will be able to take as a tax deduction nearly the entire amount of their investment. They will also benefit materially should the Optimistic program be successful. However, should the program fail, the investors could lose all of their money. These investors are also locked into the investment. They are able to sell only if and when the general partner allows them to sell. However, Optimistic Pharmaceutical happens to be listed on the New York Stock Exchange. An investor who believes in the R&D program could buy common stock in the company. Doesn't it stand to reason that if the company discovers a cure for cancer, the stock will go up? And if it doesn't, or if the R&D program looks as if it is going sour, the stock investor can sell. When you own the stock you have greater control.

Real estate investors can consider the shares of the publicly owned syndicators. Angeles Corporation (apartments, mobile-home parks), Equitec Financial Group (office buildings), and Integrated Resources (commercial office buildings and apartments) are three such syndicators. There are real estate developers including the Rouse Company, Koger Properties, and Cousins Properties. And there are real estate investment trusts that trade on the major exchanges. REITs are professionally managed pools of real estate that generally pay attractive dividends as well since they are required to pay out 95 percent of their operating earnings to shareholders. Among the most seasoned are the Washington REIT, BankAmerica Realty Investors, Hotel Investors Trust, Santa Anita Realty, and First Union Realty. Most REITs sell at a discount to the value of their real estate holdings, somewhat like closed-end mutual funds. For that reason it is not unusual to be able to buy $1.25 of real estate for every dollar. In a limited partnership, $1 will usually buy you $.50 to $.75 of real estate.

A number of oil and gas syndicators are public companies. They include Forest Oil, Apache Corporation, Dyco Petroleum, Unit Drilling and Exploration, and Woods Petroleum. If you are impressed with the performance record of a syndicator but are reluctant to invest in a limited partnership, check to see if the company's stock is publicly traded.

There are also royalty trusts. Through the trust mechanism an oil company is able to assign some of its oil-producing properties directly to its shareholders. The company continues to manage the wells and acreage, but because the shareholders now own them, the shareholders receive the tax deductions. They also receive larger dividends because a trust, unlike a corporation, pays no income taxes. Just as oil-income-program limited partners, royalty-trust shareholders will do well or poorly depending on the oil and gas reserves in the properties and the quality of management.

There are even a dozen or so public horse-companies. They include Thoroughbred Breeders, of East Windsor, NJ; Standard Breed Pacers and Trotters, of Great Neck, NY; and Spendthrift Farm, of Lexington, KY.

The point is that there is sometimes more than one way to take advantage of a good idea. Buying the common stock of a tax-shelter syndicator may be like following the advice of the fellow who said, "When all the world is searching for gold, I want to be the one selling the picks and shovels."

8

Invest in Your IRA
If You Sincerely
Want to Be Rich

A HEADLINE THIS BOLD WILL nearly always point us to some flimsy get-rich-quick scheme that has as much chance of working as the Russian economy. But what I'm talking about as your road to riches is an Individual Retirement Account (IRA). It can neither be called a scheme nor thought of as something that will work quickly. IRAs allow us to accumulate money over our working lifetime before it is taxed by the IRS, in accounts that are further tax sheltered. You can take full advantage of the power of compound interest in these accounts because not a single dollar is subtracted to pay taxes. Your initial investment earns interest, your interest earns interest, and the interest on the interest earns even more interest. At 12 percent for example, money doubles every six years and quadruples in thirteen. Still there are people who don't invest in IRAs. William G. Flanagan, writing in *Forbes*, said that, "It can be downright frustrating writing about IRA accounts. Here is a gift from Uncle Sam, the kindest thing the government has done for the working stiff since repealing Prohibition, and most American families still have not taken advantage of it."

American corporate leaders agree. Charles L. Brown, chairman of the board of AT&T said, "I don't think that, under current IRS rules, there is any question that an Individual

Retirement Account should be part of the investment program of everyone who qualifies." Vernon R. Loucks, Jr., president and chief executive officer of the highly respected Baxter Travenol Labs, told me: "Too many Americans are entering their retirement years inadequately prepared to financially sustain their standard of living. The government cannot be expected to carry the full burden of responsibility to provide for such an open-ended deficiency. In the spirit of American self-determination, IRAs present an ideal way for most of us to take a major role in preparing for our postretirement years."

And William K. Coors, chairman of the board of Adolph Coors Company, told me:

"I believe that IRA programs are essential to any individual's long-term well-being, unless, of course, that individual has sufficient private income to carry him through his lifetime. Employer-funded pension plans are an acceptable alternative, assuming steady employment from career start to retirement. This, of course, is not necessarily a reliable proposition.

"Finally, Social Security is in so much trouble that I cannot see it as surviving into the indefinite future. There is simply no way that unfunded pension plans can be made financially viable."

Any working person can take advantage of an IRA by depositing up to $2000 of his or her income from wages into an IRA. A working couple can invest up to $4000. A couple with only one spouse working outside the home can invest up to $2250. Each person of the couple must have an IRA account, but the $2250 contribution can be split any way they choose. Congress is likely to raise these amounts even further—just as it has steadily increased the amount of money we are allowed to contribute to Keogh accounts.

An IRA is as certain a way to get rich as any of us are likely to find, because it helps us fight against the four problems that Richard Russell, editor of the *Dow Theory Letters,* says plague investors:

"They are (a) impatience, (b) our own stupidity, (c) taxes, and, last but certainly not least, (d) time. Let me explain. If we want to get rich, all we have to do is buy long-term Treasury bonds yielding 11 percent and reinvest each year and wait.

"Let me give you an example. If you start with $1000 (at 11 percent interest) and add $1000 each year plus interest (all at 11 percent), in ten years you will have $16,700. In fifteen years you will have $34,405. In twenty years you will have $64,202. And in thirty years you will have $199,000.

"So that's the way to get rich. But there are two problems in this guaranteed way to get rich. First, taxes. It doesn't look that good if you pay the taxes on the interest. But there is a way to get around the taxes or at least defer them. And that is the IRAs.

"Next you have the problems of impatience and stupidity. And here I can't really help you. All I can say is that anyone who doesn't have a tax-deferred plan is stupid, and anyone who doesn't have patience simply must learn how to become patient. Let me put it another way: if you're stupid and you lack patience, you'll never get rich the sure way—which is the compounding way.

"Then there is one last problem, and that is TIME. If you are under the age of thirty, you still have plenty of time to get rich. But if you are, say, fifty-five or sixty-five or seventy-five you don't have enough time to get rich through compounding and waiting." Now that is as colorful an argument in support of IRAs as you are likely to find. An IRA investment can be almost as flexible as you want it to be. It can be at a bank, with an insurance company, a mutual fund, or an account that you manage yourself at a stockbrokerage firm.

The investment choices in fact include most of those that are written about in this book.

To date most IRA investors are using some form of bank savings plan or savings certificate. If that is your choice, be sure to shop around, because now that banks can compete for your deposits the rates vary significantly. Take a few minutes and call around to find out what the various savings institutions are offering. While you are at it don't forget to call the stockbrokerage firms. They can also offer insured savings certificates and money-market accounts. Sometimes their rates are higher than traditional savings institutions.

When you ask about the interest rate being offered, be sure to ask how much your $2000 deposit will be worth at the end of the term in dollars and cents. I advise you to do that because interest rates are compounded differently by different institutions. For example, 15 percent interest looks higher than 12 percent, and of course it is, if the compounding feature is identical. But if the 15 percent is a simple interest rate, added only at the end of the term, and the 12 percent is compounded daily, 12 percent might be a better deal for you. I suggest asking the bank to tell you what your deposit will be worth, because you shouldn't have to go to the trouble of figuring it out yourself. And that will avoid the problem of misinterpreting the bank's computation method. The way interest is compounded can make a big difference in the return you get from your investment.

As you can see from Chart 8-1, the difference between an investment paying a rate of 9 percent compounded annually and one paying 9 percent compounded daily is .42 percent. When interest is compounded daily, the interest you earn each day is reinvested each day so as to become, itself, a source of further income. When shopping for a place to put your money, be sure to compare the "effective yield" of one investment to another. The effective yield is what you can expect to get after compounding.

CHART 8-1. Compounding Rates

Compounded Annually	Compounded Quarterly	Compounded Monthly	Compounded Daily
8%	8.24%	8.30%	8.33%
8.5	8.77	8.84	8.87
9	9.31	9.38	9.42
9.5	9.84	9.92	9.96
10	10.38	10.47	10.52
10.5	10.92	11.02	11.07
11	11.46	11.57	11.63

Other popular IRA investments include money-market funds and zero-coupon bonds including the Treasury-backed issues called TIGERS, Bengals, CATS, and Cougars. The list of choices will continue to expand. *Business Week* predicts that "the IRA market will get more complicated, more interesting and more rewarding." You will confront new types of limited partnerships that emphasize income, and mutual funds especially designed for IRAs. As I mentioned earlier, *Business Week* figures you have 1430 different types of IRA savings certificates to choose from. That is one of the reasons I call the growing importance of your IRA one of the major money trends of this decade. The other reason is that the government will continue to raise the amount we will be allowed to contribute to our IRA plans. Some part of that contribution may be voluntary and not deductible, but I think it is only a matter of time before each of us is able to contribute as much as 10 to 15 percent of our gross income to our IRA.

WHAT COMPOUNDING CAN DO TO YOUR CONTRIBUTIONS

Little IRA accounts can mushroom into six-figure totals, and middle-sized Keogh plans into millions. Chart 8-2 shows the effect of contributing a given amount at the beginning of each year, compounded at a given yield. Let's say that a doctor with twenty-five years to go feels he or she can set aside a tax-

CHART 8-2

Years to retirement	Compounding factor if annual yield is:					
	6%	7%	8%	9%	12%	15%
1	1.06	1.07	1.08	1.09	1.12	1.15
2	2.18	2.21	2.25	2.28	2.37	2.47
3	3.37	3.44	3.51	3.57	3.78	3.99
4	4.64	4.75	4.87	4.98	5.35	5.74
5	5.98	6.15	6.34	6.52	7.12	7.75
6	7.39	7.65	7.92	8.20	9.09	10.07
7	8.90	9.26	9.64	10.03	11.30	12.73
8	10.49	10.98	11.49	12.02	13.78	15.79
9	12.18	12.82	13.49	14.19	16.56	19.30
10	13.97	14.78	15.65	16.56	19.65	23.35
15	24.67	26.89	29.32	32.00	41.75	54.72
20	38.99	43.87	49.42	55.76	80.70	117.81
25	58.16	67.68	78.95	92.32	149.33	244.71
30	83.80	101.70	122.35	148.58	270.29	499.96

deferred $15,000 to earn a safe 8 percent. Multiply by the compounding factor of 78.95 and, presto, you have $1,184,250!

ALL IRAS ARE NOT CREATED EQUAL

The best advice is to be conservative with your IRA investments. Since the government will not allow you to deduct losses in this tax-sheltered account, there is no reason to take chances. This part of your investment program should be conservatively managed. *Income* rather than *capital gain* should be your goal. Remember, every dollar that will eventually come out of the account will be taxed as ordinary income. That is why taking the extra risk necessary to achieve a capital gain usually doesn't make sense. There is no capital-gain tax advantage in an IRA.

You will find a number of limited partnerships designed specifically as IRA investments. Some of them invest in mortgages for interest payments only. Some real estate partnerships lend at below market rates and take a piece of the appreciation when the properties are sold, as well as part of the rental income while the property is held. There are programs that invest in mini-warehouses, producing oil wells, and equipment leases. You should subject these programs to the same tests that you would apply to them if they were outside the IRA. In addition have your CPA check the programs to make sure they don't generate unrelated business expenses. The IRS has ruled that those kinds of expenses could make you eligible for taxes on any income in excess of $1000 per year from your investment. Be especially wary of buying a limited partnership that is not specifically designed for a tax-sheltered account or for your IRA.

OTHER IRA TIPS

Don't Wait: Invest Early

You don't need to wait to file your tax return until after you have made your IRA contribution. The IRS will allow you until April 15 to make your IRA investment. The sooner you invest your $2000 in a tax-sheltered IRA the sooner you will begin sheltering from income taxes the interest that money earns. At 10 percent interest $2000 will earn $200 a year. If that amount is taxed at 30 to 40 percent, $60 to $80 of that $200 will be sent off to the IRS next April 15. You can keep that money in your account compounding for you by starting your IRA now!

An IRA Is Even Worth Borrowing to Have

Not only will the law allow you to shelter the interest an IRA earns, but you can deduct the interest it costs you to get the money for the program. If you are in the 35 to 40 percent tax bracket or higher, that makes sense. Your $2000 earned 10 percent tax-sheltered, so you are up $200. If the $2000 costs 15 percent to borrow, that amounts to $300 of deductible interest expense. In the 35 to 40 percent tax bracket, a $300 deduction will save you $105 to $120 in taxes. Take a few minutes to work out the numbers for yourself, but for higher-bracket taxpayers it will always make sense to borrow to fund an IRA rather than not to have one at all.

This Tax Shelter Ends at Age Seventy and One Half

You don't have to contribute every year, and you don't even have to contribute the full $2000, but you do have to stop contributing at age seventy and one half. Even though you are allowed to pull your money out without a tax penalty as early as age fifty-nine and one half, an IRA may be the best form of tax shelter available to someone all the way up to the maximum age.

You May Want More Than One IRA

You can have as many different IRAs as you would like. The only limitation is that you can't invest more than $2000 in the combination of IRAs in a year. You can transfer your funds without tax penalty from one fund to another.

How to Get Money out of an IRA

If you have a large IRA, from a rollover, for example, and you are over age fifty-nine and one half, begin withdrawing a nominal amount periodically. The reason is that if you die before you start making regular withdrawals, the IRS could force your beneficiary to collect all the money in the plan and pay the taxes within five years. If you have begun a withdrawal program, the benefits could be spread over what should have been your statistical life expectancy.

At age seventy and one half, you don't have to pull it all out at once. You can withdraw it in regular annual amounts based on your life expectancy. The IRS says a seventy-and-one-half-year-old man has a life expectancy of twelve years, so one-twelfth of his IRA can be withdrawn each year. You can also transfer the money, without paying tax, into an insurance company annuity plan that will guarantee you payments as long as you live. Many of these plans provide a lump-sum payment to your survivors should you not live some minimum number of years from the date that you buy the annuity.

If you pull out the money before age fifty-nine and one half you are in deep kimchi. The IRS will hit you with a 10 percent tax penalty on the amount withdrawn and you will need to pay income tax on that amount at your regular rate.

Money says that some kimchi is less deep than other: "The tax benefits eventually outweigh the penalty. For taxpayers in the 33% bracket—$29,000 to $35,200 taxable income for a couple filing jointly—an IRA account earning 12% interest reaches the break-even point after five years." Even paying the penalty and income tax, you will have more money left than if you earned the same return outside an IRA and paid taxes annually. But the longer you leave the money in the IRA after the break-even point, the more you will benefit from the compounding.

The American Association of Individual Investors has calculated just how long it takes to break even considering the tax penalty and your tax bracket. To use the table to find your break-even holding period, find your marginal tax bracket on the left of Chart 8-3. Then look across to find the average annual return you have been earning on your IRA. The corresponding number in the chart shows how many years pass before you can withdraw your money from the IRA before you come out behind.

CHART 8-3

IRA Break-Even Holding Periods

Constant marginal tax rate* (%)	Average annual yield to withdrawal*											
	6%	7%	8%	9%	10%	11%	12%	13%	14%	15%	16%	17%
10	19.63	16.83	14.72	13.09	11.78	10.71	9.82	9.06	8.41	7.85	7.36	6.93
15	13.91	11.92	10.43	9.27	8.34	7.59	6.95	6.42	5.96	5.56	5.22	4.91
20	11.13	9.54	8.35	7.42	6.68	6.07	5.56	5.14	4.77	4.45	4.17	3.93
25	9.54	8.18	7.16	6.36	5.72	5.20	4.77	4.40	4.09	3.82	3.58	3.37
30	8.56	7.34	6.42	5.71	5.14	4.67	4.28	3.95	3.67	3.43	3.21	3.02
35	7.96	6.82	5.97	5.30	4.77	4.34	3.98	3.67	3.41	3.18	2.98	2.81
40	7.60	6.51	5.70	5.06	4.56	4.14	3.80	3.51	3.26	3.04	2.85	2.68
45	7.43	6.37	5.57	4.95	4.46	4.05	3.72	3.43	3.19	2.97	2.79	2.62
50	7.44	6.38	5.58	4.96	4.46	4.06	3.72	3.43	3.19	2.98	2.79	2.63

*Rates are continuously compounded for both taxes and average annual yield. Rates not continuously compounded can be substituted for a rough idea of the break-even point.

9

How to Use Insurance
as an Investment

TAX-DEFERRED ANNUITIES

There is no investment better designed to postpone the tax bite
on interest income or capital gain than a tax-deferred annuity.
If you will be in a lower tax bracket at some later point in your
life, it might be an ideal investment for you. That is because it
allows you to shelter investment earnings from taxes while you
are in a high tax bracket and withdraw it later when you are in a
lower tax bracket. There are two basic types of annuities. They
are usually referred to as *fixed* and *variable*. Fixed annuities
are like saving certificates. They are simply a loan that you
make to an insurance company. The company guarantees to
pay you back and to pay you interest on the amount borrowed.
Since the insurance company credits the interest to your annuity account rather than paying it out to you, you are allowed
to postpone paying any income tax on the interest until you
actually take it out of the annuity account. Variable annuities
are usually investments in a family of mutual funds. Just like a
fixed annuity, you need not pay any tax until you withdraw
capital gains, interest, and dividend income. The mutual fund
can be any type the insurance company offers—from a money-
market fund to an aggressive-growth fund. The funds are pools

of money managed by the insurance company specifically for their annuity accounts. The tax laws won't allow you to select just any mutual fund and put it into an annuity. Lipper Analytical Services, (212) 269-4080, monitors many variable annuities just as it publishes performance reports for all mutual funds. Performance varies significantly from one fund to another.

There are even annuities that will allow you to channel money into real estate. Integrated Resources calls their plan "Harvest." Along with a share of the rental income, Harvest owners share in rent increases and property appreciation. Harvest is an open-end fund with a $5000 minimum initial investment and with $1000 minimum additional investments. Harvest can be contacted at (800) 221-2644. Merrill Lynch has a real estate annuity plan called Realty Plus. It actually owns real estate rather than mortgages on property.

Not all annuity contracts are created equal. Here are some of the features that can make one an ideal investment and another a poor choice:

- *Sales charge*. Be sure you understand what it is. Some charge a commission at the time of purchase. Others can be bought without a fee but impose a surrender charge should you ever withdraw funds rather than annuitize. I'll explain what it means to annuitize in the next section. A number of plans charge a withdrawal fee that reduces annually. For example, if you cash out after one year, the penalty is 5 percent of the amount withdrawn. After the second year the percentage drops to 4 percent, and so on. Watch out for the plans that charge a fixed percentage that never disappears. There is never a reason to lock yourself into such an arrangement.
- *How long is the guaranteed return guaranteed?* Fixed-annuity contracts will usually promise a high first-year return to entice you to make the investment. After the first year or first couple of years the rate can be adjusted by the insurance company. Find out in writing what the contract promises as a minimum interest rate. Forget what the salesperson promises. Some annuity contracts guarantee only a very low interest rate after the initial rate, and believe me, they may pay it. If that happens you are stuck with having to choose between the low rate of

interest or paying the withdrawal penalty to get your money out.

• *Quality of the insurance company.* Even insurance companies can go bankrupt. The best advice is to choose a good-quality company even if the rate of return is not as high as it would be with some firm whose reputation you don't know. Insurance companies are rated, and you can find their ratings in *Best's Insurance Reports*, available in many libraries. A+ is *Best's* highest rating.

WHAT DOES IT MEAN TO ANNUITIZE?

The original idea of an annuity was to provide its owner with an income he or she couldn't outlive. One obtains that income by annuitizing. It is, in fact, one of the oldest financial arrangements in the history of civilized man, originating over 2000 years before Christ. A person who wanted to provide for his family during his old age or after his death could deposit grain with the local granary. Years later the granary would provide grain to the members of the person's family for the rest of their lives. In the middle ages the concept was expanded. People would give money to their town treasurer to provide a like income for a newborn child. If the child died, the benefits were passed on to other siblings. Until recently annuity contracts were used mainly by associations of educators. In the 1970s stockbrokers redesigned them as investments and began selling them to their clients, most of whom will never annuitize. They simply want to benefit from the attractive investment characteristics.

Let's say you buy an annuity contract and rather than cash it in and withdraw all your funds at one time, you ask the insurance company to dribble payments out to you over time. If you do that you have annuitized your investment. You can choose to have it paid out to you over the remainder of your life. The insurance company uses its actuarial tables to determine how many years you are expected to live and makes payments to you based on your life expectancy.

You may outlive their prediction, in which case you will receive more money than the insurance company expected to pay you. Or you may get hit by a car and die the day after you annuitize. In that case the insurance company wins.

If you would rather not play this form of Russian roulette, there are other choices including the *guaranteed return of your principal* to your beneficiary should you die early. *Life with a guaranteed number of years certain* is another choice that will continue to make payments to your beneficiary for at least a preselected number of years should you die before that number of years passes. *Joint and survivor* provides for payments over two lives—usually yours and your spouse's.

The amount of monthly payments from your annuity account will vary based on which option you choose. Obviously, the less time over which the insurance company needs to guarantee payments the higher the monthly income will be.

Two other important points about annuitizing. Once you begin you can't change your mind and stop the program. Make your choice carefully. And just because you have invested with a particular insurance company doesn't mean that you must accept one of their options in order to annuitize. You are permitted to transfer your annuity account without any tax penalty to another insurance company to take advantage of a better plan or higher payment rates if you choose. So shop around *before* you make your annuity selection.

For Whom Are Annuities Best?

They are ideally suited to people who want a steady income from the money they have accumulated over their lifetime.

However, unlike a bond that will also pay a steady income, there is nothing left to pass along to beneficiaries when the annuity has stopped paying. With that in mind, make sure that "steady income" is appreciably higher than it would be if the money were simply invested in bonds and then left to some favorite charity.

LIFE INSURANCE AS A TAX SHELTER

They come by different names and with different distinguishing features, but when you boil them down to their basics, most turn out to be wonderful tax shelters for most people. These flexible life or universal life insurance policies not only provide death benefits at a price that is competitive with term insurance premiums, but you can overpay the premium to have the money go into a tax-sheltered investment account.

You can adjust both the level of death benefit and investment to your changing circumstances. For example, in the early years of marriage, when your children are young and your assets are few, you need a high level of death benefit. As your children grow older and become self-dependent, and your assets, we hope, have grown, you can reduce the amount of death protection. At retirement you may need no death protection at all.

The investment part of the program is flexible. During periods in your life when you can afford to save, you are encouraged to add money to the investment portion of the universal life policy. Should you need to withdraw some of that money, you can do that too. Because of the favorable tax legislation life insurance companies have been able to wrangle from Congress, every dollar earned in the program is tax sheltered. You pay no income tax until you withdraw more money from the program than the total amount you paid in. This can be quite a benefit to you.

The major points of universal and variable life are:

1. You can pay into the program when, and in any amount you choose, subject to certain minimums. The insurance company withdraws enough money from the investment portion to pay for the insurance coverage.

2. You can withdraw funds without paying a tax on that amount as long as it doesn't exceed the amount of your contribution.

3. You can raise and lower the amount of your death benefit, although you may have to take a health exam to increase coverage.

4. Your investment portion can earn money-market rates of interest, tax sheltered. (Variable life policies will even permit you to select from a family of mutual funds for the investment portion.) This is the most attractive feature of the program. In

addition to providing a guaranteed death benefit whatever your investment experience, the policy can become one of your best tax-sheltered investment tools. In the 30 percent tax bracket, when you can earn 10 percent tax deferred, that is as good as earning 14¼ percent on which you must pay taxes.

5. Both kinds of policies provide an annual statement showing you exactly how much the policy is worth, how much cash accumulated, what the current dividend rate is, as well as the death benefit. You won't find this with traditional life insurance policies.

Money said that "if you tried to invent the ideal policy, it might closely resemble universal life." It is a combination of life insurance and a high-interest savings account, or an investment account that can be arranged and rearranged to match your family's changing responsibilities and your ability to pay insurance premiums. It is an "unbundled" insurance policy. That basically means that the cash reserves have been separated. There are some tax reasons for this.

The Wall Street Journal called these policies "a better deal" because they offer a decent investment return in addition to protection. The *Journal* also said that these policies could be some of the best tax shelters around. That is because the money that accumulates in a life insurance policy is considered tax-free. Both types allow you to take advantage of favorable tax legislation, but more about that later.

What Your Life Insurance Policy Looks Like

A traditional whole life policy could be visualized as an empty glass.

On the first day of your policy, the company is entirely at risk for the face value. The glass is empty. That is because there is no cash value. Over time the amount of cash value increases as part of your premium payment accumulates in a low-yield (3 to 7 percent) investment program. The glass is becoming full. If you want any part of your cash value you must borrow it from your policy—and pay interest. The loan reduces your death benefit (the amount in the glass). For example, if you borrowed $5000 from your $100,000 policy and died before repaying, the death benefit would be $95,000. Midway through your program the life insurance company's risk has been cut by half, because if you died, one-half of the death benefit would be your own cash value. Meanwhile, your premium has remained the same throughout. A universal or variable rate policy would look like Chart 9-1.

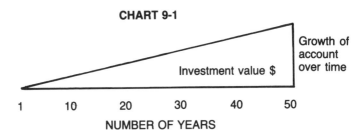

CHART 9-1

Growth of account over time

Investment value $

NUMBER OF YEARS

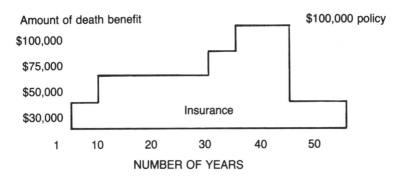

Amount of death benefit $100,000 policy

$100,000

$75,000

$50,000

$30,000   Insurance

NUMBER OF YEARS

Both policies separate the insurance from the investment. Remember, you can adjust the amount of insurance to adapt to your changing financial responsibilities. Your investment value will grow over time at a substantially higher rate than in the whole life policy. You can take the money out whenever you choose, and when you do you won't be borrowing it from your policy. Most importantly, the amount of your loan won't affect your death benefit.

Not all of these insurance products are created equal. Some programs, in fact, are probably much worse than what you own. So don't accept this as a blanket endorsement of every policy promoted to be a universal or variable life insurance product available to you. The concept makes sense. A sharp insurance specialist can show you the nuts-and-bolts difference in the actual policies.

What to Watch For

- Commissions can be high—especially the first-year fee. Shop around.
- Track records of the funds vary. Check them.
- High-tax-bracket individuals benefit most from these plans. If you are in a low tax bracket, invest elsewhere.

You Can Borrow From These Policies

Both types of policies allow you to borrow the cash value, usually at a modest rate of interest. The insurance companies will continue to credit some minimum interest on the borrowed cash even though you have it. For example, you may pay 6 percent to borrow $1000 from your policy and be credited 4 to 5 percent. Your actual cost is only 1 or 2 percent. This amount is tax deductible if you pay it in cash. The firms that are offering these plans are E.F. Hutton (Omniplan), Merrill Lynch (Prime Plan), Paine Webber (Ultraplan), and Shearson/American Express (Dynaplan).

10

How to Tailor the
Perfect Investment
Portfolio for You

KEEPING THE RECORDS STRAIGHT

Getting and staying in good financial shape takes planning. It takes some organization and it requires the discipline to keep good records. People who keep track of their financial life on paper tend to do better than those who have only a sketchy idea about how their financial life is progressing. And when those people go on to some other world, a good set of records can make life much easier for those who are left behind. The best advice is to keep every statement you receive. Someday they may be needed.

Most of us put ourselves through an unnecessary amount of pain at tax time each year as we struggle to gather together those pieces of paper that may prove to support a tax-deductible expense. That is nonsense. If you would keep a calendar in which you record tax-deductible expenses each day, the year-end chore would become a simple task of adding numbers.

Ronald B. Find, a senior associate editor of *Medical Economics,* suggests that you spend ten minutes a day, when you go through the mail, to keep your records up to date. According to Mr. Find, "All the system requires is a strongbox, a desk drawer, a file-cabinet drawer, and possibly a loose-leaf notebook (the notebook may be unnecessary if you have a personal computer).

"The strongbox, which should be fire-resistant, protects papers that don't belong in a bank safe-deposit box: passports, insurance policies, auto titles, duplicate Social Security cards, and copies of wills. It's also prudent to store an inventory of home possessions here with appraisals, photos, and receipts that document their value. If you've received an inheritance, keep a copy of the estate valuation in the strongbox.

"The desk drawer, divided into compartments, stores savings-account passbooks, CDs, monthly checking-account statements, and canceled checks that aren't needed to verify tax deductions.

"The file cabinet is used to keep folders for stocks, bonds, mutual funds, and other investments, tax records, and home improvements."

Here's how the individual files might be set up:

- Tax records. You need enough folders for each tax-deductible category. That is, business entertainment, travel, telephone and automobile expense. Set up your folders based on the major categories of deductions that you took last year. In each folder keep receipts, canceled checks, and any other materials, such as appraisals of property donated to charity, that will document deductions on your tax return for the current year. In the remaining folder keep copies of your last few annual federal and state tax returns plus the checks and documents backing up your deductions.
- Home improvements. It's wise to keep a running file of receipts and other papers that document expenditures for major home improvements. (They reduce the amount of profit you have to report to the IRS when you sell.)

Use the notebook to keep track of how your investments are performing. My advice is to write down the prices of each of your funds once a month. Pick a day and make it a ritual. The first Saturday of each month, for example. I want you to go through the physical act of *writing* the price down because it forces you to keep track. Glancing at the newspaper now and then is too casual a system. It is a slipshod method that will allow your investments to get away from you. When you spot a significant trend developing, you should sell (see chapter 5).

The notebook should also be used to record capital-gains distributions and dividends. They are taxed differently. I can't tell you how many people I've met who have no idea what their tax basis is for their mutual-fund investments. When it comes time to sell a number of years after holding the fund, they are likely to be far too generous to the IRS simply because their records are so shoddy. I've also known many people who have kept their fund long after it should have been sold because they couldn't deal with the burden of computing their tax base. A simple schedule such as Chart 10-1 could have eliminated that burden.

Keep a separate page in your notebook for each of your IRA and Keogh accounts. And make sure your spouse knows where these records are, as well as how to understand your record-keeping system.

CHART 10-1

Name of Investment		Templeton Growth Fund		
Address:				
Phone No:				
History (Dates)	Investment	Withdrawal	Dividend	Cap. Gain

This all may sound like too much of a chore for the ordinary investor, but I assure you the Internal Revenue Service *expects you to lead your life this way*. If you have ever been audited you know exactly what I mean.

Let me make another prediction. If you aren't now keeping accurate records and you make the changes that I've suggested, my guess is that you will save hundreds, perhaps even thousands, of tax dollars.

* * *

Mark Twain wrote, "The more you explain it, the more I don't understand it." This is especially true about building financial game plans. The good ones don't come out of cookie cutters. So many variables come into play, because each of us is unique. Our goals, personalities, level of investment acumen, amount of interest, motivators, family situation, age, marital status, experiences, backgrounds, education and desire to be successful as investors are different for everyone. That is why simple formulas won't work. And that is why many investors may feel precisely like Mark Twain. Good investment planning is the result of answering many questions and dealing with many explanations.

As a financial writer it would be so easy to tell you that every single, twenty-nine-year-old female earning $40,000 a year should do X, and every sixty-three-year-old couple should do Y, but as someone who works with real-life investors every day, I know that won't work. What I have tried to do is to help you think about yourself, your goals, and what motivates you. I have described the types of choices that are available for you to make. I've also identified some of the major money-trends that will affect your financial life and taught you how to turn those trends to your advantage. In this final section I want to help match you to appropriate investments. It is a matter of continually narrowing your choices to those that make the most sense to you.

One of the quickest ways to narrow them is to eliminate every one of them that makes you uncomfortable. I made the point earlier that it is important to distinguish between being uncomfortable because you don't understand an investment and being uncomfortable because the investment doesn't "feel right" to you. Every investor should have as a goal never to be intimidated by the seeming complexity of an investment. However challenging it seems, you should keep in mind that every investment boils down to this simple fact: *Someone wants some of your money to do something with.* Learn to ask enough questions so that you understand (1) who that someone is, (2) what that someone wants to do, and (3) how he or she plans to do it. If those basic questions can't be answered in a way that you and the member of your family with the most common sense understand, you have every right to reject the idea without feeling a bit sorry. Similarly, if the person who wants you to invest your money can't explain the investment to *your* satisfaction, you should walk away from it. As an investor, you are under no obligation to learn a new language just so that you can communicate with securities salespeople. If they want your money, let them speak your language! And let them do it over and over until every one of your questions is answered. On page 191 I have listed the questions that I suggest you ask.

In my opinion you have three responsibilities as a serious investor.

1. To open your mind wide enough to consider the opportunities available to you. In his book *Creating Wealth Through Real Estate*, Robert Allen made an important point about personal growth with this story:

"I'll never forget a radio interview I did in Pittsburgh. The host and I spent some time talking about the road to wealth. The host's assistant, a young woman, listened intently. After the interview she questioned me. 'Mr. Allen, all of what you say sounds interesting, even feasible. But it goes against everything my parents have always taught me!'

"I asked, 'How are your parents doing financially?' She replied, 'Terribly. They are really strapped for money.' Then she laughed at what she had just said. She understood."

If you aren't willing to grow, nothing can change and all of the time you spend reading this book might as well have been spent at some mindless task like mowing the yard.

2. Your second responsibility is to make informed choices. Abraham Lincoln said, "If I had eight hours to chop down a tree, I'd spend six sharpening my ax." That is of course why

you are reading this book and why you must constantly work to upgrade your knowledge of investments.

3. Your third responsibility as a serious investor is to make your decisions based not only on reason but on your instinct. The bottom of your stomach knows your investment comfort zone perhaps better than the left side of your brain. Some investors can't tolerate risk. Some thrive on it. Most investors can accept some measure of risk in exchange for what they consider to be a fair rate of return. Selecting the most appropriate investments for your situation involves matching the risk you are willing to take with the investments with that measure of risk.

On Chart 10-2, picture your comfort zone as an expandable set of dotted lines that run parallel with a solid line. The solid line represents no-risk investments. The larger your comfort zone, the greater the variety of higher-risk investments you probably feel at ease using. Be honest with yourself as you define your personal comfort zone, and keep in mind that it is normal for it to expand or contract as you change.

Typically, younger, higher paid, entrepreneurial people will have larger comfort zones than older, lesser paid, security-minded people. That is easy to understand, because the first group finds money easier to replace than the second.

Investments that fit in the low-risk comfort zone are money-market funds, savings certificates, short- and intermediate-term high-quality bond funds, and perhaps modest amounts of good-quality mutual funds.

Medium-risk comfort-zone investors would probably find a wide range of mutual funds to be acceptable investments. Some of the more conservative limited partnerships might also appeal to this group, and perhaps modest amounts of the higher-risk limited partnerships.

Higher-risk investors could invest comfortably in a diversified portfolio of every investment recommended in this book. Diversification controls risk and provides for more opportunities to be successful.

CHART 10-2.   Determining Your Own Comfort Zone

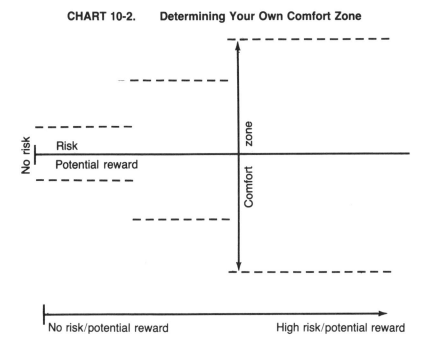

INVESTMENT PERSONALITY

Your investment personality can also affect your comfort zone. Financial basket-cases and nervous Nellies have, by definition, smaller zones than Captain America or the financial junkies. Wild Bill Hickock must constantly guard against having his zone expand and contract like an accordion. The point about comfort zones is that you recognize the limits of your own and try to invest within those limits. Investing should be a happy experience. It should be an extension of the way you lead the rest of your life. It should allow you to make decisions as soon as you are comfortable with the facts, and live with your choice as long as the investment performs up to your expectations. Making an investment choice is not much different from buying a car. Think about both choices in similar terms and your investments are likely to be appropriate ones.

But unlike a car purchase, investing touches different emotions for many people. At its worst it plays on your fear and on your greed. Making investment choices tends to exaggerate the worst of our personality traits. Kiril Sokoloff and George Clairmont, the authors of *Street Smart Investing* wrote, "If you are greedy, the market can turn you into a pauper. If you are arrogant, the market can humble you. If you are obstinate, the market can break you." You have got to take a more businesslike approach to your investment decision-making process. How do you respond if it becomes clear that you bought the wrong car? You would probably replace it. You would do well to react to bad investment decisions the same way rather than allowing yourself to be so emotionally wrapped up that you can't deal with them routinely.

WHICH INVESTMENT CHARACTERISTICS ARE IMPORTANT TO YOU?

Investments have different characteristics. Some are easy to get in and out of. They are called *liquid* as opposed to *illiquid* investments. Some can fluctuate in value in a very wide range.

They can make your tens of dollars grow to thousands of dollars or cause the thousands to drop to tens. Some won't change in value at all. They simply generate income. Some pay no income but offer potential of rapid growth. But of course with that potential comes the corresponding potential of rapid loss. The speed with which an investment can gain or lose value (its volatility) is another characteristic.

The Most Illiquid Investments

Tax shelters are the most illiquid investments described in this book. You should put only money you won't need for several years into tax shelters. And once you commit, you might as well put them out of your mind. Aside from reading the mail from the general partner, there is little you can do with your tax-sheltered investment. You are at the mercy of the general partner. That is why making the right choice in the beginning is so important.

Aside from being illiquid, tax shelters generally offer the greatest potential reward and highest risk of any of the investments I've described.

The Most Liquid Investments

Money-market funds are the most liquid investments. Money you place in them will not fluctuate in value. The rate of interest you earn can go up and down, but your basic investment will not. You should use money-market funds to store cash you might need for emergencies and day-to-day requirements. Beyond having enough in reserve for those purposes, your money should be invested.

Is Your Objective Growth or Income?

This is a choice you must make yourself. Most people have investment programs that heavily favor one or the other. Income-oriented investors tend to be people who want to earn interest on their investment capital without exposing that capital to much fluctuation in value.

CHART 10-3. How to Select the Best for You

Objective	Type of Investment
Highest quality	U.S. Government securities or the most highly rated securities: AAA,Aaa
High tax-bracket investors (35% plus)	Tax-free securities
Maximum return	Junk bonds (low quality) Highest yields
Minimum price fluctuation of basic investment	Short- or intermediate-term notes or bonds
Maximum price-fluctuation potential	Long-term bonds (20-40 years)

QUESTIONS YOU SHOULD ASK ABOUT EVERY INVESTMENT

Every time you evaluate an investment I'd like you to ask these questions and write down the answers to each in your own language. I suggest you write them because if you are able to do that it means you probably understand the investment well enough to explain it. Writing forces you to confront the risks and deal with them emotionally. Writing is an emotional commitment. By inking it you are also thinking it. It does no good to leave out facts about an investment. In the end you hurt only yourself. Your written summary also forces you to deal with a finite number of issues, whereas when we try to deal in our mind with an investment, it seems almost abstract. The task can seem overwhelming. The variables and unknowns seem without limit. The investment is almost impossible to evaluate. When we write down our concerns and questions they become orderly. On paper they can be dealt with one at a time.

The Questions:

1. What would it take to make this a successful investment?
2. How likely is that?
3. What could go wrong?
4. What could cause that?
5. How likely is that?
6. Where does this investment fit into my investment program?
7. How much time must I spend monitoring this investment?
8. When am I going to spend that time?
9. Is my information about this investment accurate?
10. Am I interpreting it correctly?
11. What would the person I know with the most common sense think about it?
12. Is it right for me?

Your financial life is yours alone. It is different from everyone else's. That is why *you* must take charge of it, not anyone else. It is your struggle against the odds for whatever level of financial success you really want for yourself. It can be mastered. Tens of thousands already have. They are the Captain Americas who are willing to make the effort and to try again and again every time their last best effort turns out not to be good enough.

Nearly a Thousand Mutual-Fund Choices

The following is a descriptive listing of every mutual fund avail-ble to you—as well as information about how you can contact each. It was obtained by Steve Gritzan. He is a bright, in-quisitive, young professional whose college education and work experience have been in radio and television. Steve's task was to call every mutual fund in America. He was to find out what each common-stock fund specialized in. Since most money market and bond funds have similar investment strategies, we did not ask about those funds.

What is interesting about Steve's experiences is that they would probably be identical to your own if you were to under-take the same time-consuming task. Steve is not an investment insider. He was looking for answers that he could understand as a layman. This is Steve's report of his phone contacts with the mutual-fund industry. The information is provided in hopes that Steve's efforts will save you about a month's worth of phone calls.

My assignment was clear enough: call as many major mu-tual funds in America as possible, find out what type of fund each was, and what areas of investment the fund keyed on. Wayne made it clear from the start that many funds were part of larger groups and that I could possibly reach ten funds by calling one number.

The assignment, as I said, appeared clear and easy enough. I started on a Tuesday; Wayne suggested that maybe we could get things wrapped up by Friday. I countered with a ten-day deadline. I walked back to my apartment looking at perhaps a week's work. That was the first mistake. We overrated the cooperation of the funds.

My procedure remained consistent throughout: I'd call the number, get a secretary, and ask to speak with someone who could give me more information about Fund X. Sometimes the second person I spoke to would be able to help me. But more often I was passed on to yet another person. Sometimes another. Sometimes even another. Some funds, after keeping me on the phone for twenty minutes, would then ask me to call back tomorrow, or ask for my number as a callback. All funds offered to send me "informational materials" or "a prospectus." Many sent them by U.S. mail, others via Federal Express. Some didn't send anything after saying that they would.

When I finally reached someone who seemed able to help, I still often ran into trouble. Most funds were willing to send me flyers on everything they offered, but others were hesitant to discuss their funds over the phone. Several times I was accused of working for another mutual fund, even more often I was told that mutual funds were too complex to discuss over the phone. "Wouldn't you like some pamphlets and prospectuses instead?" In all fairness, I observed that smaller funds were much more responsive and open to my questions than the biggies. I suppose that the small guys had much more to gain by being cordial. But many of the larger groups were rude and quite impatient that I didn't know about "front-end contractual plans" and "leverage funds." I explained that I was the original layperson when it came to the investment world, and sometimes this helped. Yet some fund representatives felt unable to communicate even the most general information about their funds.

Some of the problems I encountered were not because the fund representative didn't want to help me, but because he or she couldn't get his mind out of "financialese" mode. Some questions about a certain term were answered with a larger term and enough mumbo-jumbo (in my mind anyway) to fill a textbook. After much questioning, I often got an answer. But it sometimes took forty-five minutes to get ten minutes of information.

As my research came to an end and my apartment became filled with all sorts of annual reports, prospectuses, and other investment matter, I began to notice a pattern. Many of the most helpful and down-to-earth funds were also the ones with the most understandable and colorful literature. Funds that avoided my questions or were just plain nasty tended to have dry, technical, boring materials for consumer use. Ah ha! Could some funds have a different approach to customer relations and promotions? In many cases my research showed this to be true.

Examining the computer readout on which I recorded research, I realize that many funds were left out for a variety of reasons. Some of the other funds listed were either bond funds, municipal-bond funds, or even money-market funds. They are quite similar. But taking into account the funds I spoke with, here is a very general breakdown.

20% Very cooperative. Mostly smaller funds. Information gathered quickly, explanations concise.

40% Fairly cooperative. Small, medium, and medium-large funds. Information sometimes too technical and hard to understand.

20% Uncooperative. Mostly larger groups. No one could be reached who could answer my questions.

20% Uncooperative. Some information gathered, but attitude generally condescending and nasty.

EXPLANATION OF FUND DESCRIPTIONS

For obvious reasons it was very difficult to classify each fund. What is "aggressive" to one firm could be "conservative" to another. This point was drilled into my head by almost every firm that I called. So in order to have my listings make sense, I used the terms "aggressive" and "conservative" in a very general way. For example, I rarely said "very aggressive" unless the spokesman from that firm used the phrase "very aggressive." In most cases, funds were described in comparison with other funds in that group. For example, the Kemper group of funds were described as compared with one another: "Kemper's most aggressive fund . . ." Smaller groups and single mutual funds were described as best as I could. Most times I read back my description to the spokesman to get a reaction. I took their views into account and sometimes rewrote what I had written. Terms like "moderate," "volatile," and "very conservative" were often taken straight from the spokesman's mouth.

For some funds, I listed some of the more concentrated areas that they had invested in. This was a very touchy area, for as you know, such information varies from week to week. I looked for trends, that is, areas that funds had invested in for the past couple of years. Some funds (maybe 10 percent) specialized in a certain area like science or health or foreign investments. Others were very diverse and showed no trends (these occurred especially among the larger funds). For these, I simply said that they were "diverse." But it should be made very clear that much of the information I gathered could date very quickly.

TERMINOLOGY

"Specializing in" refers to a fund that (you guessed it) specializes in one specific industry or area. Many of these funds were considered aggressive because of this concentration.

"Keying on" refers to a fund that has tended to invest in certain areas over a proven length of time. This information was either procured from a fund spokesmen or from the *Weisenberger Investment Companies Service Guide*. Of course, such a listing is subject to change and should not be the sole reason why someone invests or doesn't invest.

"Including" refers to a fund that is very diverse. Industries or concentrations noted aren't stable indications at all: they are just a sampling of what the fund has invested in before. Not to be used solely in making a final decision, only for reference.

Even though I found many of the larger groups to be somewhat difficult and uncooperative, I also began to understand some of their problems. Often I spoke with representatives who sounded as though they needed to take one Valium per hour! To review a group that had twenty funds (sometimes more) would have taken quite a long time on the phone. Plus, I learned that mutual funds are often grouped or classified according to investment strategy rather than concentration in a certain industry. And, of course, nothing is ever simple in the business world. After talking with their peers and clients all day, it must have been tough to explain price-earnings ratios to a former stickball champ from New Jersey. Still, many groups were more than helpful. T. Rowe Price spent an hour on the phone patiently explaining their investment strategies with me. The GIT Fund of Arlington, VA, not only told me about their funds, but commiserated with me about the lack of good pizza in the Washington area! Now that's understanding! All kidding aside, I just want to compliment the funds that made my research easy, and I hope that my rantings and ravings over the phone at least made a few fund representatives think about their treatment of potential customers. After all, since doing this research I've been talking with friends about their investments and giving suggestions . . .

Some exceptional funds . . . on both ends of the spectrum. (Of course this only reflects their treatment of me!)

Very Helpful (without being too technical)

Axe-Houghton Group	T. Rowe Price	Templeton Group
GIT Funds	Security Group	Unified Group
Lord Abbett Group	Strong Funds	Vanguard Group

Very Uncooperative (or condescending or snotty . . .)

Federated Group	Phoenix Funds
Franklin Group	PRO Group
Massachusetts Financial Group	Putnam Group
Pennsylvania Mutual Funds	

I realize that investment firms, like all companies, are made up of many employees and that one person's attitude cannot be taken to represent an entire company. This should be kept in mind.

Note: (800) numbers are toll-free.

ABT Arbitrage Fund   OPTION
450 Australia Ave. S.
West Palm Beach, FL 33401
(305) 655-3481   (800) 327-4508

Conservative growth/income fund, specializing in technology-oriented firms. Fairly diverse.

ABT Emerging Growth Fund   CAPITAL APPRECIATION
450 Australia Ave. S.
West Palm Beach, FL 33401
(305) 655-3481   (800) 327-4508

Somewhat aggressive growth fund, keying on electronics, telecommunications, and business services.

Acorn Fund   SMALL COMPANY GROWTH
120 S. LaSalle St.
Chicago, IL 60603
(312) 621-0630

Information, finance, industrial goods and services.

ADV Fund   GROWTH & INCOME
One New York Plaza
New York, NY 10004
(212) 908-9582

Aetna Income Shares   CORPORATE BOND
151 Farmington Ave.
Hartford, CT 06156
(203) 273-0123   (800) 243-5774

Affiliated Fund   GROWTH & INCOME
63 Wall St.
New York, NY 10005
(212) 425-8720

Growth/income fund, keying on electric light/power, communications, financial. Diverse. (Lord Abbett Fund)

Afuture Fund   GROWTH
Front & Lemon St.
Media, PA 19063
(215) 565-3131

Moderately aggressive growth/income fund. Diverse.

A.G.E. High Income Fund   BOND
155 Bovet Rd.
San Mateo, CA 94402
(415) 570-3000   (800) 227-6781

Bond fund, including consumer goods, utilities.

Aggressive Growth Shares   GROWTH
One Wall St.
New York, NY 10005
(212) 269-8800   (800) 221-5757

Alliance Mortgage Securities   GROWTH
140 Broadway
New York, NY 10005
(212) 902-4126

Mortgage-backed securities.

Alliance Technology Fund   GROWTH
140 Broadway
New York, NY 10005
(212) 902-4126   (800) 221-5672

Aggressive-growth fund, keying on computers, defense electronics, medical
technology.

Alpha Fund   GROWTH
2 Piedmont Center NE
Suite 500
Atlanta, GA 30363
(404) 262-3480   (800) 241-1662

Moderately aggressive growth fund, specializing in small-to-midsized technology firms.

AMCAP Fund   GROWTH
333 S. Hope St.
Los Angeles, CA 90071
(213) 486-9200   (800) 421-0180

American Balanced Fund   BALANCED
PO Box 7650
San Francisco, CA 94120
(415) 421-9360

One of the earliest "balanced funds" (1932).

American Birthright Trust   GROWTH
450 Australia Ave. S.
Suite 300
West Palm Beach, FL 33401
(305) 655-3481   (800) 327-4508

Conservative-growth fund, keying on dividend-paying technology, consumer goods.

American Capital Bond Fund   FIXED INCOME
PO Box 3121
2777 Allen Pkwy.
Houston, TX 77253
(713) 522-1111

American Capital Comstock Fund   CAPITAL APPRECIATION
PO Box 3121
2777 Allen Pkwy.
Houston, TX 77253
(713) 522-1111

Less aggressive.

American Capital Enterprise Fund   GROWTH
PO Box 3121
2777 Allen Pkwy.
Houston, TX 77253
(713) 522-1111

American Capital Harbor Fund   GROWTH & INCOME
PO Box 3121
2777 Allen Pkwy.
Houston, TX 77253
(713) 522-1111

American Capital High Yield Invest. Fund   FIXED INCOME
PO Box 3121
2777 Allen Pkwy.
Houston, TX 77253
(713) 522-1111

American Capital Pace   CAPITAL APPRECIATION
PO Box 3121
2777 Allen Pkwy.
Houston, TX 77253
(713) 522-1111

Aggressive, will buy out-of-favor stocks.

American Capital Venture Fund   CAPITAL APPRECIATION
PO Box 3121
2777 Allen Pkwy.
Houston, TX 77253
(713) 522-1111

American Express Govt Money Fund   GOVT BONDS
PO Box 1335
Boston, MA 02205
(617) 956-9758   call collect

American Express Growth Fund   GROWTH
PO Box 1335
Boston, MA 02205
(617) 722-6870   (800) 343-1300

Moderate-growth fund, including capital goods, basic industries, consumer
durables.

American Growth Fund   GROWTH
650 17th St.
Suite 800
Denver, CO 80202
(303) 623-6137   (800) 525-2406

American Heritage Fund   CAPITAL APPRECIATION
Mr. Jefferson Bender
Menlo Management Corporation
10201 Perish Place
Cupertino, CA 95014
(408) 996-2710

American Industrial Shares   GROWTH & INCOME
PO Box 3942
St. Petersburg, FL 33731
(813) 823-8712

American Investors Fund   GROWTH
PO Box 2500
Greenwich, CT 06830
(203) 622-1600   (800) 243-5353

Moderate-growth fund, keying on communications equipment, electronics, business machines.

American Investors Income Fund   FIXED INCOME
PO Box 2500
Greenwich, CT 06830
(203) 622-1600   (800) 243-5353

Corporate bond, preferred-stock income fund. Very diverse.

American Leaders Fund   GROWTH & INCOME
421 Seventh Ave.
Pittsburgh, PA 15219
(412) 288-1900   (800) 245-4270

Very conservative, mostly blue-chip oil/gas, some utilities. May be developing new, more aggressive growth fund in future.

American Mutual Fund   GROWTH & INCOME
333 S. Hope St.
Los Angeles, CA 90071
(213) 486-9200   (800) 421-0180

American National Bond Fund   FIXED INCOME
Two Moody Plaza
Galveston, TX 77550
(409) 766-6572   (800) 231-4646

American National Growth Fund   GROWTH
Two Moody Plaza
Galveston, TX 77550
(409) 766-6572   (800) 231-4646

American National Income Fund   EQUITY INCOME
Two Moody Plaza
Galveston, TX 77550
(409) 766-6572   (800) 231-4646

Analytic Optioned Equity   OPTION FUND
2222 Martin St.
Suite 230
Irvine, CA 92715
(714) 833-0294

Armstrong Associates   GROWTH
311 N. Market St.
Suite 205
Dallas, TX 75202
(214) 744-5558

Diverse-growth fund, including business equipment, telecommunications.

Axe-Houghton Fund B   BALANCED
400 Benedict Ave.
Tarrytown, NY 10591
(914) 631-8131   (800) 526-3187

Balanced fund, diverse, slight majority of assets in bonds and preferred stocks.

Axe-Houghton Income Fund   FIXED INCOME
400 Benedict Ave.
Tarrytown, NY 10591
(914) 631-8131   (800) 526-3187

Corporate-bond fund, keying on industrial, foreign, and communications utilities.

Axe-Houghton Stock Fund   GROWTH
400 Benedict Ave.
Tarrytown, NY 10591
(914) 631-8131   (800) 526-3187

Aggressive-growth fund, keying on emerging small-to-medium retail trade, computers, electronics.

David L. Babson Growth Fund   GROWTH & INCOME
Three Crown Center
2440 Pershing Rd.
Kansas City, MO 64108
(816) 471-5200

David L. Babson Income Fund   FIXED INCOME
Three Crown Center
2440 Pershing Rd.
Kansas City, MO 64108
(816) 471-5200

Bank Stock Fund   GROWTH
PO Box 367
333 N. Tejon St.
Colorado Springs, CO 80901
(303) 473-8100

Bascom Hill Investors 402 S. Gammon Pl. Madison, WI 53719 (608) 833-6300

GROWTH & INCOME

Beacon Growth Fund 46 Homestead Park Needham, MA 02194 (617) 444-2770

GROWTH

Beacon Income Fund 46 Homestead Park Needham, MA 02194 (617) 444-2770

INCOME

Beacon Hill Mutual Fund 75 Federal St. Boston, MA 02110 (617) 482-0795

GROWTH

BLC Growth Fund 711 High St. Des Moines, IA 50307 (515) 247-5711

GROWTH

Moderately conservative growth fund, keying on electronics, home furnishings. Avoids speculation.

BLC Income Fund 711 High St. Des Moines, IA 50307 (515) 247-5711

EQUITY INCOME

Conservative income fund, mostly common stock, keying on banking, petroleum, steel, and utilities.

BMI Equity Fund 67 Wall St. New York, NY 10005 (212) 422-1619

CAPITAL APPRECIATION

Bond Fund of America 333 S. Hope St. Los Angeles, CA 90071 (213) 486-9200   (800) 421-0180

FIXED INCOME

Bond Portfolio for Endowments   FIXED INCOME
PO Box 7650
San Francisco, CA 94120
(415) 421-9360

Boston Co. Capital Appreciation Fund   GROWTH
One Boston Pl.
Boston, MA 02106
(617) 722-7250   (800) 343-6324

Conservative-growth fund—deals in blue chip stocks, keying on technology, capital goods.

Boston Co. Govt Income Fund   FIXED INCOME
One Boston Pl.
Boston, MA 02106
(617) 722-7250   (800) 343-6324

Conservative government-bond fund. Mostly U.S. Treasury notes.

Boston Co. Special Growth Fund   GROWTH
One Boston Pl.
Boston, MA 02106
(617) 722-7250   (800) 343-6324

New fund (1982). Aggressive, very diverse—invests in consumer services, capital goods.

Boston Foundation Fund   BALANCED
421 Seventh Ave.
Pittsburgh, PA 15219
(412) 288-1900   (800) 245-4270

Boston Mutual Fund   GROWTH
120 Royall St.
Canton, MA 02021
(617) 828-7000

Bowser Growth Fund   PENNY STOCK
107 N. Adams St.
Rockville, MD 20850

Specializes in stocks under two dollars.

Bruce Fund   GROWTH
200 W. Monroe St.
Chicago, IL 60606
(312) 236-9160

Bull & Bear Capital Growth   GROWTH
11 Hanover Sq.
New York, NY 10005
(212) 785-0900

Bull & Bear Equity Income Fund   EQUITY INCOME
11 Hanover Sq.
New York, NY 10005
(212) 785-0900

Bull & Bear High Yield Fund   FIXED INCOME
11 Hanover Sq.
New York, NY 10005
(212) 785-0900

Bullock Fund   GROWTH & INCOME
One Wall St.
New York, NY 10005
(212) 269-8800   (800) 221-5757

Calvert Fund—Equity Port.   GROWTH
4550 Montgomery Ave.
Suite 1000
North Bethesda, MD 20814
(301) 951-4800   (800) 368-2745

Conservative-growth fund, keying on blue-chip manufacturing.

Calvert Fund—Income Port.   FIXED INCOME
4550 Montgomery Ave.
Suite 1000
North Bethesda, MD 20814
(301) 951-4800   (800) 368-2745

Corporate, government-bond fund—some electric utilities.

Calvert Social Invest.—Growth Mngt.   PORT. GROWTH & INCOME
4550 Montgomery Ave.
Suite 1000
North Bethesda, MD 20814
(301) 951-4800   (800) 368-2745

Growth/income fund with social considerations, keying on government securities, some media.

Canadian Fund   CANADIAN
One Wall St.
New York, NY 10005
(212) 269-8800   (800) 221-5757

American fund that specializes in Canadian firms, including oil, mining—
companies chosen will benefit by Canada's growth.

Capital Preservation T-Note Trust   FIXED INCOME
755 Page Mill Rd.
Palo Alto, CA 94304
(415) 858-2400   (800) 227-8380

Cardinal Fund   GROWTH & INCOME
155 E. Broad St.
Columbus, OH 43215
(614) 464-6975

Growth/income fund—diverse.

Centennial Growth Fund   GROWTH
3600 S. Yosemite St.
Denver, CO 80237
(303) 770-2345   (800) 525-9310

Century Shares Trust   GROWTH & INCOME
50 Congress St.
Boston, MA 02109
(617) 482-3060

Chancellor New Decade Fund   GROWTH
100 Gold St.
New York, NY 10292
(212) 791-4654   (800) 221-7984

Charter Fund   CAPITAL APPRECIATION
2100 Republic Bank Tower
Dallas, TX 75201
(214) 742-6567

Buys well-established companies with accelerating earnings.

Cheapside Dollar Fund   GROWTH
One State St.
New York, NY 10015
(212) 269-6500

Chemical Fund   GROWTH
61 Broadway
New York, NY 10006
(212) 480-8600   (800) 221-5233

Growth fund that invests in high-quality stock of larger, established science
and technology-oriented companies.

CIGNA Growth Fund   GROWTH
N-73
Hartford, CT 06152
(203) 726-6000

CIGNA High Yield Fund   FIXED INCOME
N-73
Hartford, CT 06152
(203) 726-6000

CIGNA Income Fund   FIXED INCOME
N-73
Hartford, CT 06152
(203) 726-6000

Colonial Corporate Cash Trust   EQUITY INCOME
75 Federal St.
Boston, MA 02110
(617) 426-3750   (800) 225-2365

Conservative fund, keying on consumer nondurables, utilities.

Colonial Fund   GROWTH & INCOME
75 Federal St.
Boston, MA 02110
(617) 426-3750   (800) 225-2365

Conservative fund, invests in above-average stocks, including manufacturing.

Colonial Growth Shares   GROWTH
75 Federal St.
Boston, MA 02110
(617) 426-3750   (800) 225-2365

Conservative-growth fund, specializing in manufacturing, technology.

Colonial High Yield Securities   FIXED INCOME
75 Federal St.
Boston, MA 02110
(617) 426-3750   (800) 225-2365

Corporate-bond fund, keying on consumer goods/services, industrials.

Colonial Income Fund   FIXED INCOME
75 Federal St.
Boston, MA 02110
(617) 426-3750   (800) 225-2365

Bond fund, specializing in U.S. govt agencies.

Colonial Option Growth Trust   OPTION
75 Federal St.
Boston, MA 02110
(617) 426-3750   (800) 225-2365

Very aggressive stock fund, investing in U.S. and foreign emerging technology and manufacturing firms.

Colonial Option Income Fund   OPTION
75 Federal St.
Boston, MA 02110
(617) 426-3750   (800) 225-2365

Conservative common-stock fund, keying on technology and other high-
quality firms.

Colonial Tax-Managed Trust   EQUITY INCOME
75 Federal St.
Boston, MA 02110
(617) 426-3750   (800) 225-2365

Tax-free, utility-oriented income fund.

Columbia Fixed Income Securities   FIXED INCOME
PO Box 1350
1301 SW Fifth
Portland, OR 97207
(503) 222-3600   (800) 547-1037

Balanced fund, mostly bonds. U.S. govt securities.

Columbia Growth Fund   GROWTH
PO Box 1350
1301 SW Fifth
Portland, OR 97207
(503) 222-3600   (800) 547-1037

Moderately conservative growth fund, keying on consumer goods—searches for midsize emerging firms.

Combined Penny Stock Fund   CAPITAL APPRECIATION
PO Box 6429
Colorado Springs, CO 80934
(303) 636-1511

Commerce Income Shares   INCOME
333 Clay St.
Suite 4300
Houston, TX 77002
(713) 751-2400

Commonwealth Funds Plans A&B   GROWTH & INCOME
One Winthrop Sq.
Boston, MA 02110
(617) 482-6500

Commonwealth Funds Plan C   GROWTH & INCOME
One Winthrop Sq.
Boston, MA 02110
(617) 482-6500

Companion Fund   GROWTH
Connecticut General Life Insurance Co.
Hartford, CT 06152
(203) 726-6000

Companion Income Fund   FIXED INCOME
Connecticut General Life Insurance Co.
Hartford, CT 06152
(203) 726-6000

Composite Bond & Stock Fund   BALANCED
Sea First Financial Center, 9th Fl.
Spokane, WA 99201
(509) 624-4101

Bond fund, includes large communications, technology.

Composite Fund   GROWTH & INCOME
Sea First Financial Center, 9th Fl.
Spokane, WA 99201
(509) 624-4101

Growth/income fund, including consumer nondurables, banking, others.

Composite Income Fund   FIXED INCOME
Sea First Financial Center, 9th Fl.
Spokane, WA 99201
(509) 624-4101

Concord Fund   GROWTH
60 State St., Room 930
Boston, MA 02109
(617) 742-7077

Constellation Growth Fund   CAPITAL APPRECIATION
331 Madison Ave.
New York, NY 10017
(212) 557-8787

Aggressive-growth fund, two-thirds in over-the-counter stocks, well diversified.

Continental Mutual Investment Fund   GROWTH & INCOME
6631 East Ironside Dr.
Scottsdale, AZ 85253
(602) 991-1363

Convertible Yield Securities   FIXED INCOME
11 Greenway Plaza
Suite 1919
Houston, TX 77046
(713) 626-1919

Copley Tax Managed Fund   GROWTH & INCOME
109 How St.
Fall River, MA 02724
(617) 674-8459

Corporate Cash Management Fund   FIXED INCOME
PO Box 1515
580 Sylvan Ave.
Englewood Cliffs, NJ 07632
(201) 567-2375

Corporate Leaders Trust B Fund   GROWTH & INCOME
PO Box 1515
580 Sylvan Ave.
Englewood Cliffs, NJ 07632
(201) 567-2375

Country Capital Growth Fund   GROWTH
PO Box 2222
1701 Towanda Ave.
Bloomington, IL 61701
(309) 557-2670

Country Capital Income Fund   FIXED INCOME
PO Box 2222
1701 Towanda Ave.
Bloomington, IL 61701
(309) 557-2670

Dean Witter Development Growth Securities   SMALL COMPANY GROWTH
Five World Trade Center
New York, NY 10048
(212) 938-4500   (800) 621-2525

Dean Witter Dividend Growth Securities   GROWTH & INCOME
Five World Trade Center
New York, NY 10048
(212) 938-4500   (800) 621-2525

Dean Witter High Yield Fund   FIXED INCOME
Five World Trade Center
New York, NY 10048
(212) 938-4500   (800) 621-2525

Dean Witter Ind. Value Fund   GROWTH
Five World Trade Center
New York, NY 10048
(212) 938-4500   (800) 621-2525

Dean Witter—Natural Resources Division   NATURAL RESOURCES
Five World Trade Center
New York, NY 10048
(212) 938-4500   (800) 621-2525

Decatur Income Fund   EQUITY INCOME
10 Penn Center Plaza
Philadelphia, PA 19103
(215) 988-1200

Conservative-stock fund seeking high income, keying on consumer goods,
financial.

Delaware Fund   EQUITY INCOME
10 Penn Center Plaza
Philadelphia, PA 19103
(215) 988-1200

Growth/income fund, very diverse, includes transportation, technology.

Delchester Bond Fund   FIXED INCOME
10 Penn Center Plaza
Philadelphia, PA 19103
(215) 988-1200

Industrial/government-bond fund. Industrials include communications and
entertainment.

Delta Trend Fund   CAPITAL APPRECIATION
10 Penn Center Plaza
Philadelphia, PA 19103
(215) 988-1200

Moderately aggressive growth fund that specializes in emerging energy companies.

de Vegh Mutual Fund   GROWTH
140 Broadway
New York, NY 10005
(212) 635-3516   (800) 221-7780

Conservative-growth fund, keying on business equipment, defense, retailing, health care.

DFA—Inflation Hedge A   FIXED INCOME
310 S. Michigan Ave.
Chicago, IL 60603

DFA—Small Company   SMALL COMPANY GROWTH
310 S. Michigan Ave.
Chicago, IL 60603

Directors Capital Fund   OPTION
30 Broad St.
New York, NY 10004
(212) 635-0616

Dividend Growth Fund   EQUITY INCOME
11400 Rockville Pike
Suite 300
Rockville, MD 20852
(301) 770-1600

Dividend Shares   (GROWTH & INCOME
One Wall St.
New York, NY 10005
(212) 269-8800   (800) 221-5757

Dodge & Cox Balanced Fund   BALANCED
One Post St., 35th Fl.
San Francisco, CA 94104
(415) 981-1710

Dodge & Cox Stock Fund   GROWTH & INCOME
One Post St., 35th Fl.
San Francisco, CA 94104
(415) 981-1710

Drexel Burnham Fund   GROWTH & INCOME
60 Broad St.
New York, NY 10004
(212) 483-1436

Drexel Burnham Lambert Benefactor's Money Market Fund
60 Broad St.
New York, NY 10004
(212) 483-1436

Investors can designate all or part of their interest income for the hospital,
charity, or college of their choice.

Dreyfus A Bonds Plus   FIXED INCOME
767 Fifth Ave., 35th Fl.
New York, NY 10153
(212) 715-6000   (800) 645-6561

Corporate and U.S. government-bond fund.

Dreyfus Fund   GROWTH & INCOME
767 Fifth Ave., 35th Fl.
New York, NY 10153
(212) 715-6000   (800) 645-6561

Diverse, fairly conservative income/growth fund, includes banking, foreign
investments.

Dreyfus Growth Opportunity   GROWTH & INCOME
767 Fifth Ave., 35th Fl.
New York, NY 10153
(212) 715-6000   (800) 645-6561

Diverse-growth fund, includes electronics, forest/paper products.

Dreyfus Leverage Fund   CAPITAL APPRECIATION
767 Fifth Ave., 35th Fl.
New York, NY 10153
(212) 715-6000   (800) 645-6561

Aggressive-growth fund, specializing in utilities. A leverage fund.

Dreyfus Special Income   INCOME
767 Fifth Ave., 35th Fl.
New York, NY 10153
(212) 715-6000   (800) 645-6561

Bond fund—corporate, utilities.

Dreyfus Third Century Fund   GROWTH
767 Fifth Ave., 35th Fl.
New York, NY 10153
(212) 715-6000   (800) 645-6561

Somewhat socially aware growth fund, keying on railroads, financial services.

Eagle Growth Shares   GROWTH
110 Wall St.
New York, NY 10005
(212) 668-8109

Eaton & Howard Balanced Fund   BALANCED
24 Federal St.
Boston, MA 02110
(617) 482-8260   (800) 225-6265

Conservative, balanced fund. Common stocks include oil/gas, finance, insurance.

Eaton & Howard Stock Fund   GROWTH & INCOME
24 Federal St.
Boston, MA 02110
(617) 482-8260   (800) 225-6265

Growth/income fund, including insurance, consumer goods, oil/gas—bigger companies.

Eaton Vance Growth Fund   GROWTH
24 Federal St.
Boston, MA 02110
(617) 482-8260   (800) 225-6265

Moderate-growth fund, including technology, consumer goods, office equipment.

Eaton Vance High Yield Fund   INCOME
24 Federal St.
Boston, MA 02110
(617) 482-8260   (800) 225-6265

Income fund, mostly utilities.

Eaton Vance Income Fund of Boston   INCOME
24 Federal St.
Boston, MA 02110
(617) 482-8260   (800) 225-6265

Income fund.

Eaton Vance Investors Fund   BALANCED
24 Federal St.
Boston, MA 02110
(617) 482-8260   (800) 225-6265

Bond fund.

Eaton Vance Special Equities Fund   GROWTH
24 Federal St.
Boston, MA 02110
(617) 482-8260   (800) 225-6265

Aggressive-growth fund, including consumer products, technology—diverse.

Eaton Vance Tax-Managed Trust   EQUITY INCOME
24 Federal St.
Boston, MA 02110
(617) 482-8260   (800) 225-6265

Eberstadt Energy Resources   NATURAL RESOURCES
61 Broadway
New York, NY 10006
(212) 480-8600   (800) 221-5233

Diverse-growth fund that invests in companies that "are responsive to national and worldwide energy needs."

Elfun Trusts   GROWTH
PO Box 7650
112 Prospect St.
Stamford, CT 06904
(203) 357-4104

Endowments, Inc.   GROWTH & INCOME
Two Embarcadero Center
San Francisco, CA 94120
(415) 421-9360

Energy Fund   NATURAL RESOURCES
342 Madison Ave.
New York, NY 10173
(212) 850-8300

Growth fund specializing in energy and energy development concerns.

Energy & Utility Shares   SPECIALTY
PO Box 550
Axe Wood, Butler & Skippack Pikes
Blue Bell, PA 19422
(215) 542-8025

Evergreen Fund   GROWTH
550 Mamaroneck Ave.
Harrison, NY 10528
(914) 698-5711

Aims for maximum capital appreciation, looks for companies that shift suddenly into high gear.

Evergreen Total Return Fund   EQUITY INCOME
550 Mamaroneck Ave.
Harrison, NY 10528
(914) 698-5711

Explorer Fund   SMALL COMPANY GROWTH
PO Box 2600
Valley Forge, PA 19482
(215) 648-6000   (800) 523-7025

Very aggressive growth fund, keying on industrial systems, defense electronics, electronics—small firms.

Fairfield Fund   SMALL COMPANY GROWTH
605 Third Ave.
New York, NY 10158
(212) 661-3000

Farm Bureau Growth Fund   GROWTH & INCOME
5400 University Ave.
West Des Moines, IA 50265
(515) 225-5400   (800) 247-4170

Moderate-growth fund, including drugs, business machines, entertainment.

Federated GNMA Trust   FIXED INCOME
421 Seventh Ave.
Pittsburgh, PA 15219
(412) 288-1900   (800) 245-4270

Fixed-income government-bond fund.

Federated High Income Securities   FIXED INCOME
421 Seventh Ave.
Pittsburgh, PA 15219
(412) 288-1900   (800) 245-4270

Corporate-bond fund, invested mostly in utilities, multilined companies.

Federated Income Trust   INCOME
421 Seventh Ave.
Pittsburgh, PA 15219
(412) 288-1900   (800) 245-4270

Long-term government-securities fund—Freddy Mac—for income.

Federated Intermediate Govt   FIXED INCOME
421 Seventh Ave.
Pittsburgh, PA 15219
(412) 288-1900   (800) 245-4270

Fixed-income, short-term government-securities fund.

Federated Stock Trust   GROWTH & INCOME
421 Seventh Ave.
Pittsburgh, PA 15219
(412) 288-1900   (800) 245-4270

Conservative-stock trust, specializing in high-quality energy firms.

Fidelity Contrafund   GROWTH
82 Devonshire St.
Boston, MA 02109
(617) 726-0200   (800) 225-6190

Fidelity Corporate Bond   FIXED INCOME
82 Devonshire St.
Boston, MA 02109
(617) 726-0200   (800) 225-6190

Fidelity Destiny Fund   GROWTH
82 Devonshire St.
Boston, MA 02109
(617) 726-0200   (800) 225-6190

Fidelity Equity–Income Fund   EQUITY INCOME
82 Devonshire St.
Boston, MA 02109
(617) 726-0200   (800) 225-6190

Conservative stocks, convertible bonds, and preferred stocks.

Fidelity Freedom Fund   CAPITAL APPRECIATION
82 Devonshire St.
Boston, MA 02109
(617) 726-0200   (800) 225-6190

Keogh, IRA fund.

Fidelity Fund   GROWTH & INCOME
82 Devonshire St.
Boston, MA 02109
(617) 726-0200   (800) 225-6190

Conservative, blue-chip growth fund—diverse.

Fidelity Govt Securities Fund   FIXED INCOME
82 Devonshire St.
Boston, MA 02109
(617) 726-0200   (800) 225-6190

Fidelity High Income Fund   FIXED INCOME
82 Devonshire St.
Boston, MA 02109
(617) 726-0200   (800) 225-6190

Fidelity Magellan Fund   GROWTH
82 Devonshire St.
Boston, MA 02109
(617) 726-0200   (800) 225-6190

Aggressive, diverse-growth fund that employs three or four different investment strategies.

Fidelity Mercury Fund   GROWTH
82 Devonshire St.
Boston, MA 02109
(617) 726-0200   (800) 225-6190

Aggressive, diverse-growth fund, specializing in emerging growth companies.

Fidelity Puritan Fund   EQUITY INCOME
82 Devonshire St.
Boston, MA 02109
(617) 726-0200   (800) 225-6190

Conservative stock/bond fund—diverse.

Fidelity Qualified Dividend Fund   EQUITY INCOME
82 Devonshire St.
Boston, MA 02109
(617) 726-0200   (800) 225-6190

Designed for corporations that can benefit from 85 percent dividends received deduction. Individuals are not eligible to invest in this fund.

Fidelity Select Port.—Energy   NATURAL RESOURCES
82 Devonshire St.
Boston, MA 02109
(617) 726-0200   (800) 225-6190

One of a series. An aggressive-growth fund because it concentrates on energy
firms.

Fidelity Select Port.—Financial Serv.   SPECIALTY
82 Devonshire St.
Boston, MA 02109
(617) 726-0200   (800) 225-6190

One of a series. An aggressive-growth fund because it concentrates on financial services.

Fidelity Select Port.—Health Care   SPECIALTY
82 Devonshire St.
Boston, MA 02109
(617) 726-0200   (800) 225-6190

One of a series. An aggressive-growth fund because it concentrates on health
services.

Fidelity Select Port.—Precious Metals   GOLD ORIENTED
82 Devonshire St.
Boston, MA 02109
(617) 726-0200   (800) 225-6190

One of a series. An aggressive-growth fund because it concentrates on precious metals.

Fidelity Select Port.—Technology   SPECIALTY
82 Devonshire St.
Boston, MA 02109
(617) 726-0200   (800) 225-6190

One of a series. An aggressive-growth fund because it concentrates on technology.

Fidelity Select Port.—Utilities   SPECIALTY
82 Devonshire St.
Boston, MA 02109
(617) 726-0200   (800) 225-6190

One of a series. An aggressive-growth fund that concentrates on utilities.

Fidelity Thrift Trust Fund   FIXED INCOME
82 Devonshire St.
Boston, MA 02109
(617) 726-0200   (800) 225-6190

Fidelity Trend Fund   GROWTH
82 Devonshire St.
Boston, MA 02109
(617) 726-0200   (800) 225-6190

Fiduciary Capital Growth Fund   GROWTH
222 E. Mason St.
Milwaukee, WI 53202
(414) 271-6666

Financial Bond Shares Fund   FIXED INCOME
7503 Marin Dr.
Englewood, CO 80111
(800) 525-9831

Financial Dynamics Fund   CAPITAL APPRECIATION
7503 Marin Dr.
Englewood, CO 80111
(800) 525-9831

Financial Industrial Fund   GROWTH & INCOME
7503 Marin Dr.
Englewood, CO 80111
(800) 525-9831

Financial Industrial Income Fund   INCOME
7503 Marin Dr.
Englewood, CO 80111
(800) 525-9831

Finomic Investment Fund   CAPITAL APPRECIATION
First International Plaza
1100 Louisiana
Suite 4550
Houston, TX 77002
(713) 659-2611

First Investors Bond Appreciation Fund   FIXED INCOME
120 Wall St.
New York, NY 10005
(212) 825-7900

Bond fund. Lower-rated bonds, including oil/gas, finance, merchandising.

First Investors Discovery Fund   SMALL COMPANY GROWTH
120 Wall St.
New York, NY 10005
(212) 825-7900

Aggressive-growth fund that keys on emerging furniture/home furnishings,
textiles, electronics, others.

First Investors Fund for Growth   GROWTH
120 Wall St.
New York, NY 10005
(212) 825-7900

Moderate, diverse-growth fund.

First Investors Fund for Income   INCOME
120 Wall St.
New York, NY 10005
(212) 825-7900

Income fund, can invest in stocks or bonds—diverse.

First Investors International Securities Fund   INTERNATIONAL
120 Wall St.
New York, NY 10005
(212) 825-7900

Invests in overseas companies.

First Investors Natural Resources Fund   NATURAL RESOURCES
120 Wall St.
New York, NY 10005
(212) 825-7900

Growth fund, specializing in natural resources, natural-resource-related industries.

First Investors 90-10 Fund   OPTION
120 Wall St.
New York, NY 10005
(212) 825-7900

Ninety percent in money-market investing. Ten percent in options. Minimum investment $100. Subsequent investments $50.

First Investors Option Fund   OPTION
120 Wall St.
New York, NY 10005
(212) 825-7900

Options fund.

Florida Mutual U.S. Govt 2   FIXED INCOME
One Corporate Plaza
Suite 1802
Fort Lauderdale, FL 33301
(305) 522-0200   (800) 432-1592

44 Wall Street Equity Fund   CAPITAL APPRECIATION
150 Wall St.
New York, NY 10038
(212) 267-2820

44 Wall Street Fund   CAPITAL APPRECIATION
150 Wall St.
New York, NY 10038
(212) 267-2820

Aggressive-growth stocks.

Foster & Marshall Growth Fund   GROWTH
Washington Tr. Financial Center
711 W. Sprague Ave.
Spokane, WA 99204
(509) 455-6060

Foundation Growth Stock   GROWTH
6631 E. Ironside Dr.
Scottsdale, AZ 85253
(602) 991-1363

Founders Growth Fund   GROWTH
655 Broadway
Denver, CO 80203
(303) 595-3863

Moderate-growth fund, including retail, telecommunications, aerospace.

Founders Income Fund   EQUITY INCOME
655 Broadway
Denver, CO 80203
(303) 595-3863

Diverse-income fund.

Founders Mutual Fund   GROWTH & INCOME
655 Broadway
Denver, CO 80203
(303) 595-3863

Formerly unmanaged unit trust of forty blue chips—new blue chips.

Founders Special Fund   CAPITAL APPRECIATION
655 Broadway
Denver, CO 80203
(303) 595-3863

Aggressive, diverse-growth fund, keying on smaller firms.

Franklin Dynatech Fund   CAPITAL APPRECIATION
155 Bovet Rd.
San Mateo, CA 94401
(415) 570-3000   (800) 227-6781

Franklin's most aggressive growth fund, specializing in technology.

Franklin Growth Fund   GROWTH
155 Bovet Rd.
San Mateo, CA 94401
(415) 570-3000   (800) 227-6781

Fairly conservative growth fund, keying on electrical supplies/electronics,
drugs, business machines.

Franklin Income Fund   INCOME
155 Bovet Rd.
San Mateo, CA 94401
(415) 570-3000   (800) 227-6781

Income fund, invested mostly in utilities.

Franklin Option Fund   OPTION
155 Bovet Rd.
San Mateo, CA 94401
(415) 570-3000   (800) 227-6781

Invested in stock call options in the areas of health, electronics, and leisure.

Franklin U.S. Govt Series Fund   FIXED INCOME
155 Bovet Rd.
San Mateo, CA 94401
(415) 570-3000   (800) 227-6781

Ginnie Mae fund.

Franklin Utilities Series Fund   SPECIALTY
155 Bovet Rd.
San Mateo, CA 94401
(415) 570-3000   (800) 227-6781

Invested in gas and electric utilities, plus communications.

Fund for U.S. Govt. Securities   FIXED INCOME
421 Seventh Ave.
Pittsburgh, PA 15219
(312) 288-1900   (800) 245-4270

Fund of America   GROWTH & INCOME
2777 Allen Pkwy.
Houston, TX 77019
(713) 522-1111

Fund of the Southwest   CAPITAL APPRECIATION
PO Box 2511
Houston, TX 77001
(713) 757-2131

Fundamental Investors   GROWTH & INCOME
333 S. Hope St.
Los Angeles, CA 90071
(213) 486-9200   (800) 421-0180

Gateway Option Income Fund   OPTION
1120 Carew Tower
Cincinnati, OH 45202
(513) 621-7774

General Electric S&S Program L/T   FIXED INCOME
PO Box 7900
112 Prospect St.
Stamford, CT 06904
(203) 357-4104

Fixed-income fund, offered only to GE employees & affiliates.

General Electric S&S Program   GROWTH
PO Box 7900
112 Prospect St.
Stamford, CT 06904
(203) 357-4104

Growth fund, offered only to GE employees and affiliated companies.

General Securities Fund   CAPITAL APPRECIATION
133 S. Seventh St.
Minneapolis, MN 55402
(612) 332-6000

Gintel Erisa Fund   GROWTH & INCOME
Greenwich Office Park, OP-6
Greenwich, CT 06830
(203) 622-6402

Growth/income fund, high-quality stocks—diverse: oil/gas, consumer goods.

Gintel Fund   GROWTH
Greenwich Office Park, OP-6
Greenwich, CT 06830
(203) 622-6402

Conservative-growth fund, mostly well-established firms—diverse: health care, nonresidential construction, retailing, personal care, and natural gas.

GIT Equity Fund   INCOME
1800 N. Kent St.
Arlington, VA 22209
(703) 528-6500   (800) 336-3063

GIT Income A Rated Fund   FIXED INCOME
1800 N. Kent St.
Arlington, VA 22209
(703) 528-6500   (800) 336-3063

GIT Income Trust Maximum Income Fund   INCOME
1800 N. Kent St.
Arlington, VA 22209
(703) 528-6500   (800) 336-3063

Income fund.

GIT Select Growth Fund   GROWTH
1800 N. Kent St.
Arlington, VA 22209
(703) 528-6500   (800) 336-3063

Moderate-growth fund, keying on well-established but underdeveloped retail, electronics—very diverse.

GIT Special Growth Fund   SMALL COMPANY GROWTH
1800 N. Kent St.
Arlington, VA 22209
(703) 528-6500   (800) 336-3063

Aggressive-growth fund, keying on smaller food chains, electronics, building, defense.

Golconda Investors   GOLD ORIENTED
11 Hanover Sq.
New York, NY 10005
(212) 785-0900   (800) 847-4200

Invests in gold bullion and international mining concerns.

Good & Bad Times Fund   GROWTH & INCOME
PO Box 29467
San Antonio, TX 78229
(512) 696-1234

Very conservative income fund, investing in a diverse range of stable companies including food processing, textiles/apparel.

Gradison Emerging Growth Fund   SMALL COMPANY GROWTH
580 Walnut St.
Cincinnati, OH 45202
(513) 579-5700   (800) 543-1818

Gradison Established Growth Fund GROWTH
580 Walnut St.
Cincinnati, OH 45202
(513) 579-5700   (800) 543-1818

Greenfield Fund GROWTH & INCOME
230 Park Ave.
New York, NY 10017
(212) 986-2600

Greenway Fund CAPITAL APPRECIATION
11 Greenway Plaza
Suite 1919
Houston, TX 77046
(713) 626-1919

Growth Fund of America GROWTH
333 S. Hope St.
Los Angeles, CA 90071
(213) 486-9200   (800) 421-0180

Growth Industry Shares GROWTH
135 S. LaSalle St.
Chicago, IL 60603
(312) 346-4830

GSC Performance Fund CAPITAL APPRECIATION
PO Box 10230
Greenville, SC 29603
(803) 271-7622

G.T. Pacific Fund INTERNATIONAL
601 Montgomery St.
Suite 1400
San Francisco, CA 94111
(415) 392-6181

Guardian Bond Fund FIXED INCOME
201 Park Ave. S.
New York, NY 10003
(212) 598-8000

Guardian Mutual Fund GROWTH & INCOME
342 Madison Ave.
New York, NY 10173
(212) 850-8300

Growth/income fund, including insurance, consumer goods.

Guardian Park Ave. Fund   GROWTH
201 Park Ave. S.
New York, NY 10003
(212) 598-8000

Moderate-growth fund, including oil/gas and emerging growth companies.

Guardian Stock Fund   GROWTH
201 Park Ave. S.
New York, NY 10003
(212) 598-8000

Growth fund—diverse.

Guidance Investment, Inc.   INCOME
1110 Woodview Dr.
Libertyville, IL 60048
(312) 362-0034

Hamilton Funds   GROWTH & INCOME
PO Box 1500
Denver, CO 80201
(303) 770-2345   (800) 525-9310

Hartwell Growth Fund   CAPITAL APPRECIATION
50 Rockefeller Plaza
New York, NY 10020
(212) 247-8740

Moderate-growth fund, keying on communications, equipment, health care,
computer systems/automation.

Hartwell Leverage Fund   CAPITAL APPRECIATION
50 Rockefeller Plaza
New York, NY 10020
(212) 247-8740

Capital-gains objective—diverse.

High Income Shares   FIXED INCOME
One Wall St.
New York, NY 10005
(212) 269-8800   (800) 221-5757

High Yield Securities Fund   FIXED INCOME
11 Greenway Plaza
Suite 1919
Houston, TX 77046
(713) 626-1919

Home Investors Fund   FIXED INCOME
253 Broadway
New York, NY 10007
(800) 221-5733

Mortgage-backed securities.

Horace Mann Fund   GROWTH
One Horace Mann Plaza
Springfield, IL 62715
(217) 789-2500

Moderate-growth fund, including data processing, electronics, retail trade.

Hutton Investors Series—Bond   FIXED INCOME
One Battery Park Plaza
New York, NY 10004
(212) 742-6003

Hutton Investors Series—Emerging Growth   SMALL COMPANY GROWTH
One Battery Park Plaza
New York, NY 10004
(212) 742-6003

Hutton Investors Series—Growth   GROWTH
One Battery Park Plaza
New York, NY 10004
(212) 742-6003

IDS Bond Fund   FIXED INCOME
1000 Roanoke Bldg.
Minneapolis, MN 55402
(612) 372-3131   (800) 328-8300

IDS Discovery Fund   SMALL COMPANY GROWTH
1000 Roanoke Bldg.
Minneapolis, MN 55402
(612) 372-3131   (800) 328-8300

Most aggressive IDS growth fund, keying on small emerging electronics, business equipment, drug/health care.

IDS Growth Fund   GROWTH
1000 Roanoke Bldg.
Minneapolis, MN 55402
(612) 372-3131   (800) 328-8300

Aggressive-growth fund that searches for companies which will retain technological superiority in their fields—keying on retail trade, electronics.

IDS Life Capital Resource I   GROWTH
1000 Roanoke Bldg.
Minneapolis, MN 55402
(612) 372-3131   (800) 328-8300

IDS Life Capital Resource II   GROWTH
1000 Roanoke Bldg.
Minneapolis, MN 55402
(612) 372-3131   (800) 328-8300

IDS Life Special Income I   FIXED INCOME
1000 Roanoke Bldg.
Minneapolis, MN 55402
(612) 372-3131   (800) 328-8300

IDS Life Special Income II   FIXED INCOME
1000 Roanoke Bldg.
Minneapolis, MN 55402
(612) 372-3131   (800) 328-8300

IDS New Dimensions Funds   GROWTH
1000 Roanoke Bldg.
Minneapolis, MN 55402
(612) 372-3131   (800) 328-8300

Moderately aggressive, keying on consistently growing electrical, retail
trade, business equipment companies.

IDS Progressive Funds   CAPITAL APPRECIATION
1000 Roanoke Bldg.
Minneapolis, MN 55402
(612) 372-3131   (800) 328-8300

Aggressive-growth fund that searches for undervalued stocks, keying on utilities oil/gas/coal. (IDS will be opening Strategy Fund in future.)

Income Fund of America   EQUITY INCOME
333 S. Hope St.
Los Angeles, CA 90071
(213) 486-9200   (800) 421-0180

International Investors Fund   GOLD ORIENTED
122 E. 42nd St.
New York, NY 10017
(212) 687-5200   (800) 221-2220

Investment Company of America   GROWTH & INCOME
333 S. Hope St.
Los Angeles, CA 90071
(213) 486-9200   (800) 421-0180

Investment Quality Interest Fund   FIXED INCOME
333 Clay St.
Suite 4300
Houston, TX 77002
(713) 751-2400

Investment Trust of Boston   GROWTH & INCOME
77 Franklin St.
Boston, MA 02110
(617) 542-0213

Investors Mutual Fund   BALANCED
1000 Roanoke Bldg.
Minneapolis, MN 55402
(612) 372-3131   (800) 328-8300

Balanced fund, majority in common stock, keying on utilities, business equipment.

Investors Research Fund   CAPITAL APPRECIATION
1900 State St.
Santa Barbara, CA 93102
(805) 965-2211   (800) 328-8300

Investors Select Fund   FIXED INCOME
1000 Roanoke Bldg.
Minneapolis, MN 55402
(612) 372-3131   (800) 328-8300

Investors Stock Fund   GROWTH & INCOME
1000 Roanoke Bldg.
Minneapolis, MN 55402
(612) 372-3131   (800) 328-8300

Conservative growth/income fund, keying on electronics, drugs/health, business equipment.

Investors Variable Payment Fund   GROWTH
1000 Roanoke Bldg.
Minneapolis, MN 55402
(612) 372-3131   (800) 328-8300

Diverse, moderate-growth fund, keying on drugs, health care, business equipment, electronics.

IRI Stock Fund   GROWTH
One Appletree Sq.
Minneapolis, MN 55420
(612) 853-0700

ISI Growth Fund   GROWTH
PO Box 2330
1608 Webster St.
Oakland, CA 94623
(415) 832-1400

Varied-growth fund, includes U.S. govt issues, some stocks.

ISI Income Fund   GROWTH
PO Box 2330
1608 Webster St.
Oakland, CA 94623
(415) 832-1400

Income fund.

ISI Trust Fund   INCOME
PO Box 2330
1608 Webster St.
Oakland, CA 94623
(415) 832-1400

Income fund, some U.S. govt bonds.

Istel Fund   GROWTH & INCOME
345 Park Ave.
New York, NY 10154
(212) 644-2800

IVEST Fund   GROWTH
PO Box 2600
Valley Forge, PA 19482
(215) 648-6000   (800) 523-7025

International growth fund, keying on Japan and some U.S. companies.

Ivy Fund   GROWTH
201 Devonshire St.
Boston, MA 02110
(617) 426-0636

Jana Growth Fund   SPECIALTY
344 E. 49th St.
Suite 3-B
New York, NY 10017
(212) 750-9007

Janus Fund   CAPITAL APPRECIATION
789 Sherman St.
Suite 300
Denver, CO 80203
(303) 837-1810

Larger companies, growth oriented, can go into each if market looks weak.

John Hancock Bond Fund   FIXED INCOME
Hancock Place, PO Box 111
Boston, MA 02117
(617) 421-8740

Bond fund, corporate and some utilities.

John Hancock Growth Fund   GROWTH
Hancock Place, PO Box 111
Boston, MA 02117
(617) 421-8740

Growth fund, including office equipment, electronics, others.

John Hancock U.S. Govt Securities Fund   FIXED INCOME
Hancock Place, PO Box 111
Boston, MA 02117
(617) 421-8740

Fixed-income, govt-securities fund.

JP Growth Fund   GROWTH
PO Box 21008
Greensboro, NC 27420
(919) 378-2453

JP Income Fund   FIXED INCOME
PO Box 21008
Greensboro, NC 27420
(919) 378-2453

Kemper Growth Fund   GROWTH
120 S. LaSalle St.
Chicago, IL 60603
(312) 781-1121   (800) 621-1048
Aggressive-growth fund, keying on transportation, electronic components, and oil/gas—somewhat speculative.

Kemper High Yield Fund   FIXED INCOME
120 S. LaSalle St.
Chicago, IL 60603
(312) 781-1121   (800) 621-1048
Mainly a corporate-bond fund.

Kemper Income & Capital Preservation Fund   FIXED INCOME
120 S. LaSalle St.
Chicago, IL 60603
(312) 781-1121   (800) 621-1048
High-quality, conservative-bond fund, some U.S. govt securities, some corporate.

Kemper International Fund   INTERNATIONAL
120 S. LaSalle St.
Chicago, IL 60603
(312) 781-1121   (800) 621-1048
Aggressive, diverse fund that invests in foreign countries, keying on Japan and U.K.

Kemper Investments Portfolio   FIXED INCOME
120 S. LaSalle St.
Chicago, IL 60603
(312) 781-1121   (800) 621-1048

Kemper Option Income Fund   OPTION
120 S. LaSalle St.
Chicago, IL 60603
(312) 781-1121   (800) 621-1048
Hybrid fund, conservative—deals in consumer nondurable goods and electronics/communications.

Kemper Summit Fund   GROWTH
120 S. LaSalle St.
Chicago, IL 60603
(312) 781-1121   (800) 621-1048
Kemper's most aggressive growth fund. Invests in small companies with new ideas. Keys on electronic data processing.

Kemper Technology Fund   GROWTH
120 S. LaSalle St.
Chicago, IL 60603
(312) 781-1121   (800) 621-1048

Moderate-growth fund, invests in technology corporations—keys on electronic data processing.

Kemper Total Return Fund   BALANCED
120 S. LaSalle St.
Chicago, IL 60603
(312) 781-1121   (800) 621-1048

Hybrid fund that can easily switch from common stocks to bonds, depending on market conditions. Conservative, keying on electronics.

Kemper U.S. Govt Securities   FIXED INCOME
120 S. LaSalle St.
Chicago, IL 60603
(312) 845-1810   (800) 621-1048

Conservative-bond fund.

Keystone B-1 (Investment-Grade Bond Fund)   FIXED INCOME
99 High St.
Boston, MA 02104
(617) 338-3200   (800) 225-1587

Bond fund for fixed-income corporate bonds, some utilities, U.S. govt issues.

Keystone B-2 (Med.-Grade Bond)   FIXED INCOME
99 High St.
Boston, MA 02104
(617) 338-3200   (800) 225-1587

Bond fund.

Keystone B-4 (Discount Bond)   FIXED INCOME
99 High St.
Boston, MA 02104
(617) 338-3200   (800) 225-1587

Bond fund, lower-rated bonds.

Keystone K-1 (Income Fund)   INCOME
99 High St.
Boston, MA 02104
(617) 338-3200   (800) 225-1587

Income fund that invests in all types of securities.

Keystone K-2 (Growth Fund)   GROWTH
99 High St.
Boston, MA 02104
(617) 338-3200   (800) 225-1587

Diverse-growth fund, including retail, electronics, office/business equipment.

Keystone S-1 (High Grade)   GROWTH & INCOME
99 High St.
Boston, MA 02104
(617) 338-3200   (800) 225-1587

Blue-chip growth/income fund.

Keystone S-3 (Growth)   GROWTH
99 High St.
Boston, MA 02104
(617) 338-3200   (800) 225-1587

Growth fund that invests in high-quality common stock, including retail, office/business machines.

Keystone S-4 (Lower Prices)   GROWTH
99 High St.
Boston, MA 02104
(617) 338-3200   (800) 225-1587

Aggressive-growth fund, including office/business machines, retail, others.

LBKL Capital Opportunity Fund   GROWTH
55 Water St.
New York, NY 10041
(212) 558-3288   (800) 221-5350

Moderately aggressive growth fund, specializing in smaller communications/technology firms.

Legg Mason Value Trust   GROWTH
421 Seventh Ave.
Pittsburgh, PA 15219
(412) 288-1900   (800) 245-4270

Lehman Bros. Kuhn Loeb Inc.—Capital   CAPITAL APPRECIATION
Opportunity
55 Water St.
New York, NY 10041
(212) 558-3288   (800) 221-5350

Lehman Capital Fund   CAPITAL APPRECIATION
55 Water St.
New York, NY 10041
(212) 558-3288   (800) 221-5353

Moderately aggressive growth fund, invests in smaller capital goods, technology firms.

Leverage Fund of Boston   CAPITAL APPRECIATION
24 Federal St.
Boston, MA 02110
(617) 482-8260   (800) 225-6265

Lexington GNMA Income Fund   FIXED INCOME
PO Box 1515
580 Sylvan Ave.
Englewood Cliffs, NJ 07632
(201) 567-2000   (800) 526-4791

GNMA fund.

Lexington Gold Fund   GOLD ORIENTED
PO Box 1515
580 Sylvan Ave.
Englewood Cliffs, NJ 07632
(201) 567-2000   (800) 526-4791

Gold fund.

Lexington Growth Fund   GROWTH
PO Box 1515
580 Sylvan Ave.
Englewood Cliffs, NJ 07632
(201) 567-2000   (800) 526-4791

Conservative-growth fund, including emerging telecommunications, electronics, banking.

Lexington Research Fund   GROWTH
PO Box 1515
580 Sylvan Ave.
Englewood Cliffs, NJ 07632
(201) 567-2000   (800) 526-4791

Conservative growth/income fund, keying on banking/insurance, telecommunications.

LG Fund for Growth   GROWTH
522 Dixie Terminal Bldg.
Cincinnati, OH 45202
(513) 579-1110   (800) 543-8721

Moderate-growth fund, invests in identifiable communications, technology firms. Blue chip.

LG Fund for Income   EQUITY INCOME
522 Dixie Terminal Bldg.
Cincinnati, OH 45202
(513) 579-1110   (800) 543-8721

Conservative-income fund, keying on communications/technology.

Liberty Fund   FIXED INCOME
342 Madison Ave.
New York, NY 10173
(212) 853-8300

Lower-rated-bond fund.

The Libra Fund
52 Vanderbilt Ave.
New York, NY 10017
(212) 687-2322   (800) 221-3081

Designed for women investors.

Lindner Fund   GROWTH
200 S. Bemiston
St. Louis, MO 63105
(314) 727-5303

Best in down markets, can be heavily in cash, disciplined investment approach.

Lindner Fund for Income   EQUITY INCOME
200 S. Bemiston
St. Louis, MO 63105
(314) 727-5303

LMH Fund   CAPITAL APPRECIATION
PO Box 830
Westport, CT 06851
(203) 226-4768

Loomis-Sayles Capital Development Fund   GROWTH
225 Franklin St., 27th Fl.
Boston, MA 02110
(617) 482-2450

Common-stock growth fund—diverse.

Loomis-Sayles Mutual Fund   BALANCED
225 Franklin St., 27th Fl.
Boston, MA 02110
(617) 482-2450

Balanced fund, does seek growth—diverse.

Lord Abbett Bond-Debenture Fund   FIXED INCOME
PO Box 29467
San Antonio, TX 78229
(512) 696-1234   (800) 531-5777

Bond fund, convertible/nonconvertible corporate bonds. Lord Abbett will be
introducing a tax-free-income fund.

Lord Abbett Developing Growth Fund   SMALL GROWTH
63 Wall St.
New York, NY 10005
(212) 425-8720

Very aggressive growth fund, dealing in OTC stocks, keying on magnetic
memory devices, retail trade.

Lord Abbett Income Fund   INCOME
63 Wall St.
New York, NY 10005
(212) 425-8720

Income fund, mostly corporate bonds—keying on banking and financial services.

Lord Abbett Value Appreciation Fund   GROWTH
63 Wall St.
New York, NY 10005
(212) 425-8720

Fairly conservative growth fund that seeks undervalued stocks, keying on
companies affected by deregulation (airlines), lower inflation and interest
rates (financial corporations).

Lowry Fund SPECIALTY
419 Boylston St.
Suite 312
Boston, MA 02116
(617) 434-4606
Shuttle between bonds & equities based on *Lowry Report*'s signals.

Lowry Market Timing Fund GROWTH
419 Boylston St.
Suite 312
Boston, MA 02116
(617) 434-4606

MagnaCap Fund GROWTH
222 Bridge Plaza S.
Fort Lee, NJ 07024
(201) 461-7500

Magna Income Trust FIXED INCOME
222 Bridge Plaza S.
Fort Lee, NJ 07024
(201) 461-7500

Manhattan Fund CAPITAL APPRECIATION
342 Madison Ave.
New York, NY 10173
(212) 850-8300
Moderately conservative, diverse-growth fund, including office equipment,
consumer goods.

Massachusetts Capital Development Fund GROWTH
200 Berkeley St.
Boston, MA 02116
(617) 423-3500

Massachusetts Emerging Growth GROWTH
200 Berkeley St.
Boston, MA 02116
(617) 423-3500
Half high-tech companies.

Massachusetts Financial Bond Fund FIXED INCOME
200 Berkeley St.
Boston, MA 02116
(617) 423-3500
Bond fund—utilities, municipals, corporate.

Massachusetts Financial Development Fund GROWTH & INCOME
200 Berkeley St.
Boston, MA 02116
(617) 423-3500

Massachusetts Financial Emerging Growth Fund SMALL GROWTH
200 Berkeley St.
Boston, MA 02116
(617) 423-3500

Massachusetts Financial High Income Fund FIXED INCOME
200 Berkeley St.
Boston, MA 02116
(617) 423-3500

Most bonds in portfolio have low credit ratings—managers look for turn-around companies.

Massachusetts Int'l Trust—Bond Port. INTERNATIONAL OR U.S.
200 Berkeley St.
Boston, MA 02116
(617) 423-3500

Can invest in foreign fixed-income securities, dollars, or foreign currencies, and up to 20 percent in gold-mining shares.

Massachusetts Financial Special Fund CAPITAL APPRECIATION
200 Berkeley St.
Boston, MA 02116
(617) 423-3500

Massachusetts Fund BALANCED
99 High St.
Boston, MA 02104
(617) 423-6464 (800) 225-1587

Massachusetts Income Development Fund INCOME
200 Berkeley St.
Boston, MA 02116
(617) 423-3500

Conservative, diverse-income fund.

Massachusetts Investors Growth Fund GROWTH
200 Berkeley St.
Boston, MA 02116
(617) 423-3500

Massachusetts Investors Trust Fund   GROWTH & INCOME
200 Berkeley St.
Boston, MA 02116
(617) 423-3500

Mathers Fund   GROWTH
125 S. Wacker Dr.
Chicago, IL 60606
(312) 236-8215

Maxim Bond Fund   FIXED INCOME
Great West Life Insurance Co.
7400 E. Orchard
Englewood, CO 80111
(303) 793-2000

Medical Technology Fund   SPECIALTY
1107 Bethlehem Pike
Flourtown, PA 19031
(215) 836-1300   (800) 523-0864

Growth fund that specializes in medical technology industries.

Merrill Lynch Basic Value Fund   GROWTH & INCOME
633 Third Ave.
New York, NY 10017
(212) 692-2939   (800) 631-0749

Very diverse growth/income fund—securities for out-of-favor companies.

Merrill Lynch Capital Fund   GROWTH & INCOME
633 Third Ave.
New York, NY 10017
(212) 692-2939   (800) 631-0749

Diverse, conservative growth/income fund.

Merrill Lynch Corp. Bond Fund—High Income   FIXED INCOME
633 Third Ave.
New York, NY 10017
(212) 692-2939   (800) 225-5150

Income fund (bonds).

Merrill Lynch Corp. Bond Fund—High Quality   FIXED INCOME
633 Third Ave.
New York, NY 10017
(212) 692-2939   (800) 225-5150

Fixed-income bond fund that invests in A-rated or better bonds.

Merrill Lynch Corp. Bond Fund—Intermediate   FIXED INCOME
633 Third Ave.
New York, NY 10017
(212) 692-2939   (800) 225-5150

Bond fund that invests in top four categories of bonds.

Merrill Lynch Equity-Bond Fund   GROWTH
633 Third Ave.
New York, NY 10017
(212) 692-2939   (800) 631-0749

Bond fund.

Merrill Lynch Pacific Fund   INTERNATIONAL
633 Third Ave.
New York, NY 10017
(212) 692-2939   (800) 225-5150

Growth fund that invests in Far Eastern/Western Pacific-based companies, keying on Japan, Australia, and Hong Kong.

Merrill Lynch Phoenix Fund   GROWTH & INCOME
633 Third Ave.
New York, NY 10017
(212) 692-2939   (800) 631-0749

Merrill Lynch Special Value Fund   GROWTH
633 Third Ave.
New York, NY 10017
(212) 692-2939   (800) 631-0749

Diverse-growth fund that invests in emerging growth firms, regardless of size.

MidAmerica High Growth Fund   SPECIALTY
4333 Edgewood Rd., NE
Cedar Rapids, IA 52499
(319) 398-8511

MidAmerica Mutual Fund   GROWTH
4333 Edgewood Rd., NE
Cedar Rapids, IA 52499
(319) 398-8511

Midwest/Bartlett Value Fund   GROWTH & INCOME
522 Dixie Terminal Bldg.
Cincinnati, OH 45202
(513) 579-1110   (800) 543-8721

Young (summer 1983), moderately conservative, diverse-growth fund keying on apparel, banking.

Midwest Income Trust—Intermediate-Term Govt Fund   FIXED INCOME
522 Dixie Terminal Bldg.
Cincinnati, OH 45202
(513) 579-1110   (800) 543-8721

U.S. govt-bond fund.

Money Market/Options Investments, Inc.   OPTION
99 High St.
Boston, MA 02110
(617) 338-3200   (800) 225-1587

Monthly Income Shares   FIXED INCOME
One Wall St.
New York, NY 10005
(212) 269-8800   (800) 221-5757

Morgan, W.L., Growth Fund   GROWTH
PO Box 2600
Valley Forge, PA 19482
(215) 964-2600

Three-tiered growth fund, very diverse stock fund.

Mutual Benefit Fund   GROWTH
520 Broad St.
Newark, NJ 07101
(201) 481-8000

Mutual of Omaha America Fund   FIXED INCOME
10235 Regency Circle
Omaha, NE 68114
(402) 397-8555   (800) 228-9393

Bond fund, mostly govt.

Mutual of Omaha Growth Fund   GROWTH
10235 Regency Circle
Omaha, NE 68114
(402) 397-8555   (800) 228-9393

Conservative-growth fund, including banks, home furnishings, office equipment.

Mutual of Omaha Income Fund   INCOME
10235 Regency Circle
Omaha, NE 68114
(402) 397-8555   (800) 228-9393

Income fund, mostly bonds (govt, utilities).

Mutual Qualified Income Fund   CAPITAL APPRECIATION
26 Broadway
New York, NY 10004
(212) 908-4048

Mutual Shares Corporation   GROWTH & INCOME
26 Broadway
New York, NY 10004
(212) 908-4048

Naess & Thomas Special Fund   SMALL COMPANY GROWTH
One State St.
New York, NY 10004
(212) 269-6500

Aggressive-growth fund that keys on small-to-medium consumer-related, defense, health, telecommunications.

National Aviation & Technology Corp.   GROWTH
50 Broad St.
New York, NY 10004
(212) 482-8100   call collect

Growth fund specializing in the areas of aviation and technology—only such mutual fund in existence.

National Balanced Fund   BALANCED
605 Third Ave.
New York, NY 10158
(212) 661-3000

National Bond Fund   FIXED INCOME
605 Third Ave.
New York, NY 10158
(212) 661-3000

Corporate-bond fund, diverse.

National Growth Fund   GROWTH
605 Third Ave.
New York, NY 10158
(212) 661-3000
Moderate-growth fund, keying on high-tech, health care, consumer services.

National Income Fund   EQUITY INCOME
605 Third Ave.
New York, NY 10158
(212) 661-3000
Diverse-income fund.

National Industries Fund   GROWTH & INCOME
605 Third Ave.
New York, NY 10158
(212) 661-3000

National Preferred Fund   FIXED INCOME
605 Third Ave.
New York, NY 10158
(212) 661-3000

National Stock Fund   GROWTH & INCOME
605 Third Ave.
New York, NY 10158
(212) 661-3000
Diverse, fairly conservative growth/income fund.

National Telecom. & Tech.   GROWTH
50 Broad St.
New York, NY 10004
(212) 482-8100   —collect
Growth fund that specializes in telecommunications and technology.

National Total Return   EQUITY INCOME
605 Third Ave.
New York, NY 10158
(212) 661-3000
Diverse-growth/income fund, including food/tobacco, advertising/leisure,
others.

Nationwide Bond Fund   FIXED INCOME
Box 1492
One Nationwide Plaza
Columbus, OH 43216
(614) 227-7855   (800) 848-0920

Diverse-corporate/U.S. government-bond fund.

Nationwide Fund   GROWTH
Box 1492
One Nationwide Plaza
Columbus, OH 43216
(614) 227-7855   (800) 848-0920

Diverse-growth/income fund.

Nationwide Growth Fund   GROWTH
One Nationwide Plaza
Columbus, OH 43216
(614) 227-8707   (800) 848-0920

Moderate, diverse-growth fund.

Nation-Wide Securities   BALANCED
One Wall St.
New York, NY 10005
(212) 269-8800   (800) 221-5757

NEL Equity Fund   GROWTH & INCOME
501 Boylston St.
Boston, MA 02117
(617) 267-6600   (800) 225-7670

Moderately conservative growth/income fund, keying on office equipment,
auto, food/beverage.

NEL Growth Fund   GROWTH
501 Boylston St.
Boston, MA 02117
(617) 267-6600   (800) 225-7670

NEL's most aggressive, but still conservative. Keying on auto, airline, office
equipment (a growth fund).

NEL Income Fund   FIXED INCOME
501 Boylston St.
Boston, MA 02117
(617) 267-6600   (800) 225-7670

Bond fund, mostly U.S. govt bonds.

NEL Retirement Equity Fund   GROWTH
501 Boylston St.
Boston, MA 02117
(617) 267-6600   (800) 225-7670

Keoghs, IRAs—investments made in large food/beverages, auto, office
equipment.

Neuwirth Fund   GROWTH
140 Broadway
New York, NY 10005
(212) 635-3516   (800) 221-7780

Aggressive-growth fund, keying on emerging consumer staples, media/tele-
communications, other areas.

New Alternatives Fund   NATURAL RESOURCES
295 Northern Blvd.
Great Neck, NY 11021
(516) 466-0808

"New Beginnings" Growth Fund   SMALL COMPANY GROWTH
1714 First Bank Place W.
Minneapolis, MN 55402
(612) 332-3223

"New Beginnings" Income Fund   GROWTH & INCOME
1714 First Bank Place W.
Minneapolis, MN 55402
(612) 332-3223

New Economy Fund
333 S. Hope St.
Los Angeles, CA 90071
(213) 486-9200   (800) 421-0180

Invested in leisure, tourism, telecommunications, and financial services.
Minimum investment of $1000.

New Perspective Fund   GROWTH
333 S. Hope St.
Los Angeles, CA 90071
(213) 486-9200   (800) 421-0180

Newton Growth Fund   GROWTH
733 N. Van Buren St.
Milwaukee, WI 53202
(414) 271-0040

Education-related companies.

Newton Income Fund   FIXED INCOME
733 N. Van Buren St.
Milwaukee, WI 53202
(414) 271-0040

New York Venture Fund   GROWTH
309 Johnson St.
Santa Fe, NM 87501
(505) 983-4335   (800) 545-2098

Venture's most aggressive growth fund, keying on financial, insurance, consumer goods/services.

Nicholas Fund   GROWTH
312 E. Wisconsin Ave.
Milwaukee, WI 53202
(414) 272-6133

Banks & savings and loans, insurance, food & beverage.

Nicholas Fund II   GROWTH
312 E. Wisconsin Ave.
Milwaukee, WI 53202
(414) 272-6133

Nicholas Income Fund   INCOME
312 E. Wisconsin Ave.
Milwaukee, WI 53202
(414) 272-6133

Northeast Investors Growth Fund   GROWTH
50 Congress St.
Boston, MA 02109
(617) 523-3588

Northeast Investors Trust Fund   FIXED INCOME
50 Congress St.
Boston, MA 02109
(617) 523-3588

North Star Bond Fund   FIXED INCOME
PO Box 1160
1100 Dain Tower
Minneapolis, MN 55440
(612) 371-7772

North Star Regional Fund   GROWTH
PO Box 1160
1100 Dain Tower
Minneapolis, MN 55440
(612) 371-7772

North Star Stock Fund   CAPITAL APPRECIATION
PO Box 1160
1100 Dain Tower
Minneapolis, MN 55440
(612) 371-7772

Nova Fund   GROWTH
303 Wyman St.
Waltham, MA 02154
(617) 890-4415

Ohio National—Bond   FIXED INCOME
237 Wm. Howard Taft Rd.
Cincinnati, OH 45219
(513) 861-3600

Ohio National—Equity   CAPITAL APPRECIATION
237 Wm. Howard Taft Rd.
Cincinnati, OH 45219
(513) 861-3600

Omega Fund   CAPITAL APPRECIATION
77 Franklin St.
Boston, MA 02110
(617) 357-8480

One Hundred Fund   GROWTH
899 Logan St.
Denver, CO 80203
(303) 837-1810

One Hundred & One Fund   GROWTH & INCOME
899 Logan St.
Denver, CO 80203
(303) 837-1810

One William Street Fund   GROWTH & INCOME
55 Water St.
New York, NY 10041
(212) 558-3288   (800) 221-5350

Conservative-growth fund, mostly NYSE blue-chip, keying on office equipment, electronics.

Oppenheimer A.I.M. Fund   CAPITAL APPRECIATION
3410 S. Galena St.
Denver, CO 80231
(303) 671-3200   (800) 221-9839

Moderate-growth fund, keying on consumer and industrial products/services.

Oppenheimer Directors Fund   CAPITAL APPRECIATION
3410 S. Galena St.
Denver, CO 80231
(303) 671-3200   (800) 525-7048

Aggressive-growth fund, keying on smaller companies, consumer products/services.

Oppenheimer Equity Income Fund   EQUITY INCOME
3600 S. Yosemite
Denver, CO 80237
(303) 770-2345   (800) 525-7048

Fairly conservative fund, keying on consumer and industrial products/services.

Oppenheimer Fund   GROWTH
3410 S. Galena St.
Denver, CO 80231
(303) 671-3200   (800) 525-7048

Well-balanced growth/income fund keying on consumer and industrial goods/services.

Oppenheimer Gold & Special Minerals Fund   GOLD ORIENTED
3410 S. Galena St.
Denver, CO 80231
(303) 671-3200   (800) 525-7048

Gold/special minerals fund, new September 1983.

Oppenheimer High Yield Fund   FIXED INCOME
3410 S. Galena St.
Denver, CO 80231
(303) 671-3200   (800) 525-7048

Bond fund, convertible and nonconvertible.

Oppenheimer Option Income Fund   OPTION
3410 S. Galena St.
Denver, CO 80231
(303) 671-3200   (800) 525-7048

Oppenheimer Regency Fund   CAPITAL APPRECIATION
3410 S. Galena St.
Denver, CO 80231
(303) 671-3200   (800) 525-7048

New fund (Jan. 1984)—for IRAs, etc. Aggressive.

Oppenheimer Special Fund   CAPITAL APPRECIATION
3410 S. Galena St.
Denver, CO 80231
(303) 671-3200

Aggressive-growth fund, specializing in industrial products/services.

Oppenheimer Target Fund   CAPITAL APPRECIATION
3410 S. Galena St.
Denver, CO 80231
(303) 671-3200   (800) 525-7048

Very aggressive growth fund, speculates on technology and consumer products/services.

Oppenheimer Time Fund   CAPITAL APPRECIATION
3410 S. Galena St.
Denver, CO 80231
(303) 671-3200   (800) 525-7048

Fairly aggressive growth fund, keying on consumer products/services.

Over-the-Counter Securities Fund   SPECIALTY
Plymouth & Walnut Aves.
Oreland, PA 19075
(215) 887-3011

Eighty percent over-the-counter stocks, 20 percent fund manager's areas of growth opportunities. Minimum investment $500.

Paramount Mutual Fund   GROWTH & INCOME
10301 W. Pico Blvd.
Los Angeles, CA 90064
(213) 277-4900

Partners Fund   GROWTH
342 Madison Ave.
New York, NY 10173
(212) 850-8300

Conservative-growth fund, invests without tax considerations. Big companies—diverse.

Pax World Fund   BALANCED
606 Milo Dr.
Bethesda, MD 20816
(301) 229-2647

P-C Capital Fund   CAPITAL APPRECIATION
One American Row
Hartford, CT 06115
(203) 278-8050   (800) 243-1574

Penn Square Mutual Fund   GROWTH
PO Box 1419
101 N. Fifth St.
Reading, PA 19603
(215) 376-6771

Pennsylvania Mutual Fund   SMALL COMPANY GROWTH
1414 Avenue of the Americas
New York, NY 10019
(212) 355-7311   (800) 221-4268

Conservative-growth fund that invests in small companies, not because of
industry, but based on balance sheets.

Penny Fund of North America   CAPITAL APPRECIATION
PO Box 3059
Colorado Springs, CO 80934
(303) 636-1511

Permanent Portfolio Fund   CAPITAL APPRECIATION
PO Box 5847
Austin, TX 78763
(800) 531-5142

Aggressive—short selling, options, to put together a balanced portfolio—
gold, silver, Swiss francs, inflation-related stocks, T-bills.

Philadelphia Fund   GROWTH & INCOME
110 Wall St.
New York, NY 10005
(212) 668-8107

Phoenix Balanced Fund Series   BALANCED
One American Row
Hartford, CT 06115
(203) 278-8050   (800) 243-1574

Moderately balanced, growth and income fund, convertible bonds in financial services, mining, and common stock in drugs and consumer goods.
Conservative.

Phoenix Convertible Fund Series   INCOME
One American Row
Hartford, CT 06115
(203) 278-8050   (800) 243-1574

Fairly balanced growth and income fund, majority of convertible bonds, keying on drugs, oil/gas.

Phoenix Growth Fund Series   GROWTH
One American Row
Hartford, CT 06115
(203) 278-8050   (800) 243-1574

Moderately aggressive, diverse-growth fund, keying on consumer goods, electronics.

Phoenix High Quality Bond Fund   FIXED INCOME
One American Row
Hartford, CT 06115
(203) 278-8050   (800) 243-1574

High-quality bonds, majority in nonconvertible, keying on utilities, oil/gas.

Phoenix High Yield Fund Series   FIXED INCOME
One American Row
Hartford, CT 06115
(203) 278-8050   (800) 243-1574

Somewhat more aggressive than Phoenix High Quality Bond Fund. Mostly nonconvertible bonds, keying on finance, communications.

Phoenix Stock Fund   CAPITAL APPRECIATION
One American Row
Hartford, CT 06115
(203) 278-8050   (800) 243-1574

Phoenix's most aggressive growth fund, keying on emerging consumer goods, technology.

Pilgrim Adjustable Rate Fund   FIXED INCOME
222 Bridge Plaza S.
Fort Lee, NJ 07024
(201) 461-7500

Invests in adjustable-rate preferred stocks. Dividends qualify for 85 percent deduction for corporations. Rate of the preferred stocks in the fund adjusts with various U.S. Treasury instruments.

Pilgrim Fund   GROWTH
222 Bridge Plaza S.
Fort Lee, NJ 07024
(201) 461-7500

Aggressive-growth fund, including smaller, emerging natural resources, insurance and others.

Pilot Fund   CAPITAL APPRECIATION
333 Clay St.
Suite 4300
Houston, TX 77002
(713) 751-2400

Pine Street Fund   GROWTH & INCOME
140 Broadway
New York, NY 10271
(212) 635-3516   (800) 221-7780

Diverse, conservative fund, with interests in consumer staples, health care, media, many other areas.

Pioneer Bond Fund   FIXED INCOME
60 State St.
Boston, MA 02109
(617) 742-7825   (800) 225-6292

Corporate/government bond fund.

Pioneer Fund   GROWTH & INCOME
60 State St.
Boston, MA 02109
(617) 742-7825   (800) 225-6292

Diverse growth/income fund, keying on blue-chip electronic/finance, insurance.

Pioneer II   GROWTH & INCOME
60 State St.
Boston, MA 02109
(617) 742-7825   (800) 225-6292

Moderately conservative growth/income fund, keying on medium-to-large consumer goods/services, energy.

Pioneer III   GROWTH & INCOME
60 State St.
Boston, MA 02109
(617) 742-7825   (800) 225-6292

Pioneer's most aggressive growth/income fund, keying on smaller industrial
equipment, mining/metals.

Planned Investment Fund   GROWTH
60 State St.
Boston, MA 02109
(617) 742-7900

PLITREND Fund   GROWTH
PO Box 2511
Houston, TX 77001
(713) 757-2131

Precious Metals Holdings   GOLD ORIENTED
One Post Sq.
Boston, MA 02109
(617) 338-4220   (800) 251-4653

T. Rowe Price Growth & Income Fund   GROWTH & INCOME
100 E. Pratt St.
Baltimore, MD 21202
(301) 547-2308   (800) 638-1527

Conservative growth/income fund, keying on petroleum, insurance, utilities.

T. Rowe Price Growth Stock Fund   GROWTH
100 E. Pratt St.
Baltimore, MD 21202
(301) 547-2308   (800) 638-1527

Moderately conservative growth fund specializing in technology firms.

T. Rowe Price International Fund   INTERNATIONAL
100 E. Pratt St.
Baltimore, MD 21202
(301) 547-2308   (800) 638-1527

Growth fund, can be volatile due to foreign currency fluctuations. Money
invested overseas in Japan and Netherlands, other countries.

T. Rowe Price New Era Fund   NATURAL RESOURCES
100 E. Pratt St.
Baltimore, MD 21202
(301) 547-2308   (800) 638-1527

Moderately aggressive growth fund, keying on natural resources: petroleum, energy.

T. Rowe Price New Horizons Fund   SMALL COMPANY GROWTH
100 E. Pratt St.
Baltimore, MD 21202
(301) 547-2308   (800) 638-1527

Price's most aggressive growth fund, very diverse, keying on technology, consumer services, business services.

T. Rowe Price New Income Fund   FIXED INCOME
100 E. Pratt St.
Baltimore, MD 21202
(301) 547-2308   (800) 638-1527

Bond fund, fixed-income securities.

Principal Equity Fund   GROWTH
6310 N. Scottsdale Rd.
Scottsdale, AZ 85253
(602) 998-5557

Principal Preservation Tax Exempt Fund   FIXED INCOME
215 N. Main St.
West Bend, WI 53095
(412) 334-5521

Principal World Fund   INTERNATIONAL
6310 N. Scottsdale Rd.
Scottsdale, AZ 85253
(602) 998-5557

Pro Fund   GROWTH
1107 Bethlehem Pike
Flourtown, PA 19031
(215) 836-1300   (800) 523-0864

Pro Income Fund   FIXED INCOME
1107 Bethlehem Pike
Flourtown, PA 19031
(215) 836-1300   (800) 523-0864

Prospector Fund   GOLD ORIENTED
PO Box 29467
San Antonio, TX 78229

Invests in new and developing gold/silver mines in North America and Australia. High risk.

Provident Fund for Income   INCOME
2777 Allen Pkwy.
Houston, TX 77019
(713) 522-1111

Prudential-Bache Equity Fund   GROWTH
100 Gold St.
New York, NY 10292
(212) 791-4654   (800) 221-7984

Diverse, conservative-growth fund.

Prudential-Bache Govt Investment   FIXED INCOME
100 Gold St.
New York, NY 10292
(212) 791-4654   (800) 221-7984

Govt securities.

Prudential-Bache High Yield   FIXED INCOME
100 Gold St.
New York, NY 10292
(212) 791-4654   (800) 221-7984

High-yield corporate-bond fund.

Prudential-Bache Option Growth   OPTION
100 Gold St.
New York, NY 10292
(212) 791-4654   (800) 221-7984

Moderate-growth fund, including electrical equipment, drugs, aerospace.

Prudential-Bache Telecommunications Fund   GROWTH AND INCOME
100 Gold St.
New York, NY 10292
(212) 791-4654   (800) 221-7984

Bond fund, diverse.

Prudential-Bache Research Fund   GROWTH
100 Gold St.
New York, NY 10292
(212) 791-4654   (800) 221-7984

Diverse growth/income fund.

Prudential-Bache Tax-Managed Fund   EQUITY INCOME
100 Gold St.
New York, NY 10292
(212) 791-4654   (800) 221-7984

Putnam Convertible Fund   FIXED INCOME
One Post Office Sq.
Boston, MA 02109
(617) 292-1000   (800) 225-1581

Bond fund/stock fund—diverse.

Putnam, George, Fund of Boston   BALANCED
One Post Office Sq.
Boston, MA 02109
(617) 292-1000   (800) 225-1581

Balanced, high-quality fund—bigger companies.

Putnam Growth Fund   GROWTH
One Post Office Sq.
Boston, MA 02109
(617) 292-1000   (800) 225-1581

Broad, diverse-growth fund—well-established technology, consumers, others.

Putnam Health Science Trust   SPECIALTY
One Post Office Sq.
Boston, MA 02109
(617) 292-1000   (800) 225-1581

Growth fund specializing in health-oriented companies, including medical technologies, services.

Putnam High Yield Trust   FIXED INCOME
One Post Office Sq.
Boston, MA 02109
(617) 292-1000   (800) 225-1581

Diverse, lower-rated-bond fund. Income oriented—high income.

Putnam Income Fund   FIXED INCOME
One Post Office Sq.
Boston, MA 02109
(617) 292-1000   (800) 225-1581

Income fund, some stocks, some U.S. govt obligations and foreign bonds.
High quality.

Putnam Info Science   CAPITAL APPRECIATION
One Post Office Sq.
Boston, MA 02109
(617) 292-1000   (800) 225-1581

Growth fund specializing in information-science industries, computers,
broadcasting, electronics.

Putnam International Equities Fund   INTERNATIONAL
One Post Office Sq.
Boston, MA 02109
(617) 292-1000   (800) 225-1581

International growth fund that invests up to 70 percent in foreign firms—
Japan, Germany, others.

Putnam Investors Fund   GROWTH
One Post Office Sq.
Boston, MA 02109
(617) 292-1000   (800) 225-1581

High-quality, diverse-growth fund, including consumer goods.

Putnam Option Income Fund   OPTION
One Post Office Sq.
Boston, MA 02109
(617) 292-1000   (800) 225-1581

Income fund, option-writing fund.

Putnam Vista Fund   CAPITAL APPRECIATION
One Post Office Sq.
Boston, MA 02109
(617) 292-1000   (800) 225-1581

Aggressive-growth fund, keying on consumer goods, business equipment.
Diverse.

Putnam Voyager Fund   CAPITAL APPRECIATION
One Post Office Sq.
Boston, MA 02109
(617) 292-1000   (800) 225-1581

Aggressive-growth fund, diverse, includes business equipment, health care, retail.

Qualified Dividend Portfolio I   EQUITY INCOME
PO Box 1100
Valley Forge, PA 19482
(215) 964-2600

Qualified Dividend Portfolio II   FIXED INCOME
PO Box 1100
Valley Forge, PA 19482
(215) 964-2600

Quasar Associates   GROWTH
140 Broadway
New York, NY 10005
(212) 902-4126   (800) 221-7780

Conservative-growth fund, dealing in drugs, cosmetics, broadcasting, retail, others.

Quest for Value Fund   CAPITAL APPRECIATION
One New York Plaza
New York, NY 10004
(212) 825-4000   (800) 221-5833

Rainbow Fund   CAPITAL APPRECIATION
60 Broad St.
New York, NY 10004
(212) 558-1585

Rea-Graham Fund   GROWTH & INCOME
19066 Challon Rd.
Los Angeles, CA 90024
(213) 471-1917

Research Capital Fund   GOLD ORIENTED
155 Bovet Rd.
San Mateo, CA 94402
(415) 570-3000   (800) 227-6781

Research Equity Fund   GROWTH
155 Bovet Rd.
San Mateo, CA 94402
(415) 570-3000   (800) 227-6781

Retirement Plan Am-Bond Fund   FIXED INCOME
PO Box 1688
Santa Fe, NM 87501
(800) 545-2098

Retirement Plan Am-Equity   EQUITY INCOME
PO Box 1688
Santa Fe, NM 87501
(800) 545-2098

Rochester Growth Fund   GROWTH
183 E. Main St.
Suite 942
Rochester, NY 14604
(716) 232-3320

Rochester Tax-Managed Fund   GROWTH
183 E. Main St.
Suite 942
Rochester, NY 14604
(716) 232-3320

Royce Value Fund   SMALL COMPANY GROWTH
1414 Avenue of the Americas
New York, NY 10019
(212) 355-7311

SAFECO Equity Fund   GROWTH & INCOME
SAFECO Plaza
Seattle, WA 98185
(206) 545-5000   (800) 426-6730

Conservative-growth fund, very diverse, keying on food, energy, retail.

SAFECO Growth Fund   GROWTH
SAFECO Plaza
Seattle, WA 98185
(206) 545-5000   (800) 426-6730

Aggressive-growth fund, emerging electric, banking and business/consumer
firms. Invests primarily in Northwestern U.S.

SAFECO Income Fund   EQUITY INCOME
SAFECO Plaza
Seattle, WA 98185
(206) 545-5000   (800) 426-6730

Conservative-income fund, primarily common stock, but some bonds.
Mostly banking.

SAFECO Special Bond Fund   FIXED INCOME
SAFECO Plaza
Seattle, WA 98185
(206) 545-5000   (800) 426-6730

Bond fund, ¾ government securities, ¼ corporate bonds.

SAFECO Tax-Free California Income Fund   INCOME
SAFECO Plaza
Seattle, WA 98185
(206) 545-5000   (800) 426-6730

Income fund, double tax free (state and federal).

St. Paul Capital Fund   GROWTH & INCOME
PO Box 43284
Minneapolis, MN 55164
(612) 738-4271   (800) 328-1064

Conservative fund, mostly blue chip in retail trade.

St. Paul Fiduciary Fund   CAPITAL APPRECIATION
PO Box 43284
Minneapolis, MN 55164
(612) 738-4271   (800) 328-1064

Clone of St. Paul Capital Fund, for tax-exempt investors, keying on retail
trade, finance, insurance.

St. Paul Growth Fund   CAPITAL APPRECIATION
PO Box 43284
Minneapolis, MN 55164
(612) 738-4265   (800) 328-1064

Moderately aggressive growth fund, keying on office equipment, electronics.

St. Paul Income Fund   FIXED INCOME
PO Box 43284
Minneapolis, MN 55164
(612) 738-4271   (800) 328-1064

High-grade govt/corporate bond fund.

St. Paul Special Fund   CAPITAL APPRECIATION
PO Box 43284
Minneapolis, MN 55164
(612) 738-4271   (800) 328-1064

Moderately aggressive stock fund, for employees, registered stockholders, and registered representatives of the St. Paul Investment Company only.

Sci/Tech Holdings   GROWTH
633 Third Ave.
New York, NY 10017
(212) 692-2939   (800) 221-2990

Merrill Lynch—high-technology companies.

Scudder Capital Growth Fund   GROWTH
175 Federal St.
Boston, MA 02110
(617) 482-3990   (800) 225-2470

Moderate-growth fund, specializing in technology, producer durables.

Scudder Common Stock Fund   GROWTH
175 Federal St.
Boston, MA 02110
(617) 482-3990   (800) 225-2470

Very conservative, blue-chip fund, keying on technology and producer durables.

Scudder Development Fund   SMALL COMPANY GROWTH
175 Federal St.
Boston, MA 02110
(617) 482-3990   (800) 225-2470

Scudder's most aggressive growth fund, specializing in emerging technology, media, and service companies.

Scudder Income Fund   FIXED INCOME
175 Federal St.
Boston, MA 02110
(617) 482-3990   (800) 225-2470

Bond fund, 86 percent corporate.

Scudder International Fund   INTERNATIONAL
175 Federal St.
Boston, MA 02110
(617) 482-3990   (800) 225-2470

Moderate-growth fund, invests overseas, keying on Japan and U.K.

Scudder Target General 1984   FIXED INCOME
175 Federal St.
Boston, MA 02110
(617) 482-3990   (800) 225-2470

You pick the maturity date. Taxable or tax-free.

Scudder Target General 1985   FIXED INCOME
175 Federal St.
Boston, MA 02110
(617) 482-3990   (800) 225-2470

You pick the maturity date. Taxable or tax-free.

Scudder Target General 1986   FIXED INCOME
175 Federal St.
Boston, MA 02110
(617) 482-3990   (800) 225-2470

You pick the maturity date. Taxable or tax-free.

Scudder Target General 1987   FIXED INCOME
175 Federal St.
Boston, MA 02110
(617) 482-3990   (800) 225-2470

You pick the maturity date. Taxable or tax-free.

Scudder Target General 1990   FIXED INCOME
175 Federal St.
Boston, MA 02110
(617) 482-3990   (800) 225-2470

You pick the maturity date. Taxable or tax-free.

Scudder Target USGT 1984   FIXED INCOME
175 Federal St.
Boston, MA 02110
(617) 482-3990   (800) 225-2470

You pick the maturity date. Taxable or tax-free.

Scudder Target USGT 1985   FIXED INCOME
175 Federal St.
Boston, MA 02110
(617) 482-3990   (800) 225-2470

You pick the maturity date. Taxable or tax-free.

Scudder Target USGT 1986   FIXED INCOME
175 Federal St.
Boston, MA 02110
(617) 482-3990   (800) 225-2470

You pick the maturity date. Taxable or tax-free.

Scudder Target USGT 1987   FIXED INCOME
175 Federal St.
Boston, MA 02110
(617) 482-3990   (800) 225-2470

You pick the maturity date. Taxable or tax-free.

Scudder Target USGT 1990   FIXED INCOME
175 Federal St.
Boston, MA 02110
(617) 482-3990   (800) 225-2470

You pick the maturity date. Taxable or tax-free.

Security Action Fund   GROWTH
700 Harrison St.
Topeka, KS 66636
(913) 295-3127   (800) 255-3509

Contractual plan—growth fund includes electronics, manufacturing.

Security Bond Fund   FIXED INCOME
700 Harrison St.
Topeka, KS 66636
(913) 295-3127   (800) 255-3509

Mid-to-high-grade U.S. and Candian bonds—¼ in U.S. govt agencies.

Security Equity Fund   GROWTH
700 Harrison St.
Topeka, KS 66636
(913) 295-3127   (800) 255-3509

Conservative-growth fund, keying on communications, office/computing machines.

Security Investment Fund   GROWTH & INCOME
700 Harrison St.
Topeka, KS 66636
(913) 295-3127   (800) 255-3509

Growth/income fund, includes communications, gas, transportation.

Security Ultra Fund   CAPITAL APPRECIATION
700 Harrison St.
Topeka, KS 66636
(913) 295-3127   (800) 255-3509

Aggressive-stock fund, speculative, keying on services—very diverse.

Selected American Shares   BALANCED
111 W. Adams St.
Chicago, IL 60602
(312) 641-7957   (800) 621-7321

Selected Special Shares   GROWTH
111 W. Adams St.
Chicago, IL 60602
(312) 641-7957   (800) 621-7321

Seligman Capital Fund   CAPITAL APPRECIATION
One Bankers Trust Plaza
New York, NY 10006
(212) 488-0200   (800) 221-2450

Small, high-growth companies and larger companies whose earnings seem to
be improving.

Seligman Common Stock Fund   GROWTH & INCOME
One Bankers Trust Plaza
New York, NY 10006
(212) 488-0200   (800) 221-2450

Seligman Communications & Information   GROWTH
One Bankers Trust Plaza
New York, NY 10006
(212) 488-0200   (800) 221-2450

Communication and related industries: advertising, publicity, broadcasting.

Seligman Growth Fund   GROWTH
One Bankers Trust Plaza
New York, NY 10006
(212) 488-0200   (800) 221-2450

Seligman Income Fund   INCOME
One Bankers Trust Plaza
New York, NY 10006
(212) 488-0200   (800) 221-2450

Sentinal Balanced Fund   BALANCED
217 Broadway
Suite 610
New York, NY 10007
(212) 406-0404

Sentinal Bond Fund   FIXED INCOME
217 Broadway
Suite 610
New York, NY 10007
(212) 406-0404

Sentinal Common Stock Fund   GROWTH & INCOME
217 Broadway
Suite 610
New York, NY 10007
(212) 406-0404

Sentinal Growth Fund   GROWTH
217 Broadway
Suite 610
New York, NY 10007
(212) 406-0404

Sentry Fund   GROWTH
1800 North Point Dr.
Stevens Point, WI 54481
(715) 346-7051   (800) 826-0266

Sequoia Fund   GROWTH
1290 Avenue of the Americas
New York, NY 10104
(212) 245-4500

Shearson Appreciation Fund   GROWTH
Two World Trade Center, 106th Fl.
New York, NY 10048
(212) 321-6547

Shearson High Yield Fund   FIXED INCOME
505 Park Ave.
New York, NY 10022
(212) 826-1500

Sherman, Dean Fund   CAPITAL APPRECIATION
120 Broadway
New York, NY 10271
(212) 577-3850

Sierra Growth Fund   GROWTH
1880 Century Park E.
Suite 717
Los Angeles, CA 90067
(213) 277-1450

Sigma Capital Shares Fund   CAPITAL APPRECIATION
3801 Kennett Pike
Wilmington, DE 19807
(302) 652-3091   (800) 441-9490

Aggressive-growth fund, merchandise, drugs/health prominent.

Sigma Income Shares   FIXED INCOME
3801 Kennett Pike
Wilmington, DE 19807
(302) 652-3091   (800) 441-9490

Fixed income, invests in diverse fields, including oil/gas, utilities.

Sigma Investment Shares   GROWTH & INCOME
3801 Kennett Pike
Wilmington, DE 19807
(302) 652-3091   (800) 441-9490

Growth/income fund, keying on larger companies. Conservative. Drugs/
health, utilities.

Sigma Special Fund   GROWTH
3801 Kennett Pike
Wilmington, DE 19807
(302) 652-3091   (800) 441-9490

Diverse conservative fund, merchandise, drugs/health, electronics.

Sigma Trust Shares   BALANCED
3801 Kennett Pike
Wilmington, DE 19807
(302) 652-3091   (800) 441-9490

Balanced income/growth fund, keying on utilities, oil/gas.

Sigma Venture Shares   SPECIALTY
3801 Kennett Pike
Wilmington, DE 19807
(302) 652-3091   (800) 441-9490

Aggressive-growth fund, keying on business equipment and electronics.

Smith, Barney Equity Fund   GROWTH
1345 Avenue of the Americas
New York, NY 10105
(212) 613-2600

Smith, Barney Income & Growth Fund   GROWTH & INCOME
1345 Avenue of the Americas
New York, NY 10105
(212) 613-2600

SoGen International Fund   GROWTH
630 Fifth Ave.
New York, NY 10111
(212) 245-5011

Southwestern Investors Income Fund   INCOME
PO Box 2511
Houston, TX 77001
(713) 757-2131

Sovereign Investors   GROWTH & INCOME
3 Great Valley Parkway E.
Great Valley Corp. Center
Suite 103
Malvern, PA 19355
(215) 251-0705

State Bond Common Stock Fund   GROWTH
100-106 N. Minnesota St.
New Ulm, MN 56703
(507) 345-2144

State Bond Diversified Fund   GROWTH & INCOME
100-106 N. Minnesota St.
New Ulm, MN 56703
(507) 345-2144

State Bond Progress Fund   GROWTH
100-106 N. Minnesota St.
New Ulm, MN 56703
(507) 345-2144

State Farm Balanced Fund   BALANCED
One State Farm Plaza
Bloomington, IL 61701
(309) 766-2029

State Farm Growth Fund   GROWTH
One State Farm Plaza
Bloomington, IL 61701
(309) 766-2029

State Farm Interim Fund   FIXED INCOME
One State Farm Plaza
Bloomington, IL 61701
(309) 766-2029

State Street Investment Corporation   GROWTH & INCOME
225 Franklin St.
Boston, MA 02110
(617) 482-3290

Steadman American Industry Fund   CAPITAL APPRECIATION
1730 K St., NW
Washington, DC 20006
(202) 223-1000

Steadman Associated Fund   INCOME
1730 K St., NW
Washington, DC 20006
(202) 223-1000

Steadman Investment Fund   GROWTH
1730 K St., NW
Washington, DC 20006
(202) 223-1000

Steadman Oceanographic Fund   GROWTH
1730 K St., NW
Washington, DC 20006
(202) 223-1000

Use of ocean and its resources.

SteinRoe Discovery Fund   SMALL COMPANY GROWTH
150 S. Wacker Dr.
Chicago, IL 60606
(312) 368-7800   (800) 621-0320

Moderately aggressive growth fund, keying on technology.

SteinRoe & Farnham Balanced Fund   SMALL COMPANY GROWTH
150 S. Wacker Dr.
Chicago, IL 60606
(312) 368-7800   (800) 621-0320

Balanced fund.

SteinRoe & Farnham Bond Fund   FIXED INCOME
150 S. Wacker Dr.
Chicago, IL 60606
(312) 368-7800   (800) 621-0320

Bond fund.

SteinRoe & Farnham Capital Opportunities   SMALL COMPANY GROWTH
150 S. Wacker Dr.
Chicago, IL 60606
(312) 368-7800   (800) 621-0320

Diverse-growth fund, including technology.

SteinRoe & Farnham Stock Fund   GROWTH
150 S. Wacker Dr.
Chicago, IL 60606
(312) 368-7800   (800) 621-0320

Moderately diverse growth fund, including distribution, technology.

SteinRoe Special Fund   CAPITAL APPRECIATION
150 S. Wacker Dr.
Chicago, IL 60606
(312) 368-7800   (800) 621-0320

Moderate-growth fund, keying on technology.

SteinRoe Stock Fund   GROWTH
150 S. Wacker Dr.
Chicago, IL 60606
(312) 368-7800   (800) 621-0320

Moderate, diverse-growth fund, including distribution, technology.

SteinRoe Total Return Fund
GROWTH & INCOME
150 S. Wacker Dr.
Chicago, IL 60606
(312) 368-7800   (800) 621-0320

Growth/income fund—very diverse.

SteinRoe Universe Fund
CAPITAL APPRECIATION
150 S. Wacker Dr.
Chicago, IL 60606
(312) 368-7800   (800) 621-0320

Diverse-growth fund, including distribution.

Strategic Capital Gains
EQUITY INCOME
PO Box 20066
10110 Crestover
Dallas, TX 75220
(214) 350-2960

Strategic Investments Fund
GOLD ORIENTED
PO Box 20066
10110 Crestover
Dallas, TX 75220
(214) 350-2960   (800) 527-5027

Stratton Growth Fund
GROWTH & INCOME
Axe Wood, Butler & Skippack Pikes
Blue Bell, PA 19422
(215) 542-8025

Strong Investment Fund
BALANCED
815 Mason St.
Milwaukee, WI 53202
(414) 765-0620   (800) 558-1030

Somewhat conservative balanced fund, keying on food/lodging and financial (bonds). No more than 65 percent in equities. Aim 2 to 3 percent over inflation.

Strong Total Return Fund
CAPITAL APPRECIATION
815 Mason St.
Milwaukee, WI 53202
(414) 765-0620   (800) 558-1030

Fairly conservative growth/income fund, mostly commercial paper at press time, including financial.

Summit Cash Reserve Fund   GROWTH
633 Third Ave.
New York, NY 10017
(212) 692-2929   (800) 221-7210

Invests primarily in short-term instruments. Primary objective is current income.

Sunbelt Growth Fund   GROWTH
333 Clay St.
Suite 4300
Houston, TX 77007
(713) 751-2400

Sun Growth Fund   GROWTH
One Sun Life Executive Park
Wellesley Hills, MA 02181
(617) 237-6030

Merged with Massachusetts Financial Group.

Surveyor Fund   GROWTH
61 Broadway
New York, NY 10006
(212) 480-8600   (800) 221-5233

Aggressive-growth fund, specializing in emerging science-and-technology-oriented companies.

Tax-Managed Fund Utility Shares   EQUITY INCOME
450 Australia Ave. S.
Suite 300
West Palm Beach, FL 33401
(305) 655-3481   (800) 327-4508

ABT family, tax-free, utility-oriented fund.

Technology Fund   GROWTH
120 S. LaSalle St.
Chicago, IL 60603
(312) 781-1121   (800) 621-1048

Templeton Foreign Fund   INCOME
PO Box 3942
405 Central Ave.
St. Petersburg, FL 33731
(813) 823-8712   (800) 237-0738

Growth fund that invests solely in overseas firms, keying on Canada, Netherlands.

Templeton Global I Fund   SMALL COMPANY GROWTH
PO Box 3942
405 Central Ave.
St. Petersburg, FL 33731
(813) 823-8712   (800) 237-0738

Growth fund—however, no new shares being sold.

Templeton Global II Fund   SMALL COMPANY GROWTH
PO Box 3942
405 Central Ave.
St. Petersburg, FL 33731
(813) 823-8712   (800) 237-0738

Growth fund that invests in smaller U.S. and foreign-based firms, keying on
banking/finance, construction and housing.

Templeton Growth Fund   GROWTH
PO Box 3942
405 Central Ave.
St. Petersburg, FL 33731
(813) 823-8712   (800) 237-0738

Canadian-based fund (formerly a tax advantage) that invests in U.S. and
worldwide large firms.

Templeton World Fund   GROWTH
PO Box 3942
405 Central Ave.
St. Petersburg, FL 33731
(813) 823-8712   (800) 237-0738

Growth fund that invests in U.S. and in other countries, keying on energy.

Transamerica Capital Fund   GROWTH
PO Box 2438
Terminal Annex
1150 S. Olive
Los Angeles, CA 90051
(213) 742-4141

Transamerica New Income Fund   FIXED INCOME
PO Box 2438
Terminal Annex
1150 S. Olive
Los Angeles, CA 90051
(213) 748-4410

Transatlantic Fund   INTERNATIONAL
100 Wall St.
New York, NY 10005
(212) 747-0440

Travelers Equities Fund   GROWTH
One Tower Sq.
Hartford, CT 06115
(203) 277-6341

Trustees Commingled Equity   GROWTH & INCOME
PO Box 2600
Valley Forge, PA 19482
(215) 648-6000   (800) 523-7025

Trustees Commingled International Fund   INTERNATIONAL
PO Box 2600
Valley Forge, PA 19482
(215) 648-6000   (800) 523-7025

Tudor Fund   CAPITAL APPRECIATION
One New York Plaza, 30th Fl.
New York, NY 10004
(212) 908-9500

Emerging growth firms and those that could rebound from adversity.

Twentieth Century Gift Trust   GROWTH
PO Box 200
605 W. 47th St.
Kansas City, MO 64141
(816) 531-5575

Aggressive-growth fund for irrevocable gifts to children or charities. Recipients can't withdraw for ten years.

Twentieth Century Growth Investors   CAPITAL APPRECIATION
PO Box 200
605 W. 47th St.
Kansas City, MO 64141
(816) 531-5575

Larger companies.

Twentieth Century Select Investors   GROWTH
PO Box 200
605 W. 47th St.
Kansas City, MO 64141
(816) 531-5575

Computer selected for accelerated growth of sales and earnings, likes dividend payers.

Twentieth Century Ultra Investors   CAPITAL APPRECIATION
PO Box 200
605 W. 47th St.
Kansas City, MO 64141
(816) 531-5575

Small, expanding companies.

Twentieth Century U.S. Govt Fund   FIXED INCOME
PO Box 200
605 W. 47th St.
Kansas City, MO 64141
(816) 531-5575

Unified Accumulation Fund   CAPITAL APPRECIATION
600 Guaranty Bldg.
Indianapolis, IN 46204
(317) 634-3300   (800) 862-7283

New, tax-managed fund. One of nine in the U.S. Moderate-growth fund. Diverse, including finance, utilities.

Unified Growth Fund   GROWTH
600 Guaranty Bldg.
Indianapolis, IN 46204
(317) 634-3300   (800) 862-7283

Moderate-growth fund, very diverse, including medium-to-large health services, banking.

Unified Income Fund   INCOME
600 Guaranty Bldg.
Indianapolis, IN 46204
(317) 634-3300   (800) 862-7283

Diverse-income fund, including petroleum, oil/natural gas. Conservative.

Unified Mutual Shares   GROWTH & INCOME
600 Guaranty Bldg.
Indianapolis, IN 46204
(317) 634-3300   (800) 862-7283

Balanced fund, majority stocks, keying on banking, oil/gas. Unified will be starting an Islamic Growth Fund in 1984 that invests according to Koranic law.

United Accumulative Fund   GROWTH
PO Box 1343
One Crown Center
Kansas City, MO 64141
(816) 283-4000   (800) 821-5664

Diverse conservative-growth fund—larger companies.

United Bond Fund   FIXED INCOME
PO Box 1343
One Crown Center
Kansas City, MO 64141
(816) 283-4000   (800) 821-5664

Diverse corporate-bond fund—70 percent are rated A or better.

United Continental Income Fund   BALANCED
PO Box 1343
One Crown Center
Kansas City, MO 64141
(816) 283-4000   (800) 821-5664

Balanced fund, with common stocks in various areas.

United High Income Fund   FIXED INCOME
PO Box 1343
One Crown Center
Kansas City, MO 64141
(816) 283-4000   (800) 821-5664

United Income Fund   EQUITY INCOME
PO Box 1343
One Crown Center
Kansas City, MO 64141
(816) 283-4000   (800) 821-5664

Income fund—blue-chip companies including utilities, chemicals, retail trade.

United International Growth Fund INCOME
PO Box 1343
One Crown Center
Kansas City, MO 64141
(816) 283-4000   (800) 821-5664

Overseas fund, subject to currency fluctuations. At press time, over one-fifth of investment in U.S., slightly less in Japan.

United New Concepts Fund SMALL COMPANY GROWTH
PO Box 1343
One Crown Center
Kansas City, MO 64141
(816) 283-4000   (800) 821-5664

New (1983) fund, emerging growth-oriented. At press time, 80 percent in cash.

United Prospector Fund GOLD ORIENTED
PO Box 1343
One Crown Center
Kansas City, MO 64141
(816) 283-4000   (800) 821-5664

United Retirement Shares GROWTH & INCOME
PO Box 1343
One Crown Center
Kansas City, MO 64141
(816) 283-4000   (800) 821-5664

Growth/income fund, including large business service, electronics firms.

United Science & Energy Fund GROWTH
PO Box 1343
One Crown Center
Kansas City, MO 64141
(816) 283-4000   (800) 821-5664

Conservative-growth fund, specializing in development of energy and other sciences.

United Services Gold Shares GOLD ORIENTED
PO Box 29467
San Antonio, TX 78229
(512) 696-1234   (800) 531-5777

Gold fund, 85 percent invested in South African mining companies. High risk but successful.

United Services Growth Fund
PO Box 29467
San Antonio, TX 78229
(512) 696-1234   (800) 531-5777

Moderately aggressive growth fund, specializing in high-technology/energy common stocks.

United Vanguard Fund   GROWTH
PO Box 1343
One Crown Center
Kansas City, MO 64141
(816) 283-4000   (800) 821-5664

Aggressive-growth fund, keying on smaller business machines, electronics.

USAA Growth Fund   GROWTH
9800 Fredricksburg Rd.
San Antonio, TX 78288
(512) 690-3390   (800) 531-8181

Moderately conservative growth fund, some blue chip, mostly well-established, undervalued common stock including office equipment, communications equipment.

USAA Income Fund   INCOME
9800 Fredricksburg Rd.
San Antonio, TX 78288
(512) 690-3390   (800) 531-8181

Bond fund, majority of Fannie, Ginnie Maes.

USAA Sunbelt Era Fund   CAPITAL APPRECIATION
9800 Fredricksburg Rd.
San Antonio, TX 78288
(512) 690-3390   (800) 531-8181

Aggressive-growth fund that specializes in small, emerging companies in Sun Belt—aerospace/defense, retail stores, health care.

Valley Forge Fund   GROWTH
PO Box 262
Valley Forge, PA 19481
(215) 688-6839

Value Line Fund   GROWTH & INCOME
711 Third Ave.
New York, NY 10017
(212) 687-3965   (800) 223-0818

Moderate growth/income fund, diverse, including air transport, electronics, retail.

Value Line Bond Fund   FIXED INCOME
711 Third Ave.
New York, NY 10017
(212) 687-3965   (800) 223-0818

High-grade bond fund, keying on government-agency obligations, corporate bonds, which include utilities.

Value Line Income Fund   EQUITY INCOME
711 Third Ave.
New York, NY 10017
(212) 687-3965   (800) 223-0818

Income fund, common stocks key on established banks, utilities, retail stores. Bonds (corporate) include medical.

Value Line Leveraged Growth Investors   CAPITAL APPRECIATION
711 Third Ave.
New York, NY 10017
(212) 687-3965   (800) 223-0818

Moderate-growth fund that seeks greater than average capital appreciation. Keys on banks, insurance, retail stores.

Value Line Special Situations   GROWTH
711 Third Ave.
New York, NY 10017
(212) 687-3965   (800) 223-0818

Moderately aggressive growth fund—diverse, keying on air transport, health care products/services, housing, recreational vehicles.

Vance, Sanders Special Fund   GROWTH
24 Federal St.
Boston, MA 02110
(617) 482-8260   (800) 225-6265

Vanguard Fixed Income GNMA Portfolio   FIXED INCOME
PO Box 2600
Valley Forge, PA 19482
(215) 648-6000   (800) 523-7025

U.S. govt securities.

Vanguard Fixed Income—High Yield   FIXED INCOME
PO Box 2600
Valley Forge, PA 19482
(215) 648-6000   (800) 523-7025

Fixed-income fund—bonds.

Vanguard Fixed Income—Invest. Grade   FIXED INCOME
PO Box 2600
Valley Forge, PA 19482
(215) 648-6000   (800) 523-7025

Fixed-income fund—bonds.

Vanguard Fixed Income—Short Term   FIXED INCOME
PO Box 2600
Valley Forge, PA 19482
(215) 648-6000   (800) 523-7025

Vanguard Index Trust   GROWTH & INCOME
PO Box 2600
Valley Forge, PA 19482
(215) 648-6000   (800) 523-7025

Index fund, invests only in Standard & Poor's 500. Very diverse, an example
of "passive investing."

Vanguard Quality Dividend III   FIXED INCOME
PO Box 2600
Valley Forge, PA 19482
(215) 648-6000   (800) 523-7025

Fixed-income fund, invested in adjustable-rate preferred stocks. Vanguard is
in the process of starting Vanguard Specialized Portfolios: hi-tech, energy.

Variable Stock Fund   GROWTH
1250 State St.
Springfield, MA 01133
(413) 785-5811

Venture Income (+) Plus   FIXED INCOME
PO Box 1688
309 Johnson St.
Santa Fe, NM 87501
(505) 983-4335   (800) 545-2098

High-yield bond fund, mostly corporate bonds, keying on energy, transportation.

Wade Fund   GROWTH
Suite 2224
5100 Poplar Ave.
Memphis, TN 38137
(901) 682-4613

Wall Street Fund   GROWTH
One Wall St.
New York, NY 10005
(212) 943-1182

Washington Mutual Investors Fund   GROWTH & INCOME
1101 Vermont Ave., NW
Washington, DC 20005
(202) 842-5665

Diverse growth/income fund including data processing, merchandising.

Weingarten Equity Fund   CAPITAL APPRECIATION
331 Madison Ave.
New York, NY 10017
(212) 557-8787

Wellesley Income Fund   INCOME
PO Box 2600
Valley Forge, PA 19482
(215) 648-6000   (800) 523-7025

Income fund, mostly high-quality corporate bonds, some stocks.

Wellington Fund   BALANCED
PO Box 2600
Valley Forge, PA 19482
(215) 648-6000   (800) 523-7025

Balanced fund (income), mostly stocks, some bonds.

Westergaard Fund   CAPITAL APPRECIATION
540 Madison Ave.
Suite 805
New York, NY 10022
(212) 940-0218   —collect

Windsor Fund   GROWTH & INCOME
PO Box 2600
Valley Forge, PA 19482
(215) 648-6000   (800) 523-7025

Conservative growth/income fund.

Y.E.S. Fund
6869 Airport Dr.
Suite 402
Riverside, CA 92504
(714) 884-8663

Yield from interest-bearing investments, extra income from writing options against U.S. govt bonds, safety from underlying investments. Invests 80 percent in U.S. govt-backed securities.

Acknowledgments

No book is the product of one person alone. That is an especially true statement when that book is written by someone whose full-time occupation is something other than writing. One has to depend on many others for more help than they are usually expected to provide. I am especially grateful to my assistant, Maggie Shriver, who has kept my business running so smoothly in my absence. My literary agent, Rhoda Weyr, is undoubtedly the best in the business. Joan Sanger, my editor, made an orderly affair of these hundreds of pages and has always been full of enthusiasm for this project. My office manager, Phil Blevins, has made me the stockbroker I am. The Work Place met every deadline in preparing this manuscript from my horrible scribbling. Steve Gritzan and Laird White are responsible for the lengthy mutual-funds listing in the appendix. Martha Quick did a splendid job completing everything I hate to do in making the excellent copy editor, Fred Sawyer, and the efficient editorial assistant, Fenya Slatkin, happy, getting permission from those I quoted, and making certain that all of the phone numbers, addresses, and other details are correct. My clients have been wonderful in their support and encouragement for my writing. And my wonderful wife, Marti, is the force behind everything I've ever accomplished and will be for all my books that are yet to come.